"★ ★ ★ ★! A sometimes hilarious, sometimes shocking but definitely unforgettable tome on the history of America's most beloved vacation destination ... a fun book ... told with a jocularity that brings tears of laughter ... (a) wild ride!"
— *Ocala Star-Banner (Ocala, Fl.)*

"Delightful reading ... the second best thing to do if you cannot visit the Magic Kingdom is to read this book. You will find it fascinating."
— *Velma Daniels (syndicated columnist)*

"I've read just about everything that has ever been in print about Disneyland, but I hadn't read most of the things David chronicles in his book! This is original stuff ... this book is a must."
— *Amusement Business*

"... scrapes the fairy dust off the theatrical facade to reveal that what Walt Disney envisioned as a place free from the evils of the real world can be all too real."
— *Los Angeles Times*

"A fast-paced, objective and often hilarious look at the world-renowned theme park ... the book peels away the Disney-manufactured facade and uncovers secrets previously stored behind-the-scenes."
— *Daily Pilot (Orange County, Ca.)*

"A valuable addition to popular culture and to Disneyana."
— *Booklist*

"An unofficial history in which hundreds of hilarious events also prove that the 160-acre site near Los Angeles can be as goofy as a crazy cartoon."
— *New York Daily News*

"An amusing and nostalgic trip down Main Street that is entertaining and informative."
— *Santa Cruz Sentinel (Santa Cruz, Ca.)*

"... revealing ... entertaining ... This is the book that the folks at Disney don't want you to read, (but) even those of us who are Disneyholics would enjoy reading it."
— *San Antonio Express News*

MOUSE TALES

A BEHIND-THE-EARS LOOK AT
DISNEYLAND

by David Koenig

Foreword
by Art Linkletter

 **BONAVENTURE PRESS**

Mouse Tales: A Behind-the-Ears Look at Disneyland by David Koenig

Published by
BONAVENTURE PRESS
Post Office Box 51961
Irvine, CA 92619-1961
USA

Cover art by Ray Haller

Publisher's Cataloging in Publication Data
Koenig, David G.
    Mouse Tales: A Behind-the-Ears Look at Disneyland / by David Koenig.
        p. cm.
    Includes annotated references and index.
    1. Disneyland (Calif.) — History. 2. Amusement Parks (Calif.). I. Koenig,
        David G., 1962- II. Title.
GV1853.3.C22K   1994   791.0687949   94-70439

ISBN 0-9640605-5-8 (hardcover)

ISBN 0-9640605-6-6 (softcover)

Printed in the United States of America
15

For Laura,
Let me share a whole new world with you...

Contents

Acknowledgments

WITHOUT the help of the following friends and acquaintances, this book would have been about seven pages long. Seven very dull pages.

My biggest thanks to Laura Hamlin, Randy Skretvedt (the hardest working man in show business), Ray Haller and Sandra Fitzgibbons. Plus, Bill Bax, Charles Christ, Kevin and Cheryl Duarte, Larry and Sheryl Hamlin, David Hayes, Bill Jagielski, David Keefe, Rita Pipta, Terrie Rudolph, Patricia Vickers, Brent Walker, Jordan Young, and my family, Anne, Gerald, Joe, Paul and Maryanne Koenig and Michelle and Paul Roden.

Also to Art Linkletter, Lee Ray, Dawson Taylor, the History Room of the Anaheim Public Library; Mike Johnson, Julie Volner and the rest of the staff at the Orange County Courthouse; the private collection room at Santa Ana Public Library; Linda Abrams-Supko and Cheryl Haab of BookCrafters; Jorge Trevino at James Enterprises; Ben Palacios, Mary B. Theil and the Golden Ears Club; Doug Kruger of Disney University; Dave Smith and Robert Tieman at the Walt Disney Archives; Teressa Tucker and Margaret Adamic of the Walt Disney Co. legal department.

To the gracious cast members (this book really is *their* story) Jessie Adams, Alejandra (Muñoz) Aldecoa, Glen Alder, Sarah (Hewitt) Alevizon, Dorothy Andrews, Roger Baker, Mona Baldwin, Sandi (Rosner) Baldwin, Jeffrey Bals, Roger Bannier,

Tony Barksdale, Jim Barngrover, Margaret Barth, Elsie Bastrup, Shannon Baughman, Ed Beaver, David Belz, Mike Berry, William C. "Wild Bill" Berry, Diane Birnie, Virginia Bixler, Cap Blackburn, Linda (Hysell) Blackburn, Curtis Blakely, Bob Blanchard, Laurence Boag, Karen Bopp, Dennis Bowman, John Bradley, Vera Branigan, Dennis Brent, Patsy Brooks, Ruth Brooks, Patricia (Davila) Bryant, Don and Dayna Budde, Jeff Burdick, Arthur Burroughs, Joan (Keaney) Burt, Mike Calabrese, Dock Campbell, Craig Carman, Jim Cashin, Paul Castle, Joe Chandler, Jim Church, Alan Coats, Denise Cornwell, Chuck Corson, Brian Craig and Valerie (Watson) Curry...

...and Rob Damico, Lori David, Carol (Williamson) Davies, Zane DeArakal, Jeri Lee (Salisbury) De Bord, Mike Deck, John DeLucia, Jud Denaut, Alfred Dennison, Suzi (Petroni) Dow, Steven Dowd, Mary Druitt, Carol (Spurgeon) Dumas, Jim Dunham, Mike Eagen, Robert Elliott, Dorothy Eno, Ken Evans, Hank Filtz, Fred, Jane, Fritz and Fran Fischle, Sandra Fitzgibbons, Nell Flanagan, Fred Foss, Michelle (Everett) Foster, Tom Foster, Van France, David "Dav" Garland, Valerie George, Terry Goldfarb, Charlene (Kirkwood) Goltz, John Goodwin, Geralynn (Minto) Gorham, Nina (Mrs. John) Gray, Ella May Green, William Guard, Steve Hall, Ray Haller, Garth Hamlin, Earl Harper, Ruth Harper, Ron Harris, Elizabeth (Confer, Cooper) and Tracy Hayes, Dan Healy, Fred Hecker, Jeff Heileson, Glenn Hellyer, Kimberly (Hilston) Hensley, George Herold, Chuck Hintz, Barry Hofstetter, Homer Holland, Larry Holmes, Henry (Brownie) Hore, Beverly (Palombo) Hyndman, Sayde Iantorno, Thom Jacobs, Freda Jacobson, Randy Jett, Bob Johnson, Lyle Johnson and Bea Jones...

...and also Jack Kehoe, Ian Kessler, Kay Kilpatrick, Jonas Kloris, Susan (Van Alstine) Knowles, Peter Lacagno, Marc Lance, Todd Landgren, Kevin Larson, Casey (Dorcas) Lauer, Anne (Thomas) Lefebvre, Eugene "Doc" Lemmon, Jeff Lenburg, Gregg Leslie, Marcus Lewis, Tony Liberato, Vincent Licay, Wayne Ligthart, Richard Lovegren, Gary Lucas, Mig Lyles, Dick Mahoney, Sandy Mann, Brien Manning, Wendy Marshall, Barry Matas, Frank Matosich, Dick May, Mark McClaran, William McCormick, Marda (Ramocinski) McDermed, Kay McFaul, Terry McGrath, Frank McNell, David Miller, Larry Miller, Gregory

Mills, Ernie Moersch, John Moohr, Betty Neese, Alice Newman, Dale Nichols, Glenn Oder, Skip Palmer, Jim Paschal, Trudy Passo, Bob Penfield, Gary Perkins, Jim Persons, Lissa (Muench, Stack) Pestolesi, Tom Pletts, Mike Pratt and Jim Pruitt...

...and, of course, Donna Rochelle, Mike Rondeau, Pat Ross, Andy Sacks, Joseph St. Pierre, Terry Schaefer, Jeffrey Schlichter, Martin Schmidt, Steve Schwaer, Bob Schweppe, Ray Schwartz, Johanna Scillieri, Carole (Joel) Seifert, Rosemary Short, Dwain Smith, Mark Smith, Wendee (Werder) Smith, Louis Solorio, Tim Stanley, Richard and Susan (Van Orden) Steele, Dick Strimple, Joyce (Reed) Sunderman, Riley Sunrise, Vince Sweeney, Bonnie Thomas, Edwin Tachauer, Charleen (Romero) Thompson, Lorene Townsend, John Waite, Bert Walker, Rita Walther, Laura Ward, Bert Watkins, Bette Watson, Roberts Watters, John Watts, Bill "Charles" Wettengel, Lee Wettengel, Steve Wheeler, Tom Wheland, Linda Lea (Slifer, Reynolds) Williamson, John Willoughby, Jinx (Brookshire) Wilson, Julia Wilson, Caroline Winterberg, Jane Young and Tom Young.

And especially to Jesus Christ, my Lord and Savior. Every ability and every opportunity I have been given have come from Him.

Foreword
by Art Linkletter

I first heard about Disneyland while touring with Walt in Europe. We were going through the famous entertainment complex Tivoli Gardens in Copenhagen, and he was jotting things down in a notebook as he, his wife Lillian, my wife Lois and I were walking along. I asked him what he was doing and he said, "Someday I am going to build a family entertainment center and this place is more like what I envision than anything I have seen. It's clean, it's directed to the entire family and is a mix of fun, entertainment and education." He noted how important it was to have a lot of places to sit down and a wide variety of eating spots that were not too fancy and served excellent meals. He was struck by the fact that the park featured millions and millions of lights and that crews were constantly on patrol to service them while other workmen were repairing and replacing any scuffs or damage throughout the park.

The next time I was aware that things were beginning to happen was when Walt asked me to join him and a group from Stanford for an auto ride to look at the spot where they had decided that the future growth of population would be. We were all sworn to secrecy about this area, Anaheim, and I remember thinking to myself, "These people are crazy... we're 30 or 40 miles from the city in a sleepy backwoods. Who's going to come way out here and throw balls at targets for prizes?"

How wrong I was. I should have known that Walt's inventiveness would start him off on a wild journey during which time he would re-invent the entire landscape of family entertainment.

As time went on, I was increasingly skeptical of his plans, but I never let him know about my doubts. I also did not invest in any of the available real estate, which has increased in value at least 50 times. Just before the opening, Walt asked me to help him with the live ABC TV coverage, and I asked two of my good friends, Bob Cummings and Ron Reagan, if they would join Walt and me in a free-wheeling, off-the-cuff, ad-lib coverage of the entire park.

There were no rehearsals. Tape at that time was unheard of, so we did not have any pre-broadcast material ready to fill in and cover any transitional moments while we were on the air. Many mishaps occurred, of course, including my inability to find my microphone (under a pile of lumber) just as I was being introduced, and Walt almost came to blows with a guard who would not let him through the back lot on his way to the place in Tomorrowland where he was to broadcast.

On a personal note, Walt apologized for offering me scale ($200 in those days) for my services. I assured him that that amount would be perfectly satisfactory to me if he would give me the concession to sell all film and cameras in Disneyland for the first ten years. Surprisingly, the net returns from this valuable concession made me the highest paid broadcaster for that one show in the history of television!

Looking back through the decades since the opening of Disneyland, I am astounded at the gigantic success story and the unexpected events that have occurred since Walt's death.

Preface

GROWING up in the late Sixties in Orange County, California, I was enchanted by Disneyland. The park's reputation and popularity were at all-time highs, and, for my family, a trip to the Magic Kingdom was a huge event. Weeks in advance, we children mapped out which attractions we would spend our prized E-coupons on. Riding up the Santa Ana Freeway, we competed to see who would be the first to spot the Matterhorn.

No matter how difficult things got at home or at school, everything was wonderful at Disneyland. Clean, orderly, peaceful, perfect. Serene Storybook Land, playful Tom Sawyer Island, the exhilarating bobsleds.

Then, one day, when I was about ten, I noticed something peculiar on Adventure through Inner Space. The ride supposedly shrunk guests so they could visit the nucleus of an atom. As evidence, the freshly miniaturized passengers in their tiny vehicles passed by the waiting area through a transparent tube. Yet though many regular-sized vehicles began the journey empty, every miniature car in the tube was filled with people. Wait a minute! No one was shrinking – those were dolls! It was all an illusion.

It was like I'd just unmasked Santa Claus. But then, suddenly, everything started to make sense. The concrete mountains. The mechanical birds. The phony fish in the Submarine Lagoon. The midgets in the mouse suits. Tinkerbell "flying" down a wire. It hit me. Disneyland wasn't real.

Yet my fascination with and appreciation for the place grew. I was the boy captivated not by the magic so much as the magician because he made the tricks look so real. The Jungle Cruise became my new favorite attraction – the only place in the whole park where the hosts could be their sarcastic selves. They'd been around the river a time or two. When I grew up, I wanted to be a Jungle Boat skipper.

Instead, reality set in and I chose a different career path. I studied journalism at Cal State Fullerton, a giant labor pool for part-time park employees. I made many close friends who worked at the park, and what amazed me was their simultaneous devotion to and disdain for their jobs. "Dismal-land" was so strict and demanding that it practically became their whole lives. They grumbled about working weekends, holidays and graveyard shift Grad Nites. About the clueless supervisors and overbearing guests. Still, their allegiance to the park was astounding, like children loyal to their abusive parents.

The friction came to a head in 1984, during my final semester of college. The Disneyland employees went on strike. Most of my friends picketed. A few schoolmates refused to strike. One got a job as a scab. It was eerie watching the people who loved Disneyland the most *striking* Disneyland. It changed their relationships with the park and with each other. It changed them inside. It helped a few quit and move on. Others are still there.

As for me, I started freelance writing, doing investigative pieces for magazines like *Orange Coast*. I soon settled in as an editor at an established trade magazine. But the curious love/hate, fantasy/reality dichotomy of Disneyland stayed with me. And after helping fellow authors in researching books, I realized I had the greatest story never told. We all share a mutual fascination of what it's like to work at the Happiest Place on Earth. And I had eyewitness testimony of the most amazing adventures in the most unlikely place.

I spent two years digging through libraries and private collections and made 40 trips to the Orange County Courthouse, individually examining all 650 of the Superior Court cases brought against Disneyland. And, of course, there were scores of trips to Disneyland. I interviewed my friends and then my friends' friends. I went through old employee directories and even the Anaheim phone book to track down over 200 more employees.

Previously published books on Disneyland have all been overseen by Disney, and the company's heavy hand is evident. The books ignore or, at best, candy-coat any un-Disneylike events in a wacky "Good Old Days" tone. I knew Disney would and could not have any official association with my book. For instance, it's their official position that those costumed characters really are Mickey Mouse, Donald Duck, et al. They could never sanction a book suggesting otherwise.

Additionally, Disney is understandably protective of their characters and copyrights. And zealously litigious. Their lawyers bombarded three Florida child care centers that painted pictures of Disney characters on their walls.

Nevertheless, I wanted to be open and honest with Disneyland. Initially, Disney's publicity department was gracious, but requested that I clear all potential interview subjects with them first. Those who first "asked permission" from Disney I never heard from again.

Disney's legal department was more direct. By no means would I be permitted to write a book about Disneyland. Amused, I continued writing. Their occasional contacts since have ranged from vague offers of assistance and compromise to threats and outright lies. They were helpful, though, in helping me determine which photographs I would (and which I would not) be able to publish.

I've gone to great lengths to double and triple check my facts and make sure I don't infringe on any Disney copyrights. I also considered applying for a job at Disneyland, but thought that might be underhanded and that my brief, isolated experiences might overly influence my depiction of the park. After all, I didn't have to create a story. I already had hundreds of unbelievable tales, just waiting to be told. I hope this book answers your questions about what it's like Behind the Ears.

– David Koenig
March 1994

1

The Making of
the Mouse House

*O*NCE UPON A TIME, *in a land not so far away, there lived a kindly old inventor. The excitable little man bubbled with whimsy and goodness and everyone loved him. Yet, he was unhappy. He felt out of place in the cold, dark world around him.*

So, the inventor decided to create a kingdom of his own, a Magic Kingdom. It would be inhabited by furry, five-foot-tall mice and watched over by ever-smiling servants happy to work for free. There would be pink castles and wishing wells. Pirate ships and rocket ships. Parades and popcorn carts. Sparkling streets and the endless echoing of laughter and music. And, best of all, it would be a place where everyone is happy and nothing ever goes wrong and where you could wish upon a star and your dreams would come true. People came from faraway places to see this wonderful new world for themselves. And they went home believers.

More than a fairy tale, this is the image of Disneyland, the self-proclaimed "Happiest Place on Earth." And the Walt Disney Company has tirelessly worked to uphold the image since 1955. Squeaky clean, All American, fun for the whole family. A Twentieth Century Shangri-La. More than twelve million guests each year come sample Southern California's purest slice of paradise and, for the most part, believe the fantasy. Just like when they accept the premise of a talking mouse in a cartoon, visitors to Disneyland seem to accept the premise of a perfect playground. Only the park's visitors internalize this cunningly manufactured impression and take it home with them.

What the public doesn't know is how much really goes on behind Sleeping Beauty's Castle. How much planning goes into manufacturing the Image. How much hard work goes into recreating the Experience on a daily basis. And how many times real life invades the pixie dust boundaries of the Magic Kingdom, bringing conflicts, tragedies and other surprises into a most incongruous setting. Over the years, the park has been rocked by labor disputes, charges of discrimination, bomb threats, thievery, gang fights, a full scale riot, shootings, stabbings, attraction malfunctions and ensuing lawsuits.

Sometimes the problems are caused by the very perception that there are no problems... criminals enticed by the image; preoccupied or curious guests who grow careless; managers who blindly protect the image, and disillusioned workers who discover the truth. But after seemingly every incident, within minutes, the Disney damage control team springs into action to cover up or, at the very least, candy-coat the stories. Stories that don't always end with "Happily Ever After."

A place free from the evils of the real world was the whole idea for Disneyland. The idea was Walt Disney's. The filmmaker's work was recognized the world around for its innovations and its innocence. Disney was the first to introduce cartoons with sound, color, feature length, stereophonic sound and using other special techniques. And his movies promised wholesome family entertainment. Mickey Mouse was the ideal citizen, neighbor, friend and hero. The Disney name became synonymous with traditional values and good clean fun.

Walt first thought of a Disney Land in the 1930s while taking his two young daughters to a typical amusement park of the day –

dirty, garish, disorganized and of minimal interest to adults. His idea was a first class *theme* park, clean, tasteful, logically planned and fun for both children and adults. No one gave it much credence. They couldn't understand why Walt Disney of all people wanted to build a low brow tourist trap like Coney Island. But that was the whole idea. His wouldn't be.

Walt's wild idea remained just that for twenty years, until the early 1950s, when his brother Roy, who handled the finances, was able to work a deal with fledgling ABC Television to help fund the park. In exchange Walt agreed to produce *Disneyland*, the TV show. The program's first episode previewed the new park and promised to televise live the Opening Day festivities, set for July 17, 1955. Construction began July 16, 1954. Disney had exactly one year to transform seventeen tracts of orange groves in the small town of Anaheim, California, into his elaborate dreamland. It seemed impossible, but Walt was determined that his deadline be met. Said one construction foreman, "When Walt put a date on something, come hell or high water, it was done."

It was costly and took working around the clock. The crew made plenty of mistakes, but didn't have time to dwell on them. They fixed them immediately and moved on. A colorblind worker was put in charge of bulldozing certain trees marked with color-coded tags, and he started leveling everything in sight. When they first put water in the Rivers of America, it was instantly soaked up by the sandy soil. The river bottom had to be lined with clay.

Disney emptied nurseries from San Diego to Santa Barbara to fill his park with every imaginable type of tree and plant. Shrubs were pulled from the path of city bulldozers clearing way for the new Santa Ana Freeway. When, at the last minute, there were still patches of dirt, Walt had gardeners pull out weeds from the parking lot, replant them inside the park and attach signs marked with long, horticultural-sounding names.

Disney demanded that the entire park be surrounded by a twelve-to-twenty-foot-high, thickly forested berm to isolate his fantasies from the real world. He also made the city agree that no high-rises could ever be built that could be seen from inside the park.

Walt assembled a group of his imaginative movie men and tech-

UNDER CONSTRUCTION. Aerial photo of Disneyland months before the grand opening. (Early 1955) *Courtesy Anaheim Public Library.*

nological geniuses and formed a company, WED, Inc., to help develop the dream. These designers, or "Imagineers," reworked and reformulated the list of attractions, discarding lots of intriguing possibilities like Rock Candy Mountain, Lilliputian Land, Donald Duck bumper boats and Pinocchio Square. In the final plans, Disneyland would be laid out like a motion picture, with each scene, or land, logically flowing to the next. Sort of three-dimensional storytelling. Scene One was Main Street, USA, a recreation of the ideal small town of turn-of-the-century America. Guests could ride horse-drawn streetcars, one of those new-fangled horseless carriages or hop aboard the Disneyland Railroad. The street would be dotted with nostalgic shops, like a bakery, candy palace, ice cream parlor, market house and tobacco shop.

A hub at the end of Main Street fanned out like spokes in a wheel to the other scenes. Adventureland, inspired by Disney's True Life Adventure films, reproduced the tropical, untamed jungles of Africa and Asia. An *African Queen*-inspired Jungle Cruise with robotic wildlife served as its centerpiece.

Also to the West would be Frontierland, harking back to the pioneer days of Davy Crockett and frontier America. There would be rides on stagecoaches, mule trains and a Mark Twain Steamboat across the Rivers of America. The Golden Horseshoe Saloon offered a can-can/comedy revue. Real live Indians staged ceremonial dances at an Indian Village, temporarily near Adventureland but relocated to Frontierland a year later.

Fantasyland would bring to life the famous Disney cartoon characters. It took the traditional kiddie rides of carnivals and amusement parks a step further. Dark rides, typically filled with unrelated thrills, would have forward moving storylines, from the Disney movies *Snow White and the Seven Dwarfs*, *Peter Pan* and *The Wind in the Willow*. Mr. Toad's Wild Ride was originally planned as a roller coaster-type ride but toned down for fear that it might frighten small children. The Mad Tea Party placed the guest in control of the speed of the spinning teacups on the Tilt-A-Whirl-type turntable. Dumbo the Flying Elephant spun around like the Spider but left the height of the craft up to the passenger. Fantasyland's entrance was an elegant Sleeping Beauty Castle, leading to the King Arthur Carrousel centerpiece, an exacting restoration using original horses from Coney Island.

Last to take shape was Tomorrowland, which would feature:

● Space Station X-1, later called Satellite View of America, a look at our planet from 50 miles out in space.

● Rocket to the Moon, a simulated trip to the moon, with a 76-foot-tall TWA rocketship out front.

● Circarama Theater, which evolved into Circle-Vision 360, showing a movie on a 360 degree screen.

● Phantom Boats, sleek, high-finned, individually-powered little boats.

● Tomorrowland Autopia, individually-powered cars on a miniature freeway.

● Astro-Jets, a fast-spinning Dumbo-type ride with rockets in place of pachyderms.

Unfortunately, short on time and funds, Tomorrowland would suffer the most compromises. In desperation, Walt decided to fill up the space with a lot of corporate-sponsored county fair-type exhibits:

● Dutch Boy Paint Color Gallery, featuring "Our Future in Colors."

● Monsanto Hall of Chemistry museum.

● Richfield Oil's *World Beneath Us*, an animated history of man's quest for energy.

● American Dairy Association Dairy Bar exhibit with its own plastic cow.

● The Flight Circle, where model planes and later actual jet packs were demonstrated.

● Kaiser's Hall of Aluminum Fame.

● Crane Bathroom of Tomorrow, showcasing a modernistic john and "Fun with Water" exhibit.

The construction crews didn't begin work on any of Tomorrowland until six months into the project, meaning few were finished come Opening Day. The rest were unveiled, as ready, throughout the park's first year. Two weeks before opening, Walt proposed a *20,000 Leagues Under the Sea* exhibit. Workers tracked down many of the film's props and frantically raced to rebuild the actual mechanical squid which had been hacked to shreds in the movie. With just days until the park's unveiling, Walt decided he wanted the castle drawbridge to be lowered for the first pint-sized patrons to run across into Fantasyland. His men worked feverishly to find and install a motor on the stationary drawbridge.

For a place that would become a model of precision and perfection, Disneyland got off to a rocky start. Come Opening Day, eighteen attractions were deemed "ready," most perhaps prematurely. They sent 11,000 passes for the invitation-only premiere to people who worked on the park, their families, studio employees, the press, dignitaries, suppliers and officials of companies sponsoring exhibits. At first, the park feared few would show up and the live

TV coverage on Walt's own show would expose a deserted Disney-land. Fears of a low turnout vanished quickly, though, when people began lining up at the gate at 2:00 a.m. With the new freeway not yet reaching Harbor Boulevard, traffic backed up bumper to bumper for seven miles along two lane surface roads. The simple invitation-only tickets were so easily duplicated that people printed up thousands of forgeries. The staff also caught a man who had folded a ladder over the fence on the back side of the park and was letting people in for $5 apiece. The official attendance count was 28,154. No one was ready for that.

Every other attraction broke down under the press of the huge crowds. A power outage put the brakes to Mr. Toad's Wild Ride. Long, slow moving lines snaked in front of the few operational attractions and restrooms. Water washed up on the deck of the overcrowded Mark Twain Steamboat. It was impossible to find shade, a place to sit down or a drinking fountain. Guests staggered into First Aid, gasping for a cup of water. Others stumbled over ABC's cables and were annoyingly roped off from large areas needed by the TV crews. And as the sun grew hotter, tempers flared.

The carousel had been positioned so close to the castle, the entrance became an instant bottleneck. Some people decided to just climb over the carousel's chain fencing instead of waiting in line, and it, too, had to be shut down. But not before actors James Mason and Jeff Chandler got into a fight over a horse to see whose child would be one of the first riders.

Recalled one longtime employee, "There were two doors to inside the castle and one was left unlocked, so we had people climbing up into the castle thinking it was an attraction. But it was just superstructure in there. I've always wondered how no one got killed."

The hot sun also didn't help the asphalt on Main Street, which had been poured at 6:30 that morning. Disneyland's first female visitors made their grand entrance... and found their spiked heels sinking into the street. Some were forced to walk right out of their shoes.

Restaurants and refreshment stands ran out of food and drinks. When dishwashing machines broke down at the Red Wagon Inn,

diners had to eat off paper plates. A window fell out of the upper
deck of the Mark Twain onto a man's head. Anaheim's city manager Keith Murdoch thought it was such a mess he went home and
watched the debacle on television.

Unfortunately, the live telecast did little to mask the madness. It
only added a few miscues of its own. The 90-minute dedication
was filmed live by 22 cameras, making it the largest live TV show
to that day in terms of equipment and technicians. Hosts Art Linkletter, Bob Cummings and Ronald Reagan provided the commen-
tary. Walt Disney was joined by California Governor Goodwin
Knight for the official dedication.

Cameras captured Frank Sinatra and Sammy Davis, Jr., driving
Autopia cars, Jerry Colonna at the helm of a Casey Jr. circus train,

BLACK & WHITE. Walt Disney (left to right) with unnamed woman
accepts gift of black and white swans for his castle moat from Dore
Schary, head of MGM Studios, and director Mervyn LeRoy soon before
the opening of Disneyland. (mid-1955) *Courtesy Anaheim Public Library.*

Alan Young in a twirling teacup and Danny Thomas on a horseless carriage. Among the many other celebrities on hand were Kirk Douglas, Eve Arden, Maureen O'Hara, Gale Storm, Roy Rogers, Dale Evans, Lana Turner, Eddie Fisher, Debbie Reynolds, Marjorie Main, Bonita Granville, Don Defore, Disney's soon-to-be-famous Mouseketeers, Disneyland Hotel owner Jack Wrather and Walter Knott, founder of the competing Knott's Berry Farm.

For Fantasyland's unveiling, the castle's drawbridge was lowered for the first and last time and hordes of youngsters raced across, led by characters in primitive costumes that were supposed to look like Mickey Mouse, Donald Duck and others. From there, the flood gates also opened for on-camera chaos.

To open Frontierland, Fess Parker in character as national TV hero Davy Crockett galloped on screen before the announcer had a chance to introduce him. An off-camera technician misfired his gun and Parker thought it was his cue. Then someone accidentally turned on the sprinklers and soaked Parker, sidekick Buddy Ebsen and their steeds.

Art Linkletter called upon actress Irene Dunne to christen the Mark Twain with a bottle containing waters culled from the great rivers of the country. "My, it's listing," she noted, as a big crowd stormed on board the vessel. Dunne mistakenly called Linkletter "Walt" and Art referred to the bottle's contents as coming from "the rivers of the world – of America, that is!"

As the release of white doves signaled the opening of Tomorrowland, Bob Cummings noted, "Here in Disneyland, the year is 18 – er 1986, 1986, that's way ahead!"

Coordinating jumps between the 22 cameras wasn't any easier. Linkletter tried to cue Cummings at one point, announcing, "Right now Bob Cummings is at the – uh – where is he?" When Bob tried to return the spotlight, Art had lost his mike. As Linkletter frantically searched for a microphone in front of Mr. Toad's Wild Ride, Cummings provided the play-by-play: "He looks all confused. There's been something wrong here – just for an instant!" When Linkletter finally found his mike, he nervously introduced Captain Hook and his pirate crew as "Captain Crew."

Even Walt wasn't safe from the screw-ups. He stopped a speech in mid-sentence to begin talking to an off-camera technician.

Realizing he actually was on camera, he moaned, "I thought I got a signal!"

Disney was kept so occupied in preparations and rehearsals and filming, rushing from TV location to TV location, that he wasn't fully aware of the day's chaos. He got the news from the morning papers. Despite a few rave reviews, most headlines blasted: "Walt's Dream a Nitemare," "Park Can't Handle Opening Day Crush," "Disneyland Opens Amid Traffic Jams, Confusion," "Disneyland Shatters Illusion" and "Gripes Tarnish Disneyland's Glitter." Critics proclaimed the park "Disney's Folly" and "a Hollywood spectacular... a spectacular failure."

One harshly critical reporter was convinced the conspicuous shortage of drinking fountains was a devious ploy to sell more soda. In truth, a plumber's strike had forced the park to choose between building water fountains or restrooms. "People can buy Pepsi-Cola," Walt huffed. "But they can't pee in the street."

Many newspapers crabbed that Disneyland had given preferential treatment to television, so the park spent the next several months going out of its way giving personal tours for newspaper reporters.

Opening Day became known as "Black Sunday." But the following day, the first open to the general public, wasn't much brighter. Equally overflow crowds again packed the park. Fantasyland had to be closed because of a gas leak. Since the Mark Twain had no set load limits, operators kept waving on guests until the deck neared the water line. During one trip along the sparsely vegetated river route, the ship almost capsized as passengers stampeded from one side to the other to view the riverbanks' few attractions. Immediately, the park established maximum capacities, which are still in effect today.

The heavy crowds continued... for a month. In the last fifteen days of August a record heat wave hit and attendance evaporated. When temperatures finally cooled, the crowds remained light. People were just used to staying at home during the winter.

Those first few winters, no one knew if the park was going to make it. "In the beginning, we owed everybody," recalled old-timer Van France. "We had no money. There was always a rush from the Main Gate to the bank to meet the payroll. Management had to hold their paychecks. Everybody was on a week to week contract because nobody knew how long the damn thing was gonna last."

Everyone wanted so badly for Walt's wonderland to work, they gave it their all. "I ran my ass off," said one veteran. "I lost fifteen pounds in the first sixty days. You never walked; you got behind the scenes and you ran. There was always a fire to put out. I went fourteen months straight without a day off."

One employee worked so many late nights that his wife was convinced he was having an affair.

Walt's solution wasn't to slow down. It was to make the park better and better, to improve, to add, to refine. For that first Christmas, he wanted a circus. His staff protested, arguing that no one would spend two hours of their day at Disneyland sitting still, watching a circus. Walt won out, by persuading his studio to buy a huge red-and-white-striped tent, old wagon and other props to eventually make a circus film, *Toby Tyler* or *Ten Weeks in a Circus* – but in the meantime use them at the park. They set the tent up with a separate entrance to the left of the Main Gate and put a heating system and three rings inside.

Scheduled for a six week run, the "Mickey Mouse Club Circus" opened on Thanksgiving Day 1955, heralded by a circus parade down Main Street. But this wasn't to be the Greatest Show on Earth. It was doomed from the first performance. During the parade, a black panther grabbed the paw of a tiger in the next cage and chewed it off. When the procession of circus wagons entered the big top for the first performance, the second vehicle clipped one of the tent pegs and an entire section of the roof caved in. During the trapeze act, a well endowed artist's halter strap broke and her top fell. And since she had to hold onto the trapeze, there wasn't much she could do about it. Finally, two llamas got loose and ran through the bleachers. The crew chased them down the railroad track and captured them at the Main Street Station. Walt, sitting in the front row with the Mouseketeers, buried his face in his hands.

Then there were the temperamental camels, who loved to spit, and the surly circus performers, whose cussing, drinking and gambling proved quite un-Disneylike. Worst of all, no one cared.

There were more than 2,000 seats, but no performance filled even a fourth of them. The big top became Disneyland's biggest flop.

Not discouraged, Walt was determined to make Disneyland all that he had dreamed. By its first full summer, he had brought in rafts to take guests across the Rivers of America to Tom Sawyer Island and turned the island into a wilderness playground where kids could run wild. Frontierland also received a Mine Train ride and canoes that guests themselves paddled, led by Indian guides. He linked Fantasyland and Tomorrowland with a Skyway aerial tram system. He transformed the Canal Boats of the World, not much more than a boat tour of mud banks, into Storybook Land, by filling up the shores with miniature homes and buildings from famous Disney cartoons.

The next year the inside of Sleeping Beauty Castle was opened up to the public. Previously there were just beams and supports inside where employees would often sneak to enjoy their lunch in the top of the castle. The Imagineers turned the cramped quarters into a walk-through diorama with scenes from *Sleeping Beauty*.

Besides constantly breaking down, the Phantom Boats were impractical because each two-guest boat required a separate operator. Guest-driven Motor Boats replaced them. The sleek Viewliner train made its debut in Tomorrowland, but spent a lot of time down as well because its Corvette engines ran too hot. More impressive was the Monsanto House of the Future, a five room cantilever plastic house. The building and all the furnishings were made entirely of plastic. The visionary walk-through exhibit offered a look at a video telephone, large screen TV and a refrigeration unit that lowered out of ceiling. "The most talked about invention was the microwave oven," said one attendant. "Nobody believed you could bake a potato in three minutes."

The home was also incredibly durable. The demolition crew tried to tear it down nine years later to replace the outdated-looking structure with landscaping, and couldn't. When the wrecking ball hit it, it kept bouncing off. The workers finally had to take a blow torch to it and cut it into sections to haul it away.

One of Walt's directives was that the park never be complete, that it be constantly changing and expanding. He soon added the Sailing Ship Columbia to the Rivers of America, an Alice in Wonderland dark ride to Fantasyland and a diorama of the Grand Canyon to the Disneyland Railroad trip. Come 1959, he finally focused on the long-neglected Tomorrowland, introducing America's first daily operating Monorail system, the Voyage through Liquid Space submarine journey and a bobsled ride through a recreation of the famed Matterhorn. Walt had become so fascinated with the Swiss peak, he made a movie about it, *The Third Man on the Mountain*, and then built his own one-one hundredth scale reproduction on the site of a small wooded hill known as Lookout Mountain.

In 1960 Disneyland unveiled perhaps its most innovative and versatile invention. Walt had wanted to animate three-dimensional figures the way he'd animated cartoon characters in the movies. The Imagineers devised computer-programmed figures combining sound, animation and electronics: audio-animatronics. The first models were placed along the Mine Train and pack mule trail. Their Nature's Wonderland included 204 animals, birds and reptiles – coyotes that howled, elk stags that locked antlers in battle, bears that snatched fish that popped from their river, beavers that swam, slapped their tails and built dams. The technology was reused and refined for more lifelike characters and realistic movement in more than a dozen later attractions, such as Great Moments with Mr. Lincoln and the Pirates of the Caribbean.

Two years later, the Enchanted Tiki Room showcased 225 audio-animatronic birds, flowers, plants and fountains in a Polynesian musical show. To attract attention to the new Tiki Room, audio-animatronic parrot prototype José was perched above the Tiki Room, yelling, "Stop walking while I'm squawking!" Unfortunately, crowds would just stop to stare at the bird and clog up the Adventureland entrance, so he had to be moved. He's now on display in the Main Street Opera House. For the Adventureland expansion, they also added a second shooting gallery, improved the Jungle Cruise and built a 70-foot-high recreation of the Swiss Family Treehouse.

In 1961, the Flying Saucers landed at Disneyland. The single-rider hovercrafts whisked across an area with an intricate system of air pressure valves and motors beneath the deck. The jets of air from below propelled the saucers and riders clumsily steered by leaning, creating a combination of bumper cars and Air Hockey.

The ride was ingenious but not very practical. The intricate system of valves kept losing pressure and constantly broke down. At least you could always see it coming: the saucers would all start bouncing up and down, emit a series of woofing noises then a rattling sonic boom, and fall to the deck as everything suddenly turned off. It also couldn't be operated in bad weather because the air jets whipped the rain up into a hurricane.

Safety was another concern. Guests had to step between the awkward, heavy wooden saucers and across to a raised platform. Operators were stationed on long raised booms that swept across the blue floor to gather the crafts. "One night we were standing on the moving boom and a guy slipped," recalled an attendant. "His pole fell in one of the air valve holes and the boom sheared it off in nothing flat. Fortunately it wasn't his leg. We were very shaky men standing on that boom."

The attraction took up a lot of space and was very low in capacity. Guests would wait 90 minutes for a 90-second ride – if it didn't break down. The saucers were finally discarded in 1966 to clear the way for an all new, higher capacity Tomorrowland.

Disney could be equally creative in financing his park. When it was first under construction, he had neither the money nor the know-how to build and operate all the diverse exhibits, shops and restaurants. Corporations and entrepreneurs were invited in as lessees to run individual concessions, from the biggest restaurants down to the balloon salesmen. And over the years, one by one, the Disney company took over each concession. Large companies could also sponsor attractions without actually having to operate them. Richfield for the Autopia, Dole for the Tiki Room, Chicken of the Sea for the pirate ship restaurant, Pepsi-Cola for the Golden Horseshoe, Aunt Jemima for the pancake house.

For the 1964-65 World's Fair in New York, Walt agreed to design and produce four exhibits, then ended up getting the sponsors to then move them after the fair to become attractions at Disneyland. Ford Motor Co. sponsored a "Magic Skyway" trip showing man's development from prehistoric to modern times. General

YESTERDAYLAND. Tomorrowland before the major overhaul. Note the Flying Saucers (lower left), cross-shaped House of the Future (top left), TWA rocket and Flight Circle (center). (April 13, 1965) *Courtesy Anaheim Public Library.*

Electric's "Progressland" was a circular theater of seats that rotated around a series of stationary stages, each depicting the progress of the American home and electrical appliances. In the state of Illinois' "Great Moments with Mr. Lincoln," an audio-animatronic Abe delivered excerpts from the president's famous speeches. Pepsi-Cola's "It's a Small World" took boats past audio-animatronic dolls of the world singing the title tune in their own language. Over the following three summers, Mr. Lincoln was moved to the Opera House, Small World to the far end of Fantasyland, "Progressland" as the Carousel of Progress to Tomorrowland and the dinosaurs from "Magic Skyway" to a diorama viewed from the Disneyland Railroad.

By this time, Disneyland's growing, glowing reputation was as much as anything attributable to Walt's leadership. He was never content to sit still. In the park's first years, when the Jungle Cruise was the only maximum capacity ride, Walt wanted to extend the ride by a few minutes. Others disagreed because it would hurt capacity. "You didn't hear me," he answered. "I said extend the ride."

Other times, experiments didn't work. He had one Storybook Land boat redesigned so instead of guests sitting around the perimeter of the ship, the seats faced forward, with the hostess in front. Unfortunately, only the front row would hear her spiel and during loading, the first guests moved all the way to the far end of the row, tipping the boat up away from the dock. The old seats were soon reinstalled.

Just the same, Walt was a perfectionist. He set firm deadlines, but if an attraction wasn't ready, it didn't open. The day the Swiss Family Treehouse was to open, he wouldn't allow it. "Tear it down!" he fumed. "I asked for a tree. You gave me a bush!" They had to delay the grand opening to remodel the leaves and limbs more to his liking.

The day before the Blue Bayou restaurant was to open its doors, Walt entertained 150 reporters at a big press party. Following dinner at the French Market, he planned on taking the group to the scenic Blue Bayou for dessert. The food was all ordered, the staff trained and in place. But Walt didn't like the lighting. The Blue Bayou remained closed for months.

The amazing thing is Disneyland wasn't all Disney did. He simultaneously had dozens of important projects going on, movies, TV series, another park in Florida. Still, he was able to give each 100 percent. His energy seemed limitless. Sometimes he worked late, then spent the night in his apartment over the Main Street Fire Station. The first employees to arrive in the morning might find little notes of instructions from Walt – or even an early-rising Walt back walking the park in his bathrobe. He walked the grounds often, watching the crowds, evaluating the tiniest details. He seemed to instinctively sense what would work and what wouldn't and was unafraid to test his hunches. And he was a master at assembling the talent to make it work.

Then on December 15, 1966, the park received a call from the studio. Walt Disney was dead. Time seemed to stop. But at Disneyland things would never be the same. Leadership passed to Walt's elder brother, Roy, then after Roy's death in 1971, to a four-man council of family members and old-timers. They were competent but cautious. Don't worry, they promised, nothing will be different. That was the problem.

For the first few years after Walt, there were still enough projects already begun under him to keep the Imagineers busy. While Disney reportedly detested its seeming celebration of raping and pillaging, the Pirates of the Caribbean opened two months after his death. The boat trip past audio-animatronic buccaneers became the most popular attraction in the park. That summer Tomorrowland shed its image as Yesterdayland, with the addition of the People Mover continuously moving tramway, redesigned Rocket Jets, Carousel of Progress, Flight to the Moon's new Mission Control center staffed by audio-animatronic technicians, and Monsanto's Adventure through Inner Space, showing what it's like to shrink and travel through a molecule. In 1969, a light-hearted Haunted Mansion, on the drawing boards since the Fifties, was finally opened.

The new leadership would always ask itself, "What would Walt have done?" In fact, one of their first new attractions was the "Walt Disney Story," a retrospective on the creator's career which displaced Mr. Lincoln in the Opera House. The public, though, was furious and demanded Abe be returned. Disneyland relented, combining the two shows in one building. A similar controversy erupted sixteen years later when Disneyland considered replacing Mr. Lincoln with the Muppets.

Mostly, the council looked to rework what they had done before. In 1972, they displaced the Indian Village with Bear Country, a forgettable extension of Frontierland. Its centerpiece was the Country Bear Jamboree, a Tiki Room-type show with audio-animatronic bears instead of birds. Carousel of Progress was moved to Walt Disney World, and in its place Disneyland opened America Sings, which traced the history of music instead of the history of electrici-

1. Main Gate
T. Train Station
2. City Hall
3. Fire Station
4. Town Square
5. Great Moments with Mr. Lincoln
6. First Aid
7. Plaza (Hub)
8. Tiki Room
9. Jungle Cruise
10. Swiss Family Treehouse
11. Indiana Jones Adventure
12. Pirates of the Caribbean
13. Club 33
14. Haunted Mansion
15. Splash Mountain
16. Country Bear Playhouse
17. Davy Crockett Explorer Canoes
18. Mike Fink Keel Boats
19. Rafts to Tom Sawyer Island
20. Tom Sawyer Island
21. Mark Twain/ Sailing Ship Columbia
22. Golden Horseshoe Jamboree
23. Frontierland Shootin' Arcade
24. Big Thunder Mountain Railroad
25. Big Thunder Ranch
26. Skyway (former site)
27. Casey Jr. Circus Train
28. Dumbo the Flying Elephant

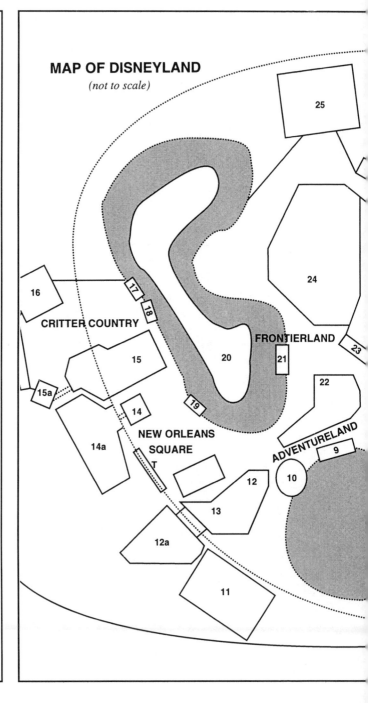

MAP OF DISNEYLAND
(not to scale)

CRITTER COUNTRY

FRONTIERLAND

ADVENTURELAND

NEW ORLEANS
SQUARE

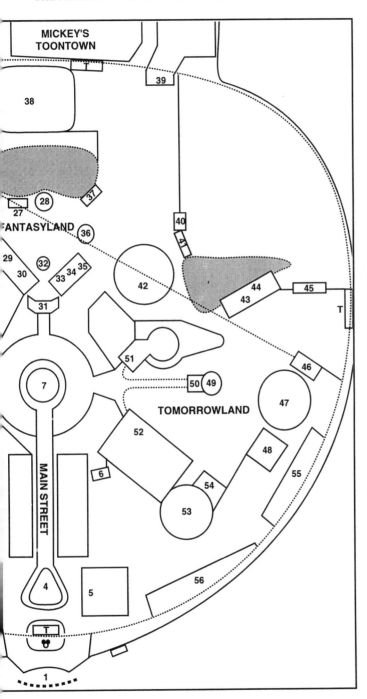

29. Pinocchio's Daring Journey
30. Snow White's Scary Adventures
31. Sleeping Beauty Castle
32. King Arthur Carrousel
33. Peter Pan's Flight
34. Mr. Toad's Wild Ride
35. Alice in Wonderland
36. Mad Tea Party
37. Storybook Land Canal Boats
38. Videopolis
39. It's a Small World
40. Motor Boats (former site)
41. Fantasyland Autopia
42. Matterhorn Bobsleds
43. Monorail
44. Submarine Voyage
45. Tomorrowland Autopia
46. Skyway (former site)
47. America Sings (former site)
48. Mission to Mars (former site)
49. Rocket Jets
50. People Mover
51. Circle-Vision
52. Star Tours
53. Space Mountain
54. Magic Eye Theater (Captain E-O)
55. Grand Canyon Diorama
56. Primeval World Diorama

ty. Flight to the Moon was minimally revamped into Mission to Mars.

Then, for the first time, Disneyland began looking at what was successful at competing parks. The rage in the amusement park industry in the mid-1970s was high speed roller coasters, so Disneyland came out with Space Mountain in 1977, a redesigned bobsled trip through the Matterhorn with an added Abominable Snowman in 1978, and Big Thunder Mountain Railroad in 1979. They didn't introduce a single new attraction for four years, until they spruced up Fantasyland, with reworked dark rides, including a lackluster Pinocchio's Daring Journey, and stylish new architecture, supposedly based on how Walt had always wanted the area to look.

Creatively and financially, the Disney company was stagnating. By 1984, attendance at Disneyland had been slipping for five consecutive years and the movie studio had become a joke in Hollywood. But with all its valuable yet underused and unused film

REFANTASIZING. In completely overhauling Fantasyland, the old carnival look gave way to a classic European motif. (Early 1983) *Photo by Ray Haller.*

library, characters and property, undervalued Disney suddenly became the target of hostile takeover attempts. Wall Street raiders could conceivably break up the company and sell off its separate parts for a quick return on their investment. Millions of shares of stock and hundreds of millions of dollars quickly changed hands between investors and when the dust settled, the old leadership had been ousted and a new team moved in, bubbling with fresh ideas to maximize profits. Disney's new chairman and chief executive officer, Michael Eisner, had been president of Paramount Pictures; president and chief operating officer Frank Wells was former co-chairman at Warner Bros.

Creativity was back. It took them fifteen weeks to transform a meadow area behind Fantasyland into Videopolis, a state-of-the-art open air amphitheater with three dance floors, stage and 1,500 seats. They teamed with movie producer George Lucas, director Francis Ford Coppola and pop singer Michael Jackson for the 70mm, 3-D rock adventure *Captain E-O*. The next year Lucas combined his *Star Wars* characters with space program flight simulator technology for Star Tours. For the grand premieres of both Captain E-O and Star Tours, Disneyland stayed open for sixty straight hours.

But, just as in the days of Walt, high energy and ambition created more room for error. Walt vowed never to have a Ferris wheel at Disneyland, but for a State Fair Days promotion starting in 1985, a Ferris wheel was placed in the middle of the hub, the center of the park. Midway games overran Town Square. They were profitable but the carnival atmosphere detracted from the innocence of Main Street USA. And the silly State Fair parade featured a cast of dancing tomatoes, carrots and broccoli.

In some ways, fresh thinking meant making old mistakes twice. Disney's circus bombed in 1955, but Circus Fantasy returned to town in 1986, anyway. Instead of a separate big top, they set up a net over Main Street and the acts were performed throughout the park, introduced by a booming voice over the park PA. "The... Globe... of... Death!" "The... Wheel... of... Destiny!" Once again, the guests didn't seem overly enamored with the circus theme, but the promotion was reused the next two years.

In 1989, Splash Mountain opened in Critter Country (formerly

Bear Country), fusing the world's steepest log flume ride with a *Song of the South*-inspired dark ride. They reused many of the audio-animatronic characters from the shutdown America Sings, even though some are quite out of place in the Old South bayou setting. Nevertheless, the project was plagued by cost over-runs and time delays. Its price tag tripled to over $80 million and its official opening was postponed for eight months to redesign the flume and boats so riders wouldn't get completely drenched.

In 1992, Disneyland's Live Entertainment division transformed the Rivers of America into the stage for Fantasmic!, a live action, laser, dancing waters, fireworks show, with incredible effects like flames leaping up from the water and movies shown on walls of water and mist. Stunning and innovative, the attraction convinced hordes to ignore the recession and visit Disneyland.

Eight months later brought Mickey's Toontown, a cramped but clever interactive land primarily for children built beyond Small World. In 1995 the park added the $100 million Indiana Jones Adventure, featuring vehicles rigged with "enhanced motion systems" to simulate being out of control. And in 1998 Tomorrowland was revamped yet again, most notably by repainting the whole area and replacing the PeopleMover with the high-speed Rocket Rods.

Eisner and Wells revitalized the entire Disney Company – movies, TV stations, magazines, video cassettes, TV series, retail shops. They brought the Disney name and characters into the Image-Is-Everything Nineties, and profits skyrocketed company-wide. But the renaissance has had its price. In 1985, for the new leadership's first summer, Disneyland planned a big gift giveaway. To mark its thirtieth anniversary, the park would give every thirtieth guest through the turnstiles a present, which might be anything from a small souvenir to a new car. A philosophical debate arose between newcomer and old guard over whether or not such an obvious ploy was Disneylike. It was settled when the promotion was an inordinate success. Giveaways would be back the next year and the next and the next.

Since 1984 admission prices have been raised *twenty* times, more than tripling. Passport prices were hiked six times in Eisner's first three years, from $13 to $21.50. "The old management style was to let the customer leave with money," said one disillusioned cast member. "The new style is take what you can get from them. Don't let them leave with anything."

With Walt, the show was always number one. Even when attendance was light, he had vendors leave out a full stand of popcorn. Now there's an Early Bird Special travel package with the Disneyland Hotel. Guests get to enter the park a couple hours before it officially opens, even though maintenance is still underway. Visitors might see workers painting Main Street or jackhammering in Tomorrowland. "Show for Dough," the old-timers call it.

The key word is marketing. There's constantly filming going on in the park, of TV talk shows, game shows, specials and commercials. And it's continually dressed up for some gimmicky promotion – State Fair Days, Circus Fantasy, Blast to the Past, Party Gras, Disney Afternoon Live.

"You can never visit the park when there's not a promotion," bemoaned one employee. "It's one promotion after another, dovetailed into each other. A favorite thing for me was just being able

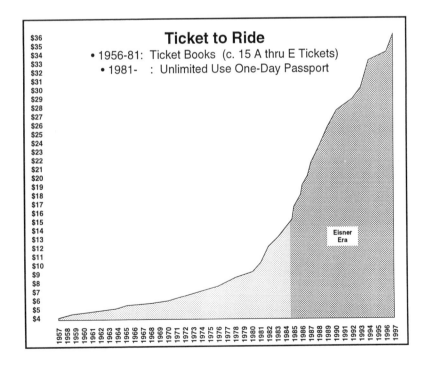

Ticket to Ride
• 1956-81: Ticket Books (c. 15 A thru E Tickets)
• 1981- : Unlimited Use One-Day Passport

Eisner Era

to see Disneyland without anything else, the temporary structures, all the glitz. People who have never been there before may never get to see it that way. There was a time when you looked forward to the summer because of the Electrical Parade. It was a summer event. It's April and they've already got it running."

The goal doesn't seem to be creating happiness, but making money by creating happiness. It's a business. An entertainment business. A capital-producing, bottom line-fixated arm of a corporate entity, that was once a labor of love.

2

Underground Disneyland

AS innocent as it seems, there's more to this stage than rides and restaurants and souvenir stores. From planning to performance, Disneyland is a complex show designed to manipulate guests both superficially and subconsciously. The Imagineers have created their own reality, covered by a peacefulness you can almost breathe. Just walking down Main Street makes you feel good. The crowds can be the same people who an hour before cut you off on the freeway, yet now you feel comfortable, safe.

It's all orchestrated. There was never a real Main Street like Disneyland's. This is the way Main Street should have been. Music is everywhere. Inconspicuous vents in front of the Candy Palace pump out the scent of vanilla or, at Christmastime, peppermint. Walt refused to allow sharp 90-degree corners on the Main Street sidewalks, too rigid, too threatening. All curbs were to be rounded at the corners. Columns on the Main Street buildings are all thin, a subliminal assurance of safety and confidence, unlike buildings fortified with thick columns to withstand attack.

To achieve intimacy, the buildings' creators employed a set design technique called forced perspective. Along Main Street the first floors are 9/10 scale, the second floors are 7/8 and the third 5/8. The decreasing heights make the shops appear taller than they really are, yet still cozy. The Sleeping Beauty Castle uses the same effect, its stones large at the base and increasingly smaller up high. On the Matterhorn, trees and shrubs halfway up are smaller than those at the base. The Mark Twain, Disneyland Railroad and Main Street vehicles are all 5/8 scale, and other structures were built in various scales based on what looked most effective to the designers.

The Imagineers have created an entire world of the make believe. They've built replica steam engines and stern wheelers, down to the most minute detail. Few of the Main Street shops have real second stories; most upper floors are just false fronts with an enclosed catwalk behind so maintenance can get to and security can peek through the upper windows. Splash Mountain looks just as real, but was built using a clay-like substance called "mud." All boulders, mountainsides, trees and mushrooms – even "wooden" boats, houses, signs and mailboxes – are actually hand-sculpted and painted mud.

For Mickey's Toontown, the Imagineers wanted the opposite effect. All the buildings had to look like they were in a cartoon, colorful, curvy, off-kilter. They had to be structurally sound, but without any straight lines. So the designers built traditional square structures and applied a clothing of plaster over them. European craftsmen who had worked on EuroDisneyland were brought in to hand-sculpt and paint the plaster into cartoon walls that curve up to three feet from the inner walls.

Even Disneyland's in-house painting department isn't made up of mere painters. They're more like artists, skilled professionals who use paint to transform a sheet of plywood into stone, gold or bark.

To lend authenticity, some of the props are genuine artifacts. The cannons in Town Square are actual French cannons used by the French Army in the Nineteenth Century. The 150-year-old street lamps on Main Street were purchased in Baltimore for three cents a pound. The Penny Arcade's nickelodeons and hand-cranked Mutascopes are authentic turn-of-the-century amusement devices. The Carrousel horses are all about 100 years old, each hand-carved and painted with no two exactly alike. The Swiss Family Treehouse is furnished with both real antiques (muskets, an

Eighteenth Century barometer, ship's wheel, sewing basket) and an organ, beds, tables and bookshelves built by the Disney crew.

In the Haunted Mansion, the organ in the ballroom is the same one used in the movie *20,000 Leagues Under the Sea*. The steam engine on display in the Big Thunder Mountain waiting area was used in the movie *Hot Lead, Cold Feet*. This bullpen area is also decorated with other authentic mining equipment from the 1800s, a stampmill, compressor, cog well, ore car, ore bucket, drill press and giant winch motor.

Due to space limitations, the Imagineers have had to get clever when adding new rides and build them around existing attractions. Much of Alice in Wonderland was built in 1958 over the single-story Mr. Toad's Wild Ride. The Submarine Voyage required a large show building to create lighting effects and house the mechanics of its animated creatures. Designers constructed the building under a section of the neighboring Autopia and land-scaped the roof, so now there are caverns for the submarines below and a forest above for the car ride.

The Pirates of the Caribbean required two massive show build-ings, but there wasn't enough room inside the twelve-foot berm. So, the second building was built outside the berm. The ride begins in the bayou section, then quickly drops below sea level to propel the boats under the railroad tracks outside and along their way through the main show building. They duplicated the tech-nique for the Haunted Mansion, using elevators to lower guests to the Doom Buggies below, which carry them under the berm, through the larger show building and drop them off at an escalator at the ride's end.

Fantasmic! required a huge nighttime amphitheater, including movie projectors, speakers, extensive lighting facilities, 30-foot-tall props, dressing rooms, fog machines, fireworks firing pads and a control room filled with high-tech computers. Only by day it all had to look like regular old, uncluttered Frontierland.

Construction crews set up green fences around the area and went to work. First, they drained the Rivers of America and dug down three stories to build a subterranean basement. Over it, they built a new stage and a Cider Mill, the technological nerve center, housing the lasers, sound system, 70mm projectors, hydraulic lifts and fog machine. A backstage marina was built for the barges used in the show. They lined the river bottom with a half-mile of natural gas tubing to create the fire effects. Speaker equipment was hidden in mock rocks, buildings and lampposts throughout the viewing area to lend a surround-sound effect. The island's Fort Wilderness is used as a backstage dressing room for the 51 performers to change into the 341 waterproof costumes. The show is controlled from a computer panel in a little room above Pirates of the Caribbean. And the 40-foot-tall lighting towers rise out from below the pavement.

The park has been equally creative and deceptive in paying tribute to the people who have helped put the place together. A movie has screen credits, but Disneyland has window credits. The names of Disney VIP's are affixed in gold leaf lettering to the second story windows above the Main Street shops. Many of the names were put up when the park first opened, as a thanks to those who helped build it. Paint Department head Larry Smith was billed as proprietor of a painting and paperhanging business, prominent designers as representatives of the Plaza School of Art, and so on. As the years passed, other names were added and the tradition was repeated above Walt Disney World's Main Street.

Names of other important Disneylanders are stenciled on crates floating in the Jungle Cruise river, boxes on the Mark Twain dock and kegs at Big Thunder Railroad. On Star Tours, designers' initials and telephone extensions are printed on the industrial pipes lining the walls near the entrance. Others who worked on the ride have their initials and birthdates on labels on baskets moving robot parts along an overhead conveyance system. Imagineers who worked on the Pirates of the Caribbean were used as the face models for the audio-animatronic figures.

Walt and Roy's initials are ornately entwined into a wrought iron rail that surrounds the balcony in front of the Disney Gallery. A placard with the Disney coat-of-arms is positioned inside the Sleeping Beauty Castle archway. The Disney "D" can also be found on the harness of the Main Street trolley horse.

The land-line telegraphy signal tapping out of the telegraph office at the Frontierland Train Station transmits Walt's opening day dedication speech. But that's just one of many links with the past. Artifacts from long-gone attractions live on in new settings. The huge microscope from Adventure through Inner Space appears in one of the opening shots of the Star Tours presentation. The Indian Burial Ground from the old Indian Village was relocated to the far end of Tom Sawyer Island. The abandoned rail track and tunnels between Big Thunder Mountain and the Rivers of America are about all that remains of the old Mine Train route. The Big Thunderscape still features the jumping fish from the Mine Train and the western store facades from the pack mule rides. Part of the original mule trail still exists in the hills of Frontierland. Some of the cannons and the rigging on the pirate ship in Peter Pan's Flight once stood aboard the old Chicken of the Sea vessel.

Disneyland is a marvel, but not all their animals are audio-animatronic. When not working their four-hours-a-day, four-days-a-week schedule, the Belgian horses that pull the streetcars were once housed in a backstage Pony Farm. In 1986, they were moved to Big Thunder Ranch, a petting zoo-type area with goats, pigs, even a cow with a Mickey Mouse-shaped spot on its side. But over the years other wild beasts have roamed the Magic Kingdom, usually unbeknownst to the visitors.

The original plans called for real wild animals to inhabit the Jungle Cruise, but zoologists convinced Walt that the beasts would probably be asleep during park operating hours. Instead, the park rented live alligators from the old Buena Park Alligator Farm, once a tiny tourist attraction near Knott's Berry Farm. The three-foot-long reptiles were placed in chicken-wire pens near the Jungle Cruise entrance to impress the people waiting in line. But since alligators make a hissing noise, many guests thought they were battery-operated and that the mechanical ones along the river were real. Children would pelt the captive creatures with popcorn and small rubber gators from the adjacent souvenir stand, and the kernels and green rubber would stick between the reptiles' teeth.

Every so often an alligator broke loose from its pen and slipped into the lagoon. Disneyland immediately called the Alligator Farm handler, who came down, stood on the dock and made funny noises with his throat, which would lure back the wayward gator. But, in the meantime, if a boat got hung up, the divers who were supposed to get them back on track would be a little hesitant knowing a real alligator was lurking somewhere out there. Tired of the alligators continually getting loose and afraid they were going to choke to death on hand-outs, management finally returned the creatures to the farm.

During its first summers, the park loaded up the Rivers of America with thousands of fish and had a red-haired, freckle-faced Tom Sawyer hand out worms, hooks and fishing poles. The fishing finally came to an end out of fear that someone might hook a cat-fish and then try to eat it.

Today the river is home to a large collection of ducks. It's pretty easy work for the birds, although a few have lost their lives in the tubes that make a section of the river look like rapids. The tubes pull water in one end and force it out the other. Unfortunate fowls have also been sucked in, only to be found with just their feathered rears sticking out into the air. When Fantasmic! was first intro-duced, rumors circulated that ducks were getting fried alive by the nightly flames that leap from the river as part of the show. Disney-land quickly dispelled the stories. It seems the water becomes so turbulent during the show that all the ducks are safely scared away well before the fiery finale.

The original black and white swans in the Sleeping Beauty Castle moat were gifts to Walt from movie producer Mervyn LeRoy. Unfortunately, the birds had bad tempers and were deter-mined to escape. They had to be penned in with a short wire fence. But that didn't stop guests from going down to try to pet them – and getting snapped at. When the first swans died off, Disneyland began renting replacements, getting a fresh batch every six months. Now the park owns its own moat team.

Over the years, the vegetation throughout the Jungle Cruise has thickened into a real jungle, attracting an assortment of creepy, crawling insects. To make the brush safe for operators and mainte-nance men who have to go behind the scenes, pistol-packing Jungle Cruise drivers used to go on Spider Patrol. "The guns we used were Smith & Wesson 48's loaded with Styrofoam-wadded plastic shells," recounted one hunter. "We'd triple and quadruple-load BB pellets from the Adventureland Shooting Gallery and pack 'em in the shells. When the crowds were low, we'd take out the maintenance skiff and go pick off garden spiders. They must have been at least four inches in diameter and we'd blow them out of their nests."

Insects are bad enough backstage, but worse if they come and bother the guests. Flies don't belong in Disneyland. On hot summer days, the Pony Farm behind Fantasyland would begin to smell like, well, a farm. A strong breeze might start blowing in towards Fantasyland, and it would take the flies with it. Disneyland solved its fly problem by bringing in thousands more flies. But these were special flies, tiny, almost invisible ones that eat the larvae of larger flies. Within days, there were no flies in sight, at least not any big enough to see.

But the worst of the animal intruders were the rats that invaded Tom Sawyer Island in the late Sixties. They were big, ugly rodents that usually came out at night to feast on the popcorn, potato chips and other treats guests had dropped behind. One night while closing up the island snack shop, the girls accidentally locked themselves in and froze in terror as rats slowly started creeping out of the darkened woodwork. The rats scurried by the girls' feet and headed for the food. The girls quickly phoned the raft operators, shrieking, "Help! They're coming!" Two operators quickly responded with canoe paddles in hand.

Later, another hostess opened a huge barrel that she'd been serving apple cider from all day to discover a dead rat floating inside.

Playful raft drivers once found a nest of baby rats behind a crate on the dock. They scooped one up in a large mint julep glass and set the glass upside down on the crate. Passersby would stop to stare at the encased rat, and the operators told them it was "Mickey's friend." Their supervisors didn't think it was too funny.

One summer the river was drained for rehab and some of the rodents got into other areas of the park. One night a hefty Monorail driver got a call from a panicky Tomorrowland hostess being terrorized by a rat. The Monorail driver cornered the rat in the submarine bullpen area, and with his big black boots, jumped on its head. Henceforth, he was known around the park as "Rat Stomper."

To get rid of the rodents, recalled one raft driver, "they used to leave out hot dogs laced with cyanide as rat bait. The rats would come out at night, eat the hot dogs, go to the river for a drink of water and fall in the river. A boat would go out in the morning and skim them off the top. During the day if we saw some floating down the river, we'd try to nonchalantly hook them from the raft. A kid picked up one of the hot dogs with cyanide and ate it. He got real sick, his family sued the park and they stopped doing that."

Management finally thought to check the rodent population by natural selection. They brought in cats to hunt them down. Wild cats still roam the park grounds to this day, appearing late at night and early in the mornings and wisely hiding from the public during business hours.

Wildlife was also discovered living inside Sleeping Beauty Castle before the diorama was put in. When the design crew went in to inspect the supposedly vacant quarters, they found dozens of wild cats – and thousands of fleas.

Visitors can bring their own animals to the Magic Kingdom, but

PET HOTEL. The park's pet center boasts a small walking area, complete with its own hydrant. (1993) *Photo by David Koenig.*

unless the pets are seeing eye dogs they have to spend the day at the Disneyland Kennels located to the right of the main entrance. Animals get room and board for $5 a day, and there's even a small exercise area with its own fire hydrant. Usually the kennels tend to dogs and cats. But over the years, it's also played pet motel to birds, snakes, iguanas, ferrets, a skunk, tiger, lion cub and even a monkey that unlocked its own door and ran wild over all the cages, terrorizing the other animals and the attendants.

Physically and psychologically, clean is comfortable, so Disneyland practices meticulous maintenance. A band of sweepers, attired in emergency room white and armed with quick-flicking brooms and dust pans, is on constant patrol. Yet most of the maintenance is never seen by the guests. After hours, an army of more than 300 comes out of the woodwork, working around the clock to have the park 100 percent safe and sterile by opening time the next morning. Every inch of counter, floor, sidewalk and window is cleaned. Every night, streets are hosed down and then scoured with special steam-cleaning guns until they look like new.

There are 48 full time electricians. With 100,000 light bulbs, one crew's sole job is changing the tiny white lights that edge every roofline. To avoid burned-out bulbs, each one is replaced when it reaches 80 percent of its life expectancy.

One man spends his entire eight hour shift polishing the brass on the Carrousel. Maintenance men clean the snow on top of the Matterhorn and brush Monstro the Whale's teeth. In the Haunted Mansion, cleaning is a little different. Since the mansion's air conditioning system keeps the place a little too tidy, custodians have to buy five pound bags of dust and spread it around with a device that looks like a grass seeder. They spray on imitation cobwebs that come in liquid form.

A 38-person landscaping staff tends to the park's 4,500 trees and 40,000 shrubs and perennials, in all 1.6 million acres of trees and grass. Flower beds are continually pulled up and replanted to keep them blooming year round. The Mickey Mouse flower portrait inside the Main Gate is replanted seven times a year. Trees and plants are treated with growth-retarding hormones to keep them from spreading beyond their assigned space. Chemicals sprayed on the olive trees prevent their messy black fruit from maturing and falling to the ground.

Supply trains drop off tons of provisions at shops and restaurants. Replenishers refill the various vehicles' fuel tanks. Three full-time divers battle the sometimes 46 degree temperatures and murky water to handle underwater maintenance in the various rivers and lagoons.

Machinists creep along the rides' tracks to check each bolt, brake and bearing for signs of wear, stress or fracture. Some use stethoscopes to check electronic motors and gears on rides for noisy bearings or improper alignment. At the first sign of noise of wear, they're replaced. Each attraction is regularly shut down, usually once a year, for a major rehab. More exacting work is performed during less frequent "dry rehabs," when the water rides are completely drained. Ever public relations friendly, Disneyland tries not to drain the rivers during a drought. But for a 1969 dry rehab of the Submarine Lagoon, the day the ride was closed a storm hit. The subs were down for ten weeks.

A complete costuming department oversees a 500,000 piece wardrobe collection. Staff members make, alter, repair and launder costumes themselves. Cast members always have to have a clean costume and can exchange theirs for a freshly cleaned outfit after or even during their shift.

Costumers also check and maintain the audio-animatronic figures' costumes, which are specially designed with zippers and Velcro to easily slip on and off. Unlike workers' outfits, theirs become worn and soiled on the inside due to moving parts and leaking oil or hydraulic fluid.

More than 20,000 gallons of paint a year are used. Sometimes it takes big fans and heaters to get the freshly-applied paint dry by opening time. In the days of the lead pellet shooting galleries, each morning five men spent half their shift retouching the chipped targets.

Separate work areas are tucked into and around the park. A roadway near the Harbor Boulevard employee entrance drops

DRY REHAB. Rivers of America drained for periodic maintenance. Note the Mark Twain's track in foreground. (Fall, 1984) *Photo by Ray Haller.*

under the railroad tracks between the Primeval World and Grand Canyon dioramas, and leads to a bustling backstage city. There are buildings for administration, security, wardrobe, lockers, cash control, storage, repairs and machinery. A service road runs around the perimeter of the park, past warehouse and parking areas, to the parade buildings, trailers and rehearsal hall, cycling shop, paint shop, machine shop, roundhouse, around to the other warehouses and staff shops off of West Street.

Other work buildings are woven into the quiltwork of the park itself. The America Sings building has been transformed into offices. The Adventureland offices are on the second story of the Safari Bazaar, the Frontierland offices tucked behind the Casa Mexicana restaurant. When the downsloping Mickey Mouse Club Theater was razed for the remodeling of Fantasyland, in its place the designers built an underground complex covered on top by the Pinocchio attraction and Village Haus restaurant. The basement features offices, storerooms, a break room and an audio/ride control room. There, engineers run the area's sound systems with computers, audio equipment and cassette tapes with labels such as "screaming" and "squeaky door." Storybook Land's Never Neverland (where they never, never take you) has another break room for Fantasyland cast members and storage docks for the boats. It opens up into a larger behind-the-scenes streetway of workshops and storage facilities.

Behind Innoventions, once home of America Sings, a backstage stairwell and freight elevator drop down to a long underground tunnel running beneath Tomorrowland to the backside of the old CircleVision building. The thick pipes along one wall would constantly regulate water in the Submarine Lagoon to keep the water pristine so visitors could view the underwater animatronics. With electrical pipes, steam pipes and water pipes running overhead and along the wall, the tunnel looks like something out of a science fiction movie. It's actually used as an accessway for maintenance and to ship supplies and equipment quickly and unseen to the dressing rooms, kitchens, food preparation, storage and equipment areas below Tomorrowland Terrace – and as a quick way to get across the park on busy days without fighting through crowds.

In the Matterhorn, an elevator climbs about ten stories high to the top of the tracks, and from there wooden stairs lead to a mountaintop attic, a break room for the mountain climbers. About the size of a basketball half-court, the attic used to have a basketball rim and net on the wall so off-duty climbers could shoot hoops.

Since such hideaways are off-limits to non-employees, conspicuous and not-so-conspicuous security officers keep visitors from going where they're not supposed to go and doing what they're not supposed to do. To make sure guests didn't join the Pirates' marauding, employees used to be stationed in dark corners along the Caribbean to tell guests to sit back down or keep their hands in their car. Unfortunately, the attraction's perpetual nighttime made it easy for workers to lose track of time and a twenty-minute shift might turn into two hours. Some lookouts fell asleep. Now there are eleven cameras hidden along the journey, televising guest activity back to separate monitors in the dispatch tower. The People Mover and Splash Mountain each have twelve hidden cameras and the Matterhorn has two. It's a Small World has a similar dispatch tower, but no cameras or monitors. Star Tours has a camera in each of its four cabins. The People Mover tracks are also lined with pressure sensitive mats to detect unidentified weight.

On the dark rides, red light sensors, when broken, trigger a high-pitched beep or recorded warning: "Please remain seated. Stay in your vehicle." Since the crafts' big sails cut down on visibility, a camera at the end of Peter Pan lets operators make sure guests have exited safely. In the old days, a big bubble mirror was used.

But some of the most interesting off-limits areas are right in front of your eyes. That fancy caboose on the Disneyland Railroad is the observation car of the original passenger train, now in moth-balls because the small-windowed cars offered a limited view of the dioramas. Christened the "Lilly Belle," after Walt's wife, Lillian, it's been transformed into a lavish VIP parlor car, the Presidential Car, with live palms, silk roses, brass fixtures, stained glass skylights, elaborate woodwork and chairs and a settee upholstered in burgundy velvet.

Above the Main Street Fire Department still sits Walt's private apartment. There's a green wooden staircase up the back and a patio to the left. The single-room apartment, decorated in pinks and reds with antiques and plush furnishings and a sofa that pulls out into a bed, is now occasionally used by Disney family members.

Walt had planned a larger private apartment above the Pirates of the Caribbean. He commissioned artist Dorothea Redmond to work up conceptual drawings. The entry would be the Royal Suite Salon with a handsome white fireplace. A men's lounge broke off to the left, other quarters to the right, all surrounding a lush, open-air patio. But Walt died before the area's completion. The 3,000-square foot apartment served as offices until 1987 when it became The Disney Gallery, a Magic Kingdom museum to show off original works of art from the Disney vaults. It premiered with an 87-piece retrospective of conceptual designs for the park.

Even more intriguing is the Disney Gallery's New Orleans Square neighbor. Most visitors have never even heard of it, let alone seen it. For them, all there is to see is an unassuming green door, tucked between the Blue Bayou Restaurant and Le Gourmet Specialty Shop. The inconspicuous entrance is identified only by a simple, mirror-backed plate reading "33." But behind the door and upstairs, extending over the quaint, bustling shops of the recreated French marketplace, is a private, members-only club.

Club 33 offers fine dining and the only alcohol available in the park to a select list of high-paying members. Only these chosen few and their guests are admitted, and the only way to become one of the approximately 400 members is if one drops out. One man said he spent fifteen years on the waiting list before he was called. And more than 25 years after its unveiling, the club's waiting list remains several years long.

Walt himself originally conceived the idea of Club 33 during the mid-1960s planning of New Orleans Square. He wanted a quiet, elegant place where he could entertain visiting dignitaries and lessees of the park away from the crowds. Artist Redmond again did the concept drawings. Then Walt, his wife and his personal interior decorator and one-time chief studio art director, Emile Kuri, traveled to New Orleans to purchase antiques and other furnishings for their showplace.

Club 33 opened five months after Disney died, as a place to entertain and thank the park's sponsors, such as Carnation, Kodak, General Electric and Frito-Lay. Some say it was named Club 33 because there were 33 original lessees. Officially, the name came from its address, 33 Royal Street.

Yet the club can't be found on any maps of the park. Perhaps presuming that the public can't feel deprived of something they don't even know about, Disneyland shrouds Club 33 with a veil of secrecy. It does no advertising and even discourages publicity of club details. It also keeps a low profile to protect members' privacy, since many are high-powered businessmen wining and dining clients.

The club has members from as far away as Florida, England and Australia. The cost to join is an initial $5,000 for individuals and up to $20,000 for corporations, plus annual dues of $2,000. Corporate memberships are transferable to all executives within the company.

A night at Club 33 begins with dinner reservations, which must be made in advance by a member, though the member himself needn't accompany his party. Reservations include free admission

MEMBERS ONLY. Club 33's ornate elevator whisks diners from the lobby to the main restaurant above. (July, 1991) *Photo by David Koenig.*

to the park for that day. Parties, often escorted by Disneyland guides through the park, arrive at the green door and press its red door bell. Years ago, diners slipped their membership card though a slot below the buzzer. Now the hostess asks for the party's name via intercom, and she checks it against her reservations list. Upon confirmation, she releases the door.

Inside the small burgundy foyer, guests are greeted by a black

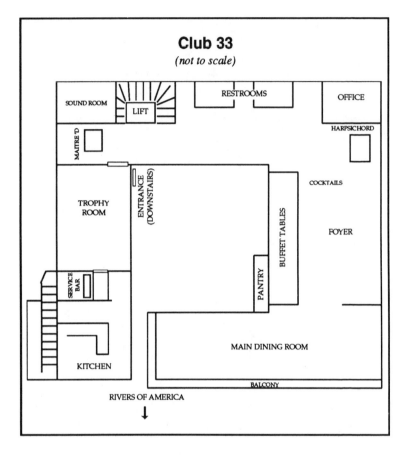

Club 33

(not to scale)

SOUND ROOM

LIFT

RESTROOMS

OFFICE

MAITRE D

HARPSICHORD

TROPHY ROOM

ENTRANCE (DOWNSTAIRS)

COCKTAILS

BUFFET TABLES

FOYER

SERVICE BAR

PANTRY

KITCHEN

MAIN DINING ROOM

BALCONY

RIVERS OF AMERICA

gowned hostess or tuxedoed host. As a "luxury formality," most diners take the antique wooden elevator with glass door upstairs rather than the spiral staircase that wraps around it. At the top of the stairs are a rare console from New Orleans and an oak telephone booth with beveled leaded glass panels adapted from the one used in the Disney movie *The Happiest Millionaire*.

Straight ahead is the Trophy Room, a richly cypress-paneled room often used as the second dining room or for larger parties or banquets. It was originally decorated with stuffed-and-mounted animals including the heads of a water buffalo and a gazelle, pheasants and a fully encased bobcat. A huge mammoth tusk unearthed in Alaska stood six feet from tip to tip, and a colorful collection of butterflies from around the world that Mrs. Disney had collected over the years adorned walls throughout the club. But after the change of leadership in 1984, she removed these and other personal treasures. The Trophy Room is now decorated with original concept drawings for the Pirates of the Caribbean. A once-audio-animatronic vulture is still perched high in a corner. "At one time Walt had talked about animating the animals on the Trophy Room walls," revealed one waitress. "But he decided that wouldn't be very elegant, so he nixed the idea."

The chandelier still has a built-in microphone, part of an aborted plan to provide better service. Diners could voice their wants and the eavesdropping staff would respond through a mounted moosehead on the wall. The idea was scrapped because they thought it might be an invasion of privacy.

The plush cocktail lounge area has other antiques, including shelves of valuable vases, a grandfather clock and a working custom-designed harpsichord trimmed in gold leaf and decorated with a hand-painted scene of Nineteenth Century New Orleans Harbor. Lounge Alley serves as a vestibule and serving site of the Sunday brunch buffet. The formal Main Dining Room features Napoleonic decor, with three chandeliers, wall sconces, French windows, parquet floors and lush green curtains. As a Club 33 tradition, a stylish black and gold pack of Club 33 matches with each party's name engraved on the back is sitting on their table when they arrive.

The service is superb. The on-duty manager appears ever on the floor, mingling with diners. Highly professional waitresses in French maid attire pour coffee from silver pots from a foot above the cup. And buspersons are ever-present to refill water glasses with Evian. Tips are hefty, so there's minimal turnover among the wait staff. "It's a pretty mature crew because nobody leaves," said one server. "The bartenders, waiters and waitresses have been there forever. I stayed there many years, working short hours, making lots of money. Nobody leaves this job. I think maybe management doesn't really like that, though, if they have 50-year-old waitresses in little French maid costumes."

Employees are provided with each artifact's background and a history of the club. And while they're discouraged from discussing club secrets away from work, servers are encouraged to answer the

questions of those who make it inside. For most everyone else,
Club 33 will remain Disneyland's best kept secret. Only one of
many at the mysterious Magic Kingdom.

3

A Cast of Characters

THEIR ever-present smiles seem so genuine. Their voices sound so sincere. In fact, Disneyland hosts and hostesses seem so pleasant, you wonder if they're not audio-animatronic. They're real, all right, all 12,000 of them, working hard to help you play and to make the make believe believable.

When the park first opened, a lot of people chose to leave steady jobs to join Walt's Dream Team. All their friends thought they were crazy, that in a few months they'd be begging for their old job back. Five years later, working at the Magic Kingdom had become the hottest, hippest job in town. Hopefuls would spend all day waiting in line to be interviewed. Before each summer, 30,000 would apply for 3,000 openings. And that gave Disneyland the luxury of selecting the best of the best. Those chosen could rightly feel special.

The personnel department looks for an attractive appearance and an engaging personality, someone whose warmth seems natural. Forget the fixed smile and the canned dialogue. Medium height and weight are desired, not just for trim looks but also because the costumes only accommodate the medium range of sizes. Oh, and they also want cleanliness, a pleasant voice, high IQ, love of people and willingness to work weekends, summer and holidays.

It's more casting than hiring. The beautiful people get the best jobs. The lucky tour guides and ride operators liked to say they played while everyone else worked. If someone with braces or pimples was hired, he'd invariably be hidden behind the scenes, usually in the food department. Disneyland naturally developed its own little class system, with class lines clearly drawn and ranked by position. People felt separate and, sometimes, alienated.

The most beautiful girls became tour guides. They had to have a sweet presence and often spoke a second language. Many were once cheerleaders, Rose Parade princesses and teenage beauty queens. "It was the best job in the park," said a former tour guide. "We did everything. It was like a sorority. We were all beautiful and we knew it. We were. What can I say?"

Naturally, other employees, particularly ticket sellers, grew jealous of the park prima donnas. Ticket sellers performed one task in one place all day. Tour guides got to roam the park and enjoy it with a small group of guests and VIP's.

Looks also played a big part in casting the other glamour position, ride operator. The cutest hostesses usually went to Storybook Land. Tall employees with the blond Prussian look were put on the Monorail. Red hair and freckles, the Tom Sawyer Island rafts. Rough and tumble jock-types were assigned to Frontierland.

Because it's a lot of physical labor, the parking lot also requires athletic types. Attendants are on the move, under pressure, having to guide in four lanes of traffic simultaneously. On hot days, it's the parking lot that's always the hottest, on cold days the coldest, on rainy days the rainiest. In Disneyland's first years, only the sections closest to the entrance were paved, meaning a lot of gravel and dirt spaces and hot, dusty conditions. The first parking lot uniforms were white short-sleeved shirts with "Disneyland" in big black letters across the back. It was so hot out there, many parking lot attendants got tanned right through their shirts and ended up with "Disneyland" in big white letters across their backs.

Because they're the ones most affected by the elements, parking lot crews are among the most tight knit in the park. The position does offer a lot of independence, especially in the afternoons, when most of the guests are inside, enjoying the park. Driving the tram could also be a thrill. "It was fun in the morning, seeing the people arriving," reminisced one driver. "They'd be so excited coming to Disneyland, some for the first time. It was also challenging – especially when the park was closing and you had 30,000 people streaming out at once – maneuvering this 120-foot-long tram with 150 people on it, weaving to get through people, traffic and lanes."

Many drivers will speed up to waiting groups of guests and slam on the brakes at the last minute. If a tram approaches too slowly, people might jump on before it comes to a complete stop.

Sweepers are even more independent and easygoing. They don't have to deal with the crowds and have the freedom to move around the park. Their custodial duties are pretty basic, but many take a special pride in their work because they realize how integral their roles are in maintaining the park's reputation. And some have refined their fancy broom and dust pan handling into an art form. In the late Seventies, a student filmmaker captured one janitor's act on film, set it to a disco soundtrack and called it *Saturday Night Sweeper.*

Most of the employees are part-timers and seasonal help, often college students or moonlighting teachers. In its first years, Disneyland also relied heavily on the nearby Marine bases for part-time help. In fact, the night crew was made up of so many servicemen that once when they had an evening alert at the El Toro Marine Base, most everyone working in Frontierland and Adventureland had to leave. Supervisors quickly had to take their places, and from then on there would be some serious changes in scheduling.

Guests wonder where the park finds all of their cheerful and caring employees. Mostly, Disneyland teaches them to be that way, using a combination of chalk dust and pixie dust. Every newcomer is put through three to five days of indoctrination at Disney University, the in-house training program. Here, they learn Disneyland isn't the normal workplace; it's a stage and their job is putting on a show. No matter who the employee, the goal isn't parking cars, selling tickets, serving food or counting money. It's creating happiness. And they can only provide this magical product through sincerity, warmth, teamwork and following Disney guidelines. It's the Disney Way. The motivational orientation program has been so successful that in 1987 other companies began hiring Disney trainers to indoctrinate their workers in the Disney Way.

Classes for new employees are held in the park's administration building, to the right of the main entrance and the kennels. Students sit at desks in a typical college-type lecture hall. Instructors are usually drawn from the ranks of veteran employees.

The freshmen hosts and hostesses first enroll in Walt Disney Traditions I, a complete orientation on the philosophy and history of Disney family entertainment. Disney University calls it "attitudinizing;" old-timers call it a "brainwash at the Mouse House." Then students take a day-long seminar on the Disney Way, starting with each pupil receiving a name tag. They learn from the beginning that everyone at Disneyland, from newly-hired janitor on up to the highest officers of the company, is on a first-name basis. Here, students discover the park has its own language, one that's both colorful and meaningful. Disneyland, for example, doesn't have *employees*, only *hosts* and *hostesses* who tend to the needs of the *guests*, not *customers*. Head hosts aren't *foremen*, they're *leads*.

DisneySpeak

English	Disneyese
Customer	Guest
Employee	Cast Member
Foreman	Lead
Crowd	Audience
Ride	Adventure
Ride Operator	Attractions Host
Guard	Security Host
At Work	On Stage or Backstage
Uniform	Costume
Position	Role
Absenteeism	Presenteeism

The class is then introduced to the detailed grooming standards, the Disney Look. Each cast member must maintain the neat and natural look with no extremes, so everyone fits in with the show. A fifteen-page handbook details precise requirements for each position's costume, hair length, style and color, sideburns, mustaches and beards (not allowed), fingernails, perfume and cologne (light), jewelry (one small ring per hand, no necklaces, bracelets or earrings), shoes, nametags, hats, sunglasses, makeup, lipstick and skirt length.

The hardline stance on grooming was especially problematic in the late Sixties and early Seventies when clothing styles were wilder and everybody except military men and Disney workers had long hair. When girls arrived at work, supervisors had to pat them on the back to make sure each one was wearing a bra. Supervisors were constantly harping on the guys about their hair, stubble or sideburns. A couple of hosts used to wear short hair wigs to hide their shoulder-length locks. After leaving Disneyland, some workers never shave again. Recalled one former ride operator, "On my last day I shaved all but above my lip and when I came in to work, my supervisor made me go back to wardrobe, where they had electric razors. I did a superficial job, so I consider it the day I started the mustache I still have today, fifteen years later."

Even after graduation from the U of D, the standards are constantly drilled into the troops though counseling and supervision. Disneyland is determined that everyone is neat, nice and smiling, every day.

The park's great demands can make for a very confining existence. Summer comes, your friends go to the beach and you work. Then comes Christmas and you work. Spring break, work. For many, Disneyland becomes their life. Work, school, social life, everything revolves around the park. It's more than a job, it's a lifestyle.

Most of them accept it. Some welcome it. They just love their jobs. They're getting paid to have fun. "It was like high school without homework," said a former tour guide. "You got to see all your friends. When people hear I worked at Disneyland, their eyes light up and they say, 'Really?' It touches the youth in everyone."

The pixie dust wears off, but for some the magic doesn't go, it just changes. "If I didn't have to make serious money, I'd go back today," said a smitten ride operator. "I'm planning on going back after I retire. And I'll work there until they won't let me work there anymore."

"It was the happiest time of my life," said a high school teacher who moonlighted as night supervisor on Main Street. "I taught to pay the bills, I worked at Disneyland to feed my soul. For a little guy who was just gonna be a little fish, I did all right. I always enjoyed it. I'd rather do that than anything. I wouldn't trade it for anything."

Even though most hire on for part-time work while at college, they usually stick around longer than they know they should. Sometimes a lot longer. When they finally do leave, there's a withdrawal period, because they're so saturated in the Disney Way. The friendships last ten years, twenty years, a lifetime. There are tour guide reunions, Jungle Cruise skipper reunions. Seventeen women who worked together as ticket sellers have been meeting for lunch once a month for the last eleven years, under the unofficial name of Terrifically Independent Ticket Sellers (T.I.T.S.). Disneyland also nurtures the bond with an intensive, multi-benefit retirement program, monthly meetings of a 900-member Mouse Ears retirement club and 3,000-member Disneyland Alumni Club.

An entire subculture has developed among the alumni. They use each other as their doctor, lawyer, real estate agent, counselor. Most of one Anaheim dentist's patients are past park co-workers, many of whose children now work there. Strangers who both worked at Disneyland can meet on the street and there's an immediate connection, an instant rapport.

They take what they've learned at Disneyland and apply it to their own businesses. Plus, Disneyland looks terrific on a resume. Personnel managers forget what the interview is for and start asking about Disneyland. It's a sure hire.

Employers know Disneyland selects and cultivates good people. "It taught me a lot," said one successful alumnus. "I didn't appreciate the place until I left, but now I always compare other companies to Disneyland. It taught us to work together, pull together and not worry about working a little late to get the job done. To have a positive attitude, even though the work gets boring. It helped me communicate with people, to manage and control huge groups and not be afraid to talk to 200 people. To take control and feel comfortable with it."

Still, working at Disneyland today is a lot different than back when Walt was alive. Everyone knew everyone and felt they were part of a family, Walt's family. He was interested in and genuinely cared about everything that was going on and, so it seemed, everyone. He corrected anyone who called him "Mr. Disney;" he was "Walt." He joined employees at the break table and solicited opinions from the sixteen-year-old balloon salesmen and the part-time souvenir stand workers. He'd be entertaining dignitaries at the Plaza Inn restaurant and sneak back to the employee cafeteria, the Inn Between, to have a cheeseburger with the crew. He led and he listened. It fostered unity, closeness and pride in one's work.

The day Walt died, shockwaves and heartache rippled through the park. Employees remember the moment as clearly as when they heard the news of John F. Kennedy's assassination. The studio called to say to keep the park open that day. That's the way Walt would have wanted it. Employees weren't to tell the guests; they were to keep smiles on their faces. That evening there was a special, touching flag ceremony. The band played "When You Wish Upon a Star." Grown-ups came to tears.

After it lost its father figure, Disneyland slowly began to lose its intimacy. It's human nature to study your father and your boss, to see what makes him successful and to model yourself after him. Now he was gone. His successors tried valiantly to carry on. They'd have the little weekly coffee chats before work with the employees to maintain the personal touch, to show they cared. For a few Christmases, Dick Nunis and the other top brass would spend the morning walking from ride to ride saying, "Merry Christmas." But that, too, faded away.

Disneyland had been one unit led by one king. Now it was fractured into many little kingdoms, each with its own king. Everyone conformed to the same general principles, but each had his own opinions, attitudes and rules as far as implementing them.

The world around Disneyland was also changing, from the We Generation to the Me Generation. The opening of Walt Disney World in Florida initially drained the usually cash-rich corporation, forcing them to take a hard look at the bottom line. Walt's motto was put on your best show and the people and the money will come, and his brother Roy would find a way to finance his dreams. In 1974, Disneyland completely streamlined management, cutting back extensively on supervision. The operating, food and merchandising divisions of each main geographic section were consolidated into three production areas. Suddenly, people who worked their way up through foods were telling attraction hosts with twenty years' experience what to do. And fewer supervisors meant less time and personal attention. Fewer supervisors but more supervision. They didn't make decisions, they just enforced those of upper management. Rules became even stricter, exceptions intolerable. Before, there had been a little leeway. You could work on your own initiative, within basic parameters. Employees were given a little rope and they could use it for a hangman's noose or a lifeline. That flexibility vanished.

Supervisors evolved into paramilitary babysitters, who seemed to delight in catching someone messing up. Some would even hide in the bushes to spy on workers. Employees called them "duck winders." Management would wind them up and they'd just waddle around the park, not really getting anything done.

No matter what the situation, everything had to go by SOP, Standard Operating Procedure. Any violations, automatic reprimand. Counseling became less constructive, even to the point of embarrassing employees by correcting them in front of co-workers.

"Management kept saying we were their greatest asset but started treating us like their biggest liability," said a longtime host. "And that generally became management's attitude."

Management continued to hire supervisors from within, usually selecting the less educated "yes men." Promotion began to be based on who you knew rather than what you knew. The lucky candidate often lacked practical experience, business sense and interpersonal skills. "A great deal of the lower level supervisors are 26-year-olds with at most two years of junior college put in a position of management," added another. "They could never ever make a lateral transfer to a business outside the walls of Disneyland. So they're managing from fear. They figure, 'I've got no BA, let alone MBA, if I don't make it at Disneyland, I won't make it anywhere.' So there's a tremendous amount of ass-covering."

Employees grew to miss the two-way communication. Walt didn't always take your advice, but he always listened, even sought out your opinion. Now when the Imagineers design a new attraction the last one to hear about it is the ride operator with 30 years of job knowledge who knows what works and what doesn't. The park did institute an I Have an Idea Program, but it's more like a suggestion box than an effective line to the decision makers. And one longtime Disneyland Railroad engineer even claims to have had his 1980 idea for Disney Dollars stolen by the park. He filed a $20 million lawsuit.

Then, in 1982, Disneyland changed admission from the long-established A through E coupon system to an all day pass. There was no need for ticket booths throughout the park or ticket takers at each ride. The move was good for business, but broke a vital contact with the guests. Eliminated were thousands of daily opportunities to show individual attention, answer questions, comfort lost children.

As money became more obviously the top priority to the park, it was also becoming increasingly important to the employees. College-age workers who graduated in the early Seventies met a recession. Jobs were hard to find and Disneyland was paying well at the time. With outside starting salaries below their Disneyland pay, these employees hung around and became lifers. Disneyland became a serious source of income for those with degrees. Every other employee seemed to be an MBA. There were three Ph.D.'s parking cars. Seniority brought with it a sense of security and it was hard to let go of that blanket.

They grew older, started families, acquired mortgages. Suddenly their families' livelihood was dependent on their Disneyland paycheck. Many women also stayed at the park after their husbands quit to add a needed second income, starting the "Disneyland Mommy" phenomenon. $10 an hour is pretty good for a part-time job.

For those who wanted to get ahead, to make Disneyland a career and move up in the organization, park politics became frustrating. Upper management at Disney had always been a Boy's Club, made up of white males who knew the right people and said the right things. Women and minorities could forget about it.

"I could not see myself staying still," said one woman who quit after years as a lead, the lowest level of management. "I either wanted to move up to upper management or nothing at all. I told one vice president that there were no women in upper management and he looked me right in the eye, totally serious, and said, 'And there never will be.' It didn't surprise me. There still aren't any."

"The reality was there were very few opportunities for blacks to move up within the system," added another lead. "I left when I discovered I would be unable to reach any higher. There was like a concrete ceiling. They let you do everything up to a certain point and then there was only horizontal movement. The frustration level got to the point where I knew it was better for me to get out. And there were a number of others who had about the same experience as I did. We continued to be recycled and left when we thought we had enough. It was part of the Disney philosophy, the Good Old Boys system, and we were not in the group."

In the late Sixties, Disneyland received mandatory hiring quotas for blacks from the ACLU, but were slow to place them in "guest contact" positions. The park even had to go to outlying areas to bus in minority kids to reach their quota.

A few years later, Disneyland came under attack concerning equal rights for women. Females thought there were too many positions reserved for men only, especially in Adventureland and Frontierland. Disneyland argued that they were casting a show. In the old days, the men captained the riverboats. But certainly female skippers were no more improbable than in the early years of the park when Storybook Land was run by all men, and football coaches and Marines gave the fairy tale spiel. The park finally relented and put female operators on rides like the canoes. Three of the top hostesses were assigned to the Jungle Cruise, ride operations' equivalent of a locker room. Neither sex took to it; the male bonding broke down and a few guys made things difficult for the women. The experiment didn't last.

But the biggest blow to the family feeling and intimacy among the workers came in 1984. Over on Wall Street, nasty takeover battles were being waged for control of the Disney empire and a new management team was on the way. But back on Main Street, the average employee had no idea what was going on. All he knew was outgoing president Ron Miller had suddenly voted himself a huge raise, in reality a defensive ploy against the hostile takeover attempts, and the corporation had reported its most profitable three quarters ever. Yet the park expected the faithful rank-and-file to take a cut in pay and benefits.

That summer, everyone anticipated that the thousands of tourists in town for the Los Angeles Olympics would pack the park. Instead, locals were so afraid of the expected mobs (which never materialized), they left town and stayed away from Disneyland in record numbers. Disneyland pointed to its slowest summer in twenty years and a decline in attendance at the park every year since 1980 in putting its initial offer on the table: an up to sixteen percent pay cut over three years for the operations, merchandising and foods divisions. The five affected unions, seeking a two year contract with four to eight percent wage increases, flatly rejected the park's proposal.

Disneyland came back with an offer of a three year wage freeze. On Monday, September 17, the unions put it to the vote of their 1,844 members. Ninety-seven percent of those voting turned it down, authorizing a strike if negotiations weren't opened and an acceptable offer made.

The strike deadline was extended one week, as Disneyland formulated one final offer, a new proposal that would freeze wages for two years, change the 26 and 52 week pay increase schedule to 30 and 80 weeks, freeze wages for new part-timers at the 80 week level, and deny benefits to new hires until they reached full-time status. That was their final offer.

On the night of September 24, workers voted 953 to 423 to strike. The next morning, ride operators, animal handlers, warehouse workers, salespersons, janitors, parking lot attendants, food servers, busboys, bakers and candymakers walked out and began pacing the park perimeter, signs in hand.

However incongruous the sight, this wasn't the first time Disneyland employees had gone on strike. Yet the previous protests had been waged by smaller, lower profile factions among the approximately 25 unions represented at the park. Back in August of 1970, about 80 members of the American Guild of Variety

Artists went on strike, including the Indian Village's ceremonial dance group, chorus girls from the Golden Horseshoe Revue, Matterhorn mountain climbers, a few characters and the Kids of the Kingdom, a Tomorrowland singing group. They demanded higher wages, comparable to the per performance pay received by Las Vegas performers.

Disneyland charged that the strike was illegal because the entertainment union's contract didn't expire until the end of the year. They promptly fired all ten Indians and the sixteen Kids of the Kingdom. Most of the strikers returned to work. But 31 disenchanted Disneylanders remained out, even though their meager daily show of force meant a thin picket line stretched across the park's outside gates. Warriors marched with signs reading "Mickey Mouse Is an Indian Giver," "Better Red Than Dead" and "Disneyland: Unfair to the Redman."

"Disneyland is a kingdom all right," a striking Brer Bear told the *Wall Street Journal*, "and we're the serfs!"

The union filed a complaint with the National Labor Relations Board accusing Disneyland of bad faith in bargaining, harassment of picketers and illegal dismissal of all strikers. They said Disneyland had even gone so far as to plant thorny rose bushes where the strikers had encamped.

To show their support, 41 members of the Operating Engineers Union decided to walk out. Disneyland quickly obtained a temporary restraining order because the engineers were violating their contract's no-strike clause and forced them to return to work.

The 1970 entertainers' strike went on for about a month and then 48 stagehands, who maintained and repaired the rides' electronics, also walked out, demanding a stiff pay hike. Disneyland had little trouble replacing singers, but finding qualified projection and sound technicians was another matter. Supervisors could fill in for a while, but lacked sufficient expertise. The park, too, was afraid that if they gave the repairmen a huge raise they would upset the eighteen other unions that had signed a less generous master agreement six months earlier. The strike lasted another month before all parties finally reached a compromise.

Then in 1979, the 500-member maintenance union voted to reject a new two-year contract because the salary and benefit

UNFAIR. Projection and sound technicians go on strike, joining a small group from the entertainment division that had been picketing the park for a month. (September, 1970) *Photo by Anaheim Bulletin. Courtesy Anaheim Public Library.*

increases were below the rate of inflation. Plumbers, carpenters, welders, masons, gardeners and truck drivers walked out. This time Disneyland was determined not to budge from its offer.

"Management, secretaries and guest relations personnel stepped in," area manager Skip Palmer recalled. "Tour guides took over landscaping, pulling weeds and planting plants. The guys who worked at WED helped with the animation. We literally maintained the park. The strikers were embarrassed the maintenance wasn't suffering."

As the strike neared two weeks, Disneyland ran a "help wanted" ad to begin replacing the striking custodians. The next morning a line of applicants circled the administration building. And after fifteen days on strike, the workers voted to approve the same contract they had rejected in the first place.

Maybe because it was so much larger, the 1984 strike at first didn't seem overly serious to the workers. After all, these were your front-line employees, the all-important guest contact positions. For them it was the Happiest Strike on Earth. There was no strategy. It was a party. Picketing strikers waved at bypassers, most of whom seemed to sympathize with the workers. Workers from the Ibis Hotel across West Street came by every morning and evening to drop off donuts and drinks. The Acapulco Restaurant invited strikers over for a free beer. Each morning, the *Los Angeles Times* threw a newspaper to each strike point. Former employees and annual pass holders joined the march. Within many couples, one would work and one would strike. With the summer over, many employees would be working reduced hours, anyway.

For most, reality just hadn't sunk in. They never imagined image-conscious, family-oriented Disney would let its children strike. "When we first went on strike, it was a joke," recalled George Herold, a longtime ride operator in Fantasyland. "I just couldn't believe that they would let this happen, and I felt really foolish walking up and down Harbor Boulevard with this stupid sign in my hand. Many people walking the picket line didn't even understand why they were there. I always felt that they paid us very well for what we did. To have a job that I enjoyed doing for $8 an hour was a lot. I didn't look at it as 'We want a raise.' What bothered me was them wanting to take away things that they had always given us, the benefits."

The difference between the two sides was immediately apparent. Whereas the employees and their powerless union representatives were largely disorganized, management had a plan and presented a united front. A week before they were about to strike, ride operators were ordered by management to train clerks, secretaries and new hires to take their places. Former ride operators and WED designers were called in to help man the attractions. The park wasn't going to budge.

Strikers immediately accused the park of unsafely operating the rides since they were manned by lesser trained crews. On Day Two of the strike, the picketers passed yellow handbills out to the guests warning that attractions might be operated by unqualified personnel. One striker held a sign reading: "I trained 32 hours to drive a Monorail. How about the scab?" Attractions operated with the minimum number of cars and frequently broke down, meaning even longer lines.

"I only went in to work one day during the strike," said a hostess with friends on both sides of the picket fence. "There were all these people in management working the rides, at very low capacity. I didn't feel it was a safe atmosphere. They weren't running the rides as they could have. They had the minimal amount of cars on so they wouldn't break down. They wore incorrect shoes which could have caused them to slip and fall. It wasn't right. I just didn't feel they were qualified to work."

But the union leaders seemed to be more harm than help. The contract usually ended in the spring, but they had negotiated the last one to run through the summer Olympics. Their contract now expired in September, as the park was winding down, and employees lost a powerful bargaining chip.

And Disneyland turned the screws. The park obtained a temporary restraining order restricting picketers from walking in front of the gate, banishing them to the sidewalks outside the perimeter of the park. After a week of no progress for the strikers, things started getting tense, tempers flaring. Bad feelings grew deeper by the day. Some began returning to work. At first those who crossed would just look the other way to avoid eye contact with the strikers when they came through the employee entrance. Eventually they began hiding in the trunks of supervisors' cars or in the backs of vans, or parking at the Disneyland Hotel and riding the Monorail in to work. Non-union workers or those in unions with contracts forbidding them to strike put up signs in their car windows: "I'm in maintenance" or "Security Guard. Please don't yell at me." One frustrated submarine operator swerved his silver Corvette at a group of picketers and a pregnant striker had to jump out of the way to narrowly avoid the vehicle. The driver sped off but returned to the scene a few minutes later and was arrested.

When the impasse reached a week-and-a-half, strikers planned a Candlelight Vigil for Day Twelve. Most of them left behind their strike signs for a night, and lined the sidewalk five-deep to hold a memorial service for Walt Disney, raising nearly 2,000 candles as they sang "When You Wish Upon a Star." Their voices were hopeful, but their minds were on the ultimatum they had received in the mail that morning: Return to work within four days or lose your job. Permanently. The workers were getting desperate. It was time for the unions to do something. Something dramatic. Something illegal.

Two days later, about 120 workers violated the restraining order and marched on the Main Gate. With "The March of the Wooden Soldiers" coincidentally blaring over the park's public address system, they stomped up to a large trash bin in front and threw in their return-to-work letters, and then joined a single file circle march out front of the ticket booths. Park officials sternly read the court order over a bullhorn and tried to force copies of the order into their hands. Most of the sheets ended up on the ground. Finally, police moved in, and the strikers scattered, leaving a half dozen union leaders to be arrested.

Two days later, on deadline day, about 500 noisy strikers again marched on the main entrance. This time they were angrier, shouting obscenities at Disneyland officials stationed near ticket booths. They walked in a circle around park public relations man Bob Roth, jeering at him with boos, hisses and chants of "Bob Roth lies!" as he tried to talk to reporters. "You think you'll enjoy seeing this every week?" yelled one picketer. "We're going to be here every week." The television crews finally had to take their cameras inside the gates to get an audible interview.

The confrontation seemed to be making headway until the morning came, when another 100 workers returned to their jobs. About 400 had now abandoned the cause. Most were afraid they were going to lose their jobs, since Disneyland had begun accepting applications and interviewing possible replacements. The park announced 1,000 new openings, and that day received 1,000 phone calls and 1,100 applications. Hopefuls lined up outside the employment offices from early morning until closing time.

Other disillusioned strikers just figured there was nothing to gain by continuing to strike. "It was doomed to be lost from the sorry little start," said Tomorrowland host Dennis Brent. "I stayed out about two weeks, after which it became apparent that nothing would be won by the employees and, in fact, the employees would even lose. It was very clear deals were being cut with the union hierarchy."

The ship was sinking fast. Each day, a few dozen more returned to work. Undercover union representatives passed safety warnings out to guests in front of the Sleeping Beauty Castle before security escorted them out of the park. Things weren't exactly ideal inside the park, either. Salaried employees were working sixteen hour days, with no overtime pay. No one had had a day off since the strike started.

Then, on Day Twenty, the two sides returned to the negotiating table. They spent all day hammering out a new deal. It looked a lot like Disneyland's last offer: a two-year wage freeze with pay and benefit restrictions, especially for new hires. In the new contract, more current employees got to retain their health benefits and fewer subcontractors could be used to replace current employees. On Day 22, about 70 percent of the 1,023 voting approved the pact.

For most of the strikers, though, the most important thing they got to keep was their pride. A huge group gathered in a vacant field across Harbor Boulevard before that first morning back to work and marched in together. They created an informal club, Club 22, open only to those who stayed out for all 22 days, with its own logo adapted from that of Club 33. They made "I survived the strike of 1984" buttons and printed shirts with an insignia of Sleeping Beauty Castle in front of a large V for Victory.

They were the idealists, vainly trying to hang on to the belief that Disneyland was still a family business. To them, those who crossed the picket line turned their backs on the family. "It was so nasty," recalled Tomorrowland's Brent, bitterly. "It divided the park. I had my car rocked and spit on. It was a bunch of young people who were all full of themselves. It was pretty pathetic. They had their big cause, but the deal was done a long time before the strike, and they came back with their tails between their legs. Those that stayed out the whole three weeks always saw themselves as much purer than everyone else. But you've got to hand it to management. They succeeded in dividing and conquering. It was just a bunch of young, innocent kids who never had a handle on what was going on."

And the family was split in two. "There are people who have never recovered from that," said one veteran. "Some crossed the lines, others didn't, and a lot of friendships were broken up over that. There are people who still don't talk to each other."

Formerly close knit friends became standoffish. Some strikers circulated "scab lists" with the names of those who crossed the line. Co-workers had to be transferred to opposite ends of the park.

For a few, the strike was a blessing in disguise. Disneyland had been a safe womb and without warning the umbilical cord was cut. The employees suddenly had to go out into the real world. Some didn't think they could do anything else. The strike pushed them to prove they could. "I think I grew up," said Fantasyland's Herold. "The strike made me realize that it was time to grow up. The park was high school. It was all playing and having parties, and life isn't supposed to be like that. It just didn't seem right. It was too much fun."

The Disney Company used the strike to divide the park. Now it could conquer and cut loose some of the holdovers who were making the maximum rate at minimum hours. "There were a bunch of us who seemed like we were going to stay there forever," said Brent. "We were C-status, meaning we were guaranteed sixteen hours at the highest pay rate. Two years earlier they'd negotiated the two-tier pay scale. So if they could replace us with seventeen-year-olds at minimum wage, they simply had to wipe us out. They took me out of my cushy job, 9-to-5 Saturdays and Sundays at the Circle-Vision Theater, and all of a sudden I found myself working private parties on Jungle Cruise and Grad Nites, which I hadn't worked in ten years. It didn't violate the terms of the contract, but they obviously were trying to get rid of us. It was pure harassment, and it worked. I left a year later."

And the chance of another strike at Disneyland is remote. "The old-timers don't want to lose their benefits. The new ones don't know anything," moaned a strike organizer. "They haven't been around, they're ignorant. There aren't enough of us. I haven't had a raise in eight years. The unions are still in existence, but they're impotent. They can raise our dues but they don't do anything for us."

Still, the strike would cost the park its full supply of quality employees both immediately and in the future. The image of Disneyland as a wonderful, caring place to work became tarnished. Employees, once the source of valuable referrals, began denigrating the park. They no longer believed in the magic. Morale began to slip, nudged further by the incoming Eisner regime's obsession with the bottom line. For the first time Disneyland found it difficult to keep a full staff.

The park now runs huge newspaper ads to attract applicants. It no longer takes years to work your way up to permanent status. Personnel has lowered the age requirement to sixteen for some positions and is also hiring a lot of retirees. College students find it lower paying and more demanding than other part-time jobs. It's just not quite as special.

Maybe the place has just grown too big for the family feeling to survive. Or people are too sophisticated for that family-style type of management. But Disneyland will do just fine. There may be too many people and too much turnover to memorize everybody's name, but you can always read their nametag. The park is still a nice place to work – it's just not home anymore.

4

Taken for a Ride

RIDE operator may be the dream job, but it's still work. Sometimes.

Hosts and hostesses are assigned to their attraction by looks and personality, though not so exclusively nowadays to permit scheduling flexibility. The class clowns end up on the Jungle Cruise. The best captains are energetic, extroverted, creative and not afraid to playfully pick on each other and the guests. Endlessly circling the lagoon can be exhausting and monotonous, but the skippers are envied among the young, college-aged cast. One 44-year-old had to temporarily fill in as a skipper, and he immediately demanded a transfer. "You had to be a young punk who didn't give a hoot," he recalled. "I wasn't gonna act like a damn fool."

Frontierland hosts are the "River Rats," the athletic, wilder jock-types. Attractions like the canoes, pack mules, rafts and boats allowed them to move around and be active. There are more trees, things are more spread out. On extra hot days, operators had a river at their disposal for cooling themselves off or even "accidentally" falling into. By consensus, the favorite ride to work in Frontierland is the Mark Twain, which mostly consists of walking the deck and talking to people for fifteen-minute stretches.

"Mark Twain was known as easy duty," said one riverboat captain. "You had a lot of independence. We'd set up lawn chairs on the back and watch the fireworks. Unbeknownst to anyone, we'd mix a batch of screwdrivers and send up a bucket of chicken or a couple of pizzas."

The "armpit" of the park was the smelly, strenuous Pack Mule ride. Eight stubborn animals were hitched together, and if all of a sudden one decided to sit down, they'd all sit down. They liked to chew on little kids' hats and were easily spooked at the sight of bright objects, like a shiny Mickey Mouse balloon. The whole line would just roll over. Rides were supposed to be about eight minutes long, but it was the mules who really decided how long each trip would last.

The old Shooting Gallery, before it became electronic, was even tougher duty. Trapped in the noisy, echoing gallery, goggle-wearing attendants had to hand load the lead BB's. "Oh, the headaches," recalled one host. "I remember taking five aspirin one night. That was the most hectic work; you had an apron full of clear plastic shells and three to four guns to keep loaded. The guns were on a horseshoe so they could only turn so much, but lots of BB's would careen off and hit you in the side of the face, though fortunately they'd lost most of their speed."

Whereas Adventureland and Frontierland are a little more laid back, Fantasyland and Tomorrowland seem a little more tense, a little more serious. There are fewer rides with spiels and more rides with small individual cars to monitor. Both lands are relatively tree-free, mostly concrete and asphalt. Especially before its remodeling, Fantasyland was extremely congested, with minimal air circulation and shade. The Mad Tea Party was set on a huge steel plate, which acted like a gigantic solar reflector. Operators would put ice cubes under their caps to avoid sunstroke.

No one likes to work the Skyway. The stations are set apart from all the other attractions, so workers are removed from all their friends. It's also physically demanding swinging the heavy cabins around from the unloading to the loading zone and then pushing them into the trip mechanism, one about every ten seconds. The industrial setting makes it seem like working at a tire factory, with the added complication that (since it's a low capacity ride) the tires will get angry at you if they're kept waiting.

Submarine duty isn't much better, going around and around in circles, trapped in claustrophobic quarters with lousy ventilation. The air conditioning system, in fact, pulls all the air from where the guests are up towards the operator in the upraised "sail." He has to remain standing and keep breathing stale air and other odors created by passengers changing a diaper or requiring a stronger deodorant.

Time goes by faster on Space Mountain, the Matterhorn and the dark rides because of the manual controls and quick pace. Working the start point of Autopia entails a lot of running around. Working the back bridge lookout section entails a lot of standing around. A little excitement comes when the electronic headsets pick up the McDonald's drive-through window across Harbor Boulevard, and operators can eavesdrop on interesting conversations that always end with, "Would you like fries with that?"

Main Street, on the other hand, is all show. Workers don't have to be as serious and conscientious about capacity. It's all about smiling and interacting with the guests.

For the park's first 30 years, it was an added privilege to work the Monorail or steam trains. Until 1982, they were owned by Retlaw, a separate company set up by Walt for his family. Employees were hand-selected and received intensified training. They had their own break area and supervisors. Even their paychecks were a different color. Along with security, they were among the first to use hand-held radios. The Monorail's shirt-and-tie outfits looked almost militaristic. Female operators had to wear their hair up, under their hats. There were minimum height requirements. They all seemed more serious, conservative and mindful of school.

The other ride operators began to grow jealous after Walt started throwing an annual Christmas party at the Studio, only for the Retlaw employees. Co-workers thought them elitists, standoffish, stuck up. They called them "Retlaws." And being branded with the Retlaw Stigma further encouraged them to congregate only with their own.

There was a certain snob appeal. "We weren't like one fish in the pond," said one Retlaw. "We were working for the Disney family."

But most of the rivalries that sprang up were in fun. High

capacity attractions like It's a Small World and the Pirates of the Caribbean would compare ride counts at the end of the night. Early one morning, a Pirate crew sneaked over to Fantasyland and photographed themselves dropping their pants in front of Small World. Small World returned the favor, inspiring a park-wide series of revealing photos: half-dressed Haunted Mansion hosts, Jungle Cruise captains, even Indians in boxers.

The Disneyland Recreation Club, now known as Cast Activities, brought organized competition to the park. Sports build team spirit and offer a chance for everyone to have a good time. There's softball, flag football, three-on-three basketball, bowling and a yearly early morning Minnie Marathon through the streets of the Magic Kingdom. The big event is the annual canoe races. As many as 400 teams enter each year, arriving at the ice cold Rivers of America as early as 6:00 a.m. for the around-the-river trials. From the first races in 1963, no one could beat the Indian Village braves, who also operated the canoe attraction. Then in the early 1970s, the lifeguards from the Disneyland Hotel were allowed to enter a team and won for four years in a row. Participants have to be gone by the time the park opens, but the first guests of the morning have been known to spot a caravan of college kids, soaking wet and smelling like duck poop, hurrying in from Frontierland.

One perk of being a ride operator is getting to sample the new attractions before anyone else. In working out the bugs before opening a ride to the public, programmers have hosts and hostesses play guests – or, more precisely, guinea pigs. That way they can see how the ride runs with weight to set the cars' speed and braking pressure and the timing of animation and circuitry.

It's fun, just don't make any plans for the evening. You might spend an hour stranded in a flying boat over Peter Pan's London, in a Skyway bucket suspended in the Matterhorn or at the edge of Splash Mountain's five-story drop.

To set the brake pressure for the zone sensors on Space Mountain, they recruited everyone in Tomorrowland weighing over 200 pounds. The heavier the sled, the faster the ride. "The first time we were flying," said one six-foot six-inch attendant. "Twelve guys over 200 pounds go a lot faster than any guests could. We were also leaning forward to make it go even faster. We

Team Disney

Team names for some of the entries in the annual employee canoe races over the years.

- Abe's Babes (Mr. Lincoln)
- The Mary Toads (Mr. Lincoln)
- Darth Vader's Raiders (Star Tours)
- Star Oars
- E-Oars (Captain E-O)
- Mickey's Masterboaters
- The Silly Seamen
- Paddle Me Hard
- Death Row
- Zoo Crew (Characters)
- Nuts, Sweets & Assorted Suckers (Main Street merchandising)
- The French Strokers (French Market Restaurant)
- UPB46AM
- Sink-Row-Nicity
- Club WED
- Rowman Empire
- Either Oar
- 9 Paddlers & a Blind Man
- Bad News Canoes
- Rock and Row
- Dead Row-It Society
- Bear Bottom Boaters
- Wicked Wiver Wenches
- P.L.O. (Parking Lot Oars)
- Oar Revoir

went right through the first brake. They pumped up the pressure. This time we stopped – practically whiplashing everyone inside. I rode it eighteen times in a row before I got off. I didn't eat anything the rest of the day. I missed the next day of work from vertigo. My balance was shot to hell. Some guys rode it 22 times. It was wild."

Technically, the basics of operating most of the rides are relatively simple. Recruits usually master them during their first week or two. Employees rotate positions on a line or even from ride to ride every fifteen minutes, with a fifteen-minute break practically every hour to keep them fresh and alert. Still the work can get quite tedious, standing there taking tickets, checking seatbelts or pushing buttons. It's hard to maintain high interest and a wide smile doing the same little task over and over again.

"Some people had the attitude that loading people in boats was like putting pickles in a jar," said Hank Filtz, a host for 32 years. "But I went away every day happy with my day's work. I got to be around people. It's not a supermarket, where they have to be. People who come to Disneyland want to be there, and I helped them have fun."

But some days could be so monotonous, so boring, with everything running so smoothly, operators would purposely try to make a ride break down. Matterhorn attendants would put four little kids in one sled and four college football players in the next. The heavy sled would quickly catch up and trigger all the brakes. Jungle Cruise drivers might load the heaviest passengers all in one corner and then turn a corner too fast so the boat would jump off the rail.

Since increasing ride capacity was an important job function, operators turned it into a contest to see how many people they could run through a ride. The adjacent Fantasyland and Tomorrowland Autopias had a competition to see who could run through the most cars, and one Tomorrowland operator decided to skew the odds in their favor by rerouting about ten of Fantasyland's drivers onto the Tomorrowland track. Back at the Fantasyland station, guests had to wait longer and longer in line, and mothers couldn't figure out what happened to their rerouted children.

Usually a Skyway cabin holds a maximum of four people. Hosts had a contest to see how many they could squeeze in. They crammed eight in a single bucket. It was so heavy, it pulled down the cable and its bottom hit the tunnel opening through the Matterhorn. It was stuck.

Another time operators tried to fill Jungle Cruise boats with as many people as possible. Thirty to 35 is capacity. Once they had a boat almost full when up came a tour group of 60 kids from Mexico. They crammed three-quarters of the group on. Kids were sitting on the engine, arms were hanging out everywhere. Packed with 70-something bodies, the boat broke down before it could leave the dock. Supervisors rushed to help unload the guests, but there were so many bodies that they filled up the next *two* boats reloading them.

One slow summer evening, an Omnibus driver decided to go for the capacity record. He told his passengers to come back at 12:30 for the last trip of the night, figuring no supervisors would be around. The double-decker bus usually seats about 35. He got 93 people on, all legal. Everyone was sitting. No one was in the aisles or stairwell. The bus creaked and listed down Main Street, with the passengers making all kinds of noise. A wide-eyed supervisor hurried to Coke Corner to see what all the commotion was about, and the driver could only hide under his hat.

One particularly busy afternoon, a supervisor promised a keg of beer to the workers on Small World if they could break the record of 40,000 riders in one day. Near the end of the night, the count had reached 39,000, but guests were growing scarce around Small World's far corner of the park. Desperate, a host ran to the Matterhorn, closed off the turnstiles and redirected everyone in line, saying, "Free rides on Small World!" Operators were literally pushing people through the turnstiles, even turning the stiles a few times themselves, but they got their beer.

Jungle Cruise skippers liked to see how many seven-minute spiels in a row they could do. One did over 60 in an eight-hour shift. He never went to lunch, the restroom or on a break. He never even got out of the boat. It's one record no one has any desire to break.

Another unusual individual has for years been spending entire afternoons riding the Teacups. He'll twirl his cup as fast as he can until the ride ends, then bound right back into line, repeating the cup-turning, stomach-churning routine for hours. Amazed guests crowd around the ride to cheer on the Master Spinner.

Everyone tried to see how fast they could run a ride, but one guy went for the record for the *longest* time to take a raft across the Rivers of America. For fifteen minutes, he took his hostages halfway down the river, spieling all the way: "Oh, look at that!" he'd stall, as the bewildered guests kept asking, "When do we get there?"

Contests even extended after hours. They'd turn off all the lights on Snow White to see who could run the fastest through the maze of animation. Running through the pitch dark could be dangerous, so the winner usually wasn't the fastest runner; he was just most familiar with where the track and figures were.

After closing time, Jungle Cruise drivers raced the eight-foot maintenance motorboats around the lagoon in the dark. "The trip took about three minutes, so we knew if he's not back in five minutes, something was wrong, like the guy ran up on shore," one skipper said. "But one guy missed the turn at the waterfall and sank the skiff. He would have been fired, so two guys, up to their waists in muck, pulled it back to the dock, dumped the water out and put it back into the boathouse like nothing happened. Of course, it didn't work the next time and no one knew why."

Before Peter Pan's Flight was rebuilt, the flying boats could swing from side to side and more daring operators would ride them standing up or even hanging off the rudder. On the Matterhorn, operators would ride sleds backwards, upside down, on the floor or in any imaginable position. A few daredevils laid out on the nose of a sled and held on for dear life, as a second operator locked onto his legs.

Autopia cars used to have governors on their engines to keep the revolutions and speed down and prevent them from over-revving. Operators figured out how to stand on the back bumper, hold up the hood and step on the governor. The cars would tear full throttle around the course, so fast that sparks would be flying out from underneath.

When ride operators have to work, they work. Come busy season in July and August, they can move thousands of guests smoothly through the attractions. But during the lulls, thoughts turn to pranks and horseplay to break up the day. Especially twenty to 30 years ago, clever pranks were common expressions of the anti-establishment mood of the country. Through the Sixties and into the Seventies, the world was a difficult, stressful place and some of that crept into the park. During the Cuban missile crisis, Disney considered buying big doors for one of the Disneyland Railroad tunnels to turn it into a massive fallout shelter. The day after Kennedy was assassinated, Disneyland made its first unscheduled closure ever. During the Watts riots, rumors were that the

Monorail had to be shut down after gunshots were fired at it. And then came the war, hitting home as many young Disneyland employees were drafted and sent off to Vietnam, some never to return.

The average attendant was a little wilder, less inhibited, more daring. Plus, there was still a family-type atmosphere, regulations were a little looser and no one was as paranoid about lawsuits. Ride operators were forever spraying each other with fire extinguishers, dousing them with five-gallon buckets of water, hitting them with water balloons, splashing them with their paddles or rudders. Every ride had two or three resident pranksters, notorious for the outrageous. They tried to keep most of it behind the scenes, turning it into a game to keep management from finding out what was going on.

Most of the pranks were directed at co-workers, just to needle or embarrass or one-up them. One slow evening, an operator disguised his voice like a distinctive-sounding supervisor and called the Fantasyland Autopia lead. "Attendance is kind of low," he mimicked. "Why don't you go ahead and shut your ride down. Early release all your people. If they want to go home, send them home. If they don't, find another ride they can work." The lead released all the workers and started refueling the cars for the next day when the supervisor walked by – and threw a fit that he was closing up early.

One Haunted Mansion attendant liked to remove his pants and run around inside the elevator as it went up to the guests to prove he could have them back on before the doors opened. Once, his buddies grabbed his pants and threw them up on one of the gargoyles, twenty feet up. The pantsless host was frantic. The elevator slowly rose closer to his trousers but also closer to the guests waiting above.

In retaliation for a joke on her, one girl brought in chocolate chip cupcakes for a break area pot luck on Small World. She baked them with Ex-Lax. Her co-workers had a difficult time trying to survive the hour until their next break without having to abandon their posts.

On the submarines, before the hatch in the sail was welded shut, pranksters would put a penny underneath so it couldn't shut completely. When the boat went under the falls, the driver would get drenched. Or they'd play hide the wing nut and the driver would frantically have to find it before he hit the falls. Or they'd stick a fire extinguisher nozzle through the sail vent and blast the driver, who had nowhere to hide.

By standing in the higher sail, well above the guests, sub drivers can see the catwalks in the caverns. Co-workers liked to stand on the catwalks and make lewd gestures to the drivers or push their bare rears against his porthole. Once two guys tried to salvage one of the plaster-of-paris mermaids to attach to one guy's submarine as he passed through the caverns. But in unclipping one of the two clips securing the underwater figure, it was so heavy, it pulled free from the second clip and sank to the bottom. The operator had to strip down to his underwear, dive in and pull up the mermaid in a cross-chest carry. But not before a submarine full of guests passed by. The passengers weren't quite sure what kind of undersea show was going on out there. In disembarking, one woman tried to report seeing a naked man with the mermaid. "Yeah, right, lady," the unknowing dock attendants laughed. "Come on, get out."

The inventive Jungle Cruise captains could also lie in wait for their co-workers' boats. One crazy drove an empty boat out to Sweitzer Falls and spilled ketchup from little packets all over his arms. He hung out over the rail with his gun around his neck. And as the following boat passed by, he cried, "Send help! Send help!" Some liked to short-circuit the animation. At the point where the driver pretends like the elephant is going to squirt the passengers but the trunk misfires, it unexpectedly would fire. Another prankster went to the Native Village and started dancing around with the natives in sunglasses and boxer shorts, holding a broom instead of a spear. Others hid behind the hippo pool armed with pistols and when a driver fired his gun, his buddies fired back at him. One driver drove extra slow through the hippo pool, but instead of shooting at them, he told his group how much he loved his pet hippos. When the driver of the next boat, following the normal spiel, proceeded to shoot the hippos, the first driver freaked out and shot at the second driver.

Skippers are supposed to stay fairly close to the set spiel, and they have to run any new jokes by their supervisors. Nobody does.

A clever new line gets around fast. Disneyland lets a little ad-libbing slide, if it's clean. Quite a few captains have been canned for making off-color comments.

The keel boat drivers would also embellish their spiel. They took the opening line – "Howdy hi, all you pioneers and buccaneers, welcome aboard the Bertha Mae" – and kept adding to it. Pretty soon guests were greeted with "Howdy hi, all you pioneers and buccaneers, souvenirs, sod busters, river rats, rif rats, polecats, card sharks, deputy sheriffs, mule skinners, Injun fighters, wild horse riders, city slickers, finger lickers, chicken pluckers, in-laws, outlaws, grandmas, grandpas, sidewinders, bear fighters, bounty hunters, square dancers, men chasers, women chasers, cabin builders, log rollers, penny pinchers, purse snatchers and all you lovely ladies... and, of course, all you other ladies, too, welcome aboard the old Bertha Mae, or May not."

Braver souls devised saltier versions to entertain late night, all adult crowds. "After-dark spiels started with a girl who worked on Storybook (Land)," revealed one cast member. "The Storybook ride usually attracted a fairly young clientele. But for a while, there were all these Marines who'd stand in line and want to go on Storybook at night, and they'd always ask for her. The other girls were wondering what was going on. What she'd do is, if she had a boatload of Marines, she'd do a dirty version. She'd sit there with her hands on her knees and tell about going into the whale's mouth, Pinocchio and the Blue Fairy, Cinderella and the ball, and Peter Pan, Tinkerbell and all the other fairies. Things like that. And the Marines would just sit there enthralled. So everyone in the park who had spiels started trying to outdo her."

Part of the spiel on Mission to Mars was an exchange between the live hostess and an audio-animatronic Mission Control technician, synchronized to deliver programmed responses. A couple hostesses liked to make up their own questions and lead-ins. "Mr. Johnson, I see your zipper is open!" she'd say. "Oh, why thank you," the robot would answer.

On their last day of work, employees usually received a traditional send-off. If you worked on the Rivers of America, you could expect to be thrown in. Jungle Cruise captains and sub drivers often ended up in their respective lagoons. One pilot couldn't find anyone to throw him into the lagoon so he jumped on top of a submarine and rode it through the falls.

The idea is to leave your mark by going out with a bang. On Small World, one guy hopped on the back of a mechanical doll and rode it around the clock tower. Another threw a rubber raft in the Small World flume and paddled it between the boats, the length of the ride. The final duty of one Frontierland host was driving a floating stage out to the middle of the river for a musical revue. In mid-revue, he removed his pants and joined the dancers. Supervisors were powerless to stop him, and he danced the rest of the half-hour show in his boxer shorts.

Ever striving at one-up-manship, the Jungle Cruise captain sees his last day as his last chance at immortality. When one arrived at the hippo pool, he ripped open his shirt, waved his rubber knife, dove in and attacked a hippo. Another tied a rope to a tree and did a Tarzan routine while a guy on board pulled out his gun and fired blanks at him. Another filled up the lagoon with bubbles. When the park found out who was responsible, they deducted the cleaning bill from his final paycheck.

A Mission to Mars hostess completely redecorated Mission Control. She littered the console with potato chip bags and paper coffee cups, then put sunglasses on the audio-animatronic host, a hat on his head, a cigarette in his ear, a T-shirt across his back and a toilet seat cover around his neck.

On one host's last day he took an entire Tom Sawyer Island raft full of people all the way around the island. A few years later, his little brother, who worked in the parking lot, hoped to outdo him. As his swan song, he planned to take a tram full of people all the way around the park, on surface streets, maybe even the freeway. The park found out and scheduled him to work the toll booth.

A restaurant worker on his last day filled up his mouth with whipped cream and, with a crazed expression on his face, chased visitors all over the park like a mad dog, foam gushing from his mouth.

A security supervisor aimed for immortality by taking Mylar letters and adding his own name to those honored in the Main Street windows. For months before management noticed, he had his own window over Main Street.

Pranks were also a good way to break in new employees. Back in the early 1970s, a band of Tomorrowland hosts thought it would be funny to welcome a new hire by tying him to the train tracks. What the new kid didn't know was the steam trains had been shut down for the construction of Bear Country. One practical joker even went to a darkened end of the track and started walking with lantern in hand toward the bound tenderfoot. The kid almost had a breakdown.

Another operator phoned a gullible Inner Space hostess, claiming to be the "guy from refrigeration." He told her the snowflakes were melting so to keep checking the temperature. When she reminded him that they were made of Styrofoam, he explained that they were Styrofoam on the outside but frozen on the inside. He kept calling back throughout the day to make sure she reported the problem to her supervisor and to say if any guests complained of getting wet to send them to First Aid.

Once a devious Matterhorn attendant found a wrapped condom on the seat of a bobsled. He brought it back to the break area, blew it up and tied it to the end of a stick. The host then carried it to a naive co-worker and asked, "Would you mind holding this balloon. I told a little boy he couldn't bring it on the ride." Stunned guests were greeted at the turnstiles by a smiling hostess clutching an inflated condom-on-a-stick. When a friend finally told her what she was holding, she burst into tears and ran to lock herself in the break room.

Extra strict supervisors and foremen who failed to earn the respect of the employees are also targets. They get locked in their offices or have black shoe polish put on their telephone receivers. One worker wallpapered a Tomorrowland office with thousands of grooming booklets. Once attendants at Fantasyland Skyway kept calling up the Tomorrowland Skyway foreman to ask him to remove Bucket Number 40 because it had a defect. After the foreman refused three times, the Fantasyland pranksters removed it, but called Tomorrowland again, saying it was an emergency and the cabin absolutely had to be taken off. Naturally, the foreman couldn't find it. "Oh, no," said the perpetrators. "It must have fallen." Hurriedly, the foreman rushed over to Fantasyland, as the operators put Bucket Number 40 back on line and sent it over to Tomorrowland. The panic-stricken foreman had no idea where the cabin had gone.

Just the same, supervisors can get revenge. One day when the park was closed to the public, two truant operators took a Monorail to the Disneyland Hotel for an extra-long lunch hour. Their boss, with keys for everything, noticed the abandoned vehicle and took it back to the park. When they finally returned, the faint-hearted twosome thought the Monorail had been stolen.

Not even maintenance is off limits. One of a closing foreman's duties is to check the attraction at the end of the night and complete a maintenance sheet for what needs repairs. Once a Mark Twain lead wrote: "Unable to steer because rope on steering wheel broken." Maintenance, evidently forgetting that the riverboat is on a track, missed the joke and had a full crew looking it over in the morning.

For the most part, employees didn't want to make the guests the butt of their jokes. "The cardinal rule," a worker said, "was to act like this was the person's first time to Disneyland. It was one of the highlights of their lives, and you didn't want to do anything to deter that."

But that didn't keep some employees from trying to have a little extra fun with the visitors. They've tried the old nail-the-quarter-to-the-floor joke and watched guests go crazy losing their fingernails trying to dig it out. The old Merlin's Magic Shop workers had the reputation of the bad boys of merchandising, entertaining and infuriating guests with the shop's gag gifts. It was one of comedian Steve Martin's first jobs. The clerks used to scare guests by lowering a big black rubber spider on a string onto them.

Matterhorn workers would inconspicuously stick doubled-up straws through the slats in the break room window into guests' sodas as they waited in line. Before the ride was remodeled in 1978, operators standing on the line could manually brake and dispatch the sleds with foot pedals. Stepping up and down on the pedals allowed them to do "Jello Tests," or bounce the riders up and down. The rippling passengers naturally thought it was just a rough ride.

Male operators especially liked to jiggle the more buxom female passengers and borrowed security's radio code "914" to point them out. 914 meant "Investigate situation." Sometimes men on the line would ask, "Would you like the ride to go faster? Then tell the guy up in that booth, '914!'" So when the chesty woman's sled pulled below the tower, she'd yell, "914! 914!" The operator would smile or nod approvingly, "I know."

"Gumby Alert" was another Matterhorn code word to signal especially overweight riders. It all started when an odd couple – a skinny little man and his humungous wife – came to ride the bobsleds. The smaller person usually sits in front of the larger, but the little man, determined to preserve his masculinity, demanded on getting in first and sitting behind his wife. The crew relented, but as she climbed in front of him, the poor man nearly vanished behind her. When the sled returned, all that was visible was one large woman with four arms. The crew had to pry her out of the sled. When she finally popped out, her flattened husband was plastered onto the seat with his arms outstretched. "He looks like Gumby," cracked one worker, and the code word stuck.

Sometimes the antics are to entertain the guests. One Frontierland operator liked to rob the Mine Train. Brandishing a pistol, he would pull over the train and hold it up. Guests would play along, handing over watches and wallets, he'd wrap them up in a handkerchief and reappear at the end of the ride to return them. But one day as he was coming in from robbing the train, he noticed a new girl from Storybook Land and instantly fell in love. He went over to talk to her, losing himself in conversation and forgetting he had the guests' goods. When the train came in, the guests became worried. One man finally asked the foreman, "Excuse me, where's my watch?" The robber would never rob again.

The People Mover spent a lot of time down during its first summer, leaving a full crew with nothing to do. A couple operators got the idea of carrying a co-worker to the front of the attraction and pretending to flip a switch on his back. He would come to life, acting like he was animated. After about five minutes, they'd shut him down and he'd hold his position frozen until they carried him off. Hundreds of amazed guests would gather to watch the incredible "robot." Supervisors put an end to the shows because no one was going on any rides.

One Mission to Mars hostess dressed up in a lab coat and pretended to be one of the audio-animatronic scientists on the Mission Control set. Two other hostesses sat among the America Sings animal cast and joined them in "Yankee Doodle Dandy."

On New Year's Eve, the girls liked to decorate the America Sings sets with balloons and put party hats on all the little animals. For Easter, one hostess gave Mr. Lincoln his own Easter basket. Others staged an egg hunt on Snow White. Another dressed a Jungle Cruise elephant in a massive diaper.

Once, someone put a black bra on one of the dolls in the Small World clock tower, bewildering the crowd that gathered to watch the dolls march out of the clock every fifteen minutes. Someone else decorated the clock with numerous empty booze bottles, and it took two weeks for management to notice. One Skyway operator put dry ice in a Skyway bucket and poured water on it as it took off over Tomorrowland. By the time it got to the Matterhorn, plumes of smoke were pouring out from the bucket. Matterhorn attendants thought the mountain was on fire and shut down the ride.

Sometimes, though, the pranks backfire or go too far. One longtime ride operator was fired after guests exiting Inner Space kept complaining that they were being pelted with hot liquid. It turns out the veteran would hide in the dark and fling soup on passengers.

A bright ride operator, now an electrician, tried to sabotage the Space Mountain brake system. He would pass a metal bar through a sensor at the fastest point on the track so it threw all the brakes in the ride.

One canoesman, when he was bored, would slap his oar at the mud hens. Once he hit one a little too hard. He decapitated the bird and the hen head went flying over a family having lunch in Bear Country. Disgusted, dad went to complain at City Hall and the oarsman wasn't around much longer.

Other canoe drivers liked to tease a certain skinnier co-worker by splashing him or forcing his canoe into the reeds or near the waterfall. Once they pushed his boat into the marsh about ten feet behind the Mark Twain, not realizing that the paddlewheeler first backs up before it leaves the dock. As the Mark Twain started backing up towards the stuck canoe, the guests went crazy. One man yelled, "We're gonna die!" and jumped out into the river with his kids. Other panicking passengers followed. The Mark Twain stopped five feet short of the canoe. Disneyland fired the four perpetrators.

Potluck parties were common during the summer on the Matterhorn. For one manager's birthday, someone secretly spiked the punch with alcohol and laced the brownies with marijuana and the guacamole dip with PCP. The crew unknowingly ate up, but then had to work the ride, potentially a hazard for the guests. The supervisor could tell everyone was "weirded out," but didn't close the attraction down right away, presumably because he was a party to the spiking. But when one operator passed out and another went into convulsions, he finally called First Aid. They had to take the convulsing host offstage and put him in a straitjacket. The ride was shut down until a whole new crew could be brought in to take over. After a lengthy investigation, two operators were terminated.

What helped keep the working relationships strong was that the friendships developed away from work. During the 1950s, crews would head after work for a drink at nearby watering holes such as The Little Gourmet, then the Clock Restaurant, Campbell's Den and Adamo's. Now workers head for Acapulco and Depot.

Disneylanders had the image that they were all clean cut, All-American kids, and at first local apartment managers were very receptive to them. But gradually working at Disneyland became more of a stigma as their true nature of rebellious college kids shone through and nightly parties got out of hand. During the summer, said a Sixties ride operator, "from 9:00 p.m. till 3:00 a.m. virtually every night there was a party somewhere. If you worked the morning shift, you'd go home, wash up and go to a 9:00 party. A little while later, the 9:00 or 10:00 p.m. shift would come in. After midnight, the parties would get new blood. They would never end." The location and time of that night's party were posted at the time shack where everyone was sure to see it.

Miraculously, most of the revelers were able to sober up by the next day's shift. Most. One morning a Jungle Cruise driver came in to work plastered and quickly became ill. Drunkenness wasn't a valid excuse to go home early, so a co-worker borrowed his name tag and went to First Aid to say he wasn't feeling well. The nurse gave him a release note. Two friends changed the drunk worker out of his uniform and carried him out of the park as if they were talking to him.

At the end of one summer in the mid-1960s, the Indians started an annual park-wide costume party, "Custer's Last Stand." They rented out a big hall, invited hundreds and filled up 50-gallon drums with mai tais. Each year they would need a bigger hall.

Jungle Cruise drivers thought they could go one better, and started staging an annual "Banana Ball." Jungle captains and tour guides spent the week before the party stealing palm branches from neighborhood trees to decorate the hall. They secretly borrowed props, barrels and costumes from the park and booked the Adventureland steel drum band. They sold tickets to cover the beer keg costs and ended up making a hefty profit. But the scenery didn't hide that the Banana Ball was nothing more than a bunch of people, many underage, getting drunk.

Other areas quickly followed suit. After a big fire on the Pirates of the Caribbean, the crew began throwing an annual "Light My Fire" party, including its own wench auction. Janitors held the "Super Sweeper Smash" and the parking lot put on "Come Park With Us."

With so many outgoing, good looking young people in one place, romance is naturally an on-the-job priority. Disneyland is a soap opera on steroids, where seemingly everyone is dating everyone. Hundreds of marriages – and quite a few divorces – have resulted. For many Disneyland-loving alumni, the best thing about the park is it's where they met their husband or wife. And sometimes they couldn't wait to get off work to make out or make love. They would get cozy in private back areas of the attractions, like the dark back corners of Inner Space or the basement of the Haunted Mansion. Other passion pits were the Sleeping Beauty Castle because it had so many dark corners and after hours in the Swiss Family Treehouse's master bedroom. Matterhorn workers playfully formed an informal Top of the Mountain Club made up of those who had made it in the ride's mountaintop attic.

There was also some action in the Mark Twain wheelhouse. "You weren't supposed to be able to lock the wheelhouse," revealed one Romeo. "But we'd put a lock on, they'd take it off, we'd put a new one on. There were more screw holes in that door..."

Guests are also fair game. There's just something about working at Disneyland that seems to attract the opposite sex. As the employee saying goes, "If you can't get a date at Disneyland, you can't get a date." Sometimes they ask them to come back to their rides, perhaps for a private, lights out trip around the Jungle. Usually they change into their street clothes and meet them after their shift. As a safeguard, some might make multiple dates, figuring there'd be a better chance one would show up. The wise ones wouldn't ask them to meet them at the same place.

"We were always on the hustle," said one host. "There were so many guests and when people are out on vacation, they figure, 'Let's have a good time.' We'd meet maybe five groups of girls and position them out front of the park in different places in order of preference. So if one didn't show up, you could go on down the line."

But even Disneyland attracts some sexually deviant employees. On Haunted Mansion, ride operators liked to hide below the track and scare guests, as a prank. But one worker liked to grab at women as their cars passed, sticking his hand halfway up their skirts. The ride operators were continually rounded up, but no one was ever missing. They finally discovered it was a maintenance man and fired him.

An older Mark Twain operator supposedly convinced maintenance that there was a leak in the wheelhouse and water would gather on the floor beneath the steering wheel. To correct the alleged "unhygienic" condition, he had them drill a hole in the floor to drain the water. He then would bring girls up to the wheelhouse to let them steer. "It's a really heavy wheel," he'd say. "So to brace yourself, make sure you spread your legs." And then he'd run down to the lower deck to look up their dresses through the hole.

When Polaroid pictures first came out, a cameraman at the Main Street Photo Stop kept a secret little photo album of snapshots of girls he persuaded to pose pulling up their tops.

Sure, Disneyland has its deviants. But there really are a lot of real All-American, straight-laced kids, too. They play their part with intense seriousness and do everything by the book. And they're always happy. Some a little too happy. They love the heck out of just being at Disneyland. They're obsessed with the place. They've got Disneyland on the brain.

One such employee would arrive at the park every morning at opening, wait around until his shift began, work and then spend the rest of the night there until the park closed. When Disneyland made a rule that employees couldn't visit the park before their shifts, the poor guy just about broke down.

Co-workers naturally like to tease and make things harder on the overly dedicated. Jungle Cruise captains will drive extra slow in front of them, just so other boats would back up behind theirs. The subs offer the option of playing a recorded spiel, but the most devoted Disneylanders love to give it live, every time. One sub pilot sped through a sightless stretch of the ride, turned the corner and smashed into the back of another boat. He heard all the seats flip up in unison as every single passenger was knocked to the floor. Without turning on his warning lights, the driver in front of him had stopped his sub to tell a story about the sea serpent.

The same operator drove his co-workers on Autopia equally crazy. He'd always jump on the side of cars to have happy little chats with the kids. One day the rest of the crew took him to the back bridge area and tied him up. They fed him lunch and kept him hostage until the end of his shift.

Such characters invariably are Disneyana collectors who seem compelled to collect everything relating to Disney and Disneyland. It's actually become a very profitable sideline. Original animation cels that artwork shops throughout the park used to sell for $1.50 apiece now fetch many thousands of dollars. In 1989, the park opened Company D, a shop exclusively for the in-house collector, carrying Disney items unavailable anywhere else. The busy little shop is housed in a trailer-turned-boutique near the employee entrance.

Some take it a step further, collecting Disney press kits, food wrappers and even bootleg tapes of the soundtracks for the rides. "It's a scary thing," said park spokesman Bob Roth. "People are so fanatical about this place you've got to lock your drawers at night."

Actually, taking home a piece of the park is practically a tradition for the Disneyland alumnus. Popular souvenirs are pieces of their costumes, from caps to liederhosen. Some prefer parts of the rides, maybe peeling a Matterhorn decal off a bobsled or hijacking a small sign. One guy was fired when they found a clock off the Mark Twain in his locker.

Things certainly aren't as wild as they used to be. Culturally, times have changed and, inside the park, supervision has grown stricter. The most innocent little prank can get you fired. Not to mention, many of today's supervisors started out as ride operators and know all the tricks. They invented them.

5

We're Entertainment

THEY ARE as much a part of Disneyland as any attraction. In fact, Mickey, Minnie, Donald and the other Disney cartoon characters are the most popular "people" in the park. Kids flock to the costumed characters. Everyone wants to pose for pictures with them. Adults even try to tip them.

Disney's official position is that their in-house costumed creatures really are the famous cartoon stars. But, believe it or not, there are *actors* inside the costumes. Behind the masks are among the park's most outgoing, expressive young employees. But even the typically reserved becomes another person on stage. "You put that head on and it's hard to verbalize but something happens to you. You do things that you'd never do with the head off," said an otherwise shy troupe member.

The characters have been an integral part of the Disneyland experience since Opening Day, though today's brightly colored Gummi Bears are a far cry from their primitive ancestors. The original outfits were Ice Capades costumes, including tights, gloves and undersized heads. As the years passed, the suits were gradually modified to make them look more like their cartoon counterparts, even if it meant harder working conditions for the actors. Paul Castle, the main Mickey at the park for 25 years, said, "The

costumes changed a lot over the years, especially in 1978 for
Mickey Mouse's Fiftieth Anniversary. They gave me these great
big shoes so I could barely walk and this big bubble for my middle,
which I think caused my back to go out. Instead of screen eyes,
they had plastic eyes with quarter-inch holes, so we'd look like
dolls. It really cut down on breathing, and we'd have to spray this
defogger on the eyes." Their own eyes were usually bloodshot,
since at night characters had to spray out their costume heads with
Lysol only to have to put them back on in the morning.

Many new characters go home after work with sore cheeks from
smiling for eight hours. They forget that their masks are already
smiling and no one can see their real faces, anyway.

In the early years, Disneyland had 30 to 40 characters on the
payroll during the summer and cut back to just a handful of regu-
lars and part-timers during the slow off-season. If one of the characters called in sick, a secretary might be dragged out of the office
to play Mickey for a few hours. Certain ride operators would also
work in character costumes, dressing as Alice in Wonderland or
Snow White when operating their namesake's attraction.

Back then, characters were predominantly played by males; now
they're mostly females. "Girls have taken over the park," sighed
Castle. "The park gets mad when I say that because they're afraid
everyone will walk up to Mickey and ask, 'Are you a girl?'"

Today the character department employs about 300 during peak
times. Most are part-timers, usually college aged and good dancers
so they can work the parades. They're assigned which characters
to play according to their height, and the average character lasts
about three to four years, while working her way through college.

Actually three years is plenty considering the rigorous working
conditions. Most characters have to carry a heavy load, literally.
The thick costumes weigh up to 40 pounds. Heads are propor-
tioned the same as in the cartoons, meaning big heads that place
pressure on the wearer's neck, back and shoulders. Local chiropractors do a healthy business treating characters with strained
backs.

The constraining costumes and oversized shoes make walking
difficult and balance precarious. When certain characters fall,
they're unable to get up and have to wait for assistance from a fel-

low cast member. It wasn't unusual to see a little pig flat on its back, wildly kicking its little legs in a vain attempt to right itself.

Calling for help is impossible because most of the characters are no longer allowed to speak. Initially all characters could talk to the guests, but in the early 1970s management ruled that "voice clearance" was reserved only for "face characters" (those like Snow White whose own faces are visible). "A new guy got into the department and said I didn't sound like the real Mickey," recalled Castle. "I couldn't get that high falsetto. And if Mickey couldn't talk then no one could. Plus, they were afraid we'd say the wrong thing."

The toughest problem for the characters is the heat. Constantly in motion under the blazing summer sun, surrounded by hordes of people, characters' costumes become like ovens, heating up to 150 degrees inside. "You'd sweat and you couldn't put your hand up to wipe your face and you couldn't take your head off," Castle said. "The worst ones were the really furry costumes, like the bears that have to breathe through their fur-covered chests."

Sweat made some of the costumes stick to the actors' skin, and they would run backstage and practically rip the suits trying to pull them off. "When you took the head off, you'd literally drip," one of the Three Little Pigs recalled. "They'd give you these salt tablets and you'd take them like candy. We had a couple of guys in dwarf suits freak out from heat prostration."

Guests fail to realize the dangers of the costumes. They'll lean on characters, adding to the weight. They yank the back of the costume, bringing the oversized head crashing down on his shoulders or pulling a bar into the actor's mouth that might crack a tooth. Visitors poke characters to see if they can feel them inside. Others forget there really is a person inside. "People would fantasize," the pig said. "They know you're not real, but they're in this Fantasyland. One woman kept grabbing at the chin of my head, which was actually near my waist. She said, 'I feel so silly!' And I said, 'A little to the right and you'll feel my nuts.'"

One lady wanted to know if Pluto was real or mechanical, so she shoved a hat pin into his shoulder. A Hispanic woman kept asking Brer Fox if inside she was a boy or a girl, "Chico or chica?" Since the character didn't have voice clearance, she couldn't respond.

So, exasperated, the woman reached out and grabbed her breasts through the costume. "Es una chica!" she proudly declared, to Brer Fox's embarrassment and Brer Bear's amusement.

One Grad Nite, the wolf from *Pinocchio* was strolling through the park when a group of teenage girls asked him to pose for a picture. They carefully positioned him, with a nearby wall as a backdrop, a girl under each arm and two kneeling in front of him. The camerawoman announced, "Ready... set... " But just as she was about to snap the photo, the girls at the wolf's sides swung around and pinned his arms against the wall and the other two reached up and fondled him. Then she quickly took the shot.

Another time Chip and Dale were posing for photos with guests at a picture booth in Frontierland. As Chip playfully put his arm around one girl, she started giggling. Her boyfriend, though, thought the character was coming on to her and punched the chipmunk in the mask. Chip fell back to the ground and the man started kicking it until he recognized the character's cries were those of a woman.

More mean spirited visitors have tried to pull the characters' heads off or stabbed the pigs with knives to see if they would deflate. They've pushed them over low fences or blown cigarette smoke into their eyes, unaware how difficult it is already to breathe inside. One visitor squirted lighter fluid on a bear and tried to set him on fire. Others have cut off Pluto's whiskers and ripped off his ears and tail. Once the dog was so tired of being vandalized, he spent the afternoon carrying his disconnected tail in one hand and rubbing his eyes with the other as if he was crying. "Poor Plutie!" the littlest kids said. "He got his tail hurt!"

One night in the early 1960s, a crazed guest pulled a six-inch switchblade on Alice in Wonderland and demanded a date with her. The Mad Hatter bounded to her rescue, and the man stabbed him in his big rubber face. Fortunately, the actor was only cut on his knuckles and the White Rabbit arrived with security to apprehend the man.

In 1986, a 21-year-old visiting from England and three friends were teasing the characters in Videopolis when he allegedly grabbed Minnie Mouse's breast. She struggled to get away from him and left the area. The man approached her again about twenty minutes later and made sexually suggestive gestures. Pluto ran to her aid and barked, "Knock it off!" Minnie fled to a break area and called security, who arrested the suspect on Main Street. He was taken to jail and held on $10,000 bail to prevent him from leaving the country. After pleading no contest to a misdemeanor count of battery, he was placed on probation and ordered to stay away from Disneyland for three years.

Children can be equally brutal, especially at the adolescent age when they're too old to believe yet too young to know better. "I got socked real hard once by a sixteen-year-old kid," said Paul Castle. "Security chased him, caught him and asked him why he did it, and he said, 'I don't know.' What can you do?"

A crocodile got punched in the stomach so hard it knocked him out. Captain Hook and Mickey Mouse had to drag him offstage as if he were a dead alligator. A boy kicked the Big Bad Wolf in the groin, crippling him so he, too, had to be helped off. Certain youngsters seem to know the most vulnerable locations. They'll sneak up behind the character and kick him in just the right place so his head falls forward. The heavy upper half of his outfit starts falling forward and he has to run for his life trying to get it back up. If he falls face first in one of the bear costumes, he'll end up lying there, helplessly suspended. And the kids run away laughing.

"I would get probably a bloody nose a week because the kids used to take Pluto's nose and smash it into my face and because it's so hot inside the head, your nose bleeds," said one worker. "But it got to the point where you went to the break area, got some ice, iced it down and you were out again. It wasn't so much kids as it was the parents. The parents would sic them on you: 'Go kick him. Go pull his tail. Go pull his ears. Go hit him in the nose.'"

So many parents would say to their kids, "Go kick the pig. I'll take your picture," that one of the Three Little Pigs wore shin-guards. Fed up, he finally pulled one boy aside and said, "Hey, kid, wanna do the pig a favor? Go kick your dad." He did and his dad clobbered him.

And the more kids, the more danger. Whenever characters sight a pack of Girl Scouts or Bluebirds in the distance, they head the other way. With maybe fifteen kids and two adults to control them, the poor animals don't stand a chance.

Most vulnerable are the Seven Dwarfs and the Three Little Pigs because they are among the smallest characters and have no working arms. For safety, they always travel in groups or are accompanied by a larger character, such as the Big Bad Wolf. Nowadays, especially since most of the characters are girls, a watchful security guard typically is close at hand.

Characters develop a sixth sense to detect potential trouble from all sides. It also helps to have a wall or railing behind them. They are not allowed to fight back but learn how to glance off punches. Others devise subtle methods of retaliation. Characters may innocently step on troublemakers' toes, turn quickly to clip them with the bill of their cap or free swinging arms, or pretend to hug them but actually squeeze their heads or rake their ears over. "Oh, I'm sorry," the character explains. "I can't see real well in this costume." Parents usually buy it.

But everyone has a boiling point, and even Mickey Mouse loses his cool. Unlike most of the wide-eyed, college-aged crew, Paul Castle was an older show business veteran before joining Disneyland to play Mickey. One day a girl kicked him in the shin and he chased her clear across the park to the Main Gate. He caught her and tried to drag her out of view, to a ticket booth, but they tripped. He landed on her and refused to get up. Hundreds of amazed witnesses couldn't believe their eyes. Mickey had gone crazy.

A few years later two kids had one of the Three Little Pigs on the ground and were shoving in her rubber face and beating her mercilessly. The Big Bad Wolf quickly ran over and pulled the boys off her. Since he didn't have voice clearance, he could only wag a disapproving finger. But as soon as he turned around, the kids were back on top of the pig. Finally, the wolf picked one of them up and stuffed him upside down in a trash barrel, with only his wildly kicking feet sticking out. Their mother ran up and went into a tirade. The characters maneuvered her backstage and explained what happened. Mom ended up thanking them for teaching her boys a lesson.

Another time the Big Bad Wolf was the target of a pre-teen attack. One boy crouched behind him and the other was going to push the wolf over him. Luckily, a little gap in his costume allowed the wolf to see the boy behind him, and he stepped back onto the boy's back, flattening him. The kid wasn't injured, but his father was incensed. Dad cocked his arm back to hit the character, so the wolf decked him. The floored father threatened to sue, but guests witnessing the scene had put their phone numbers on napkins and scraps of paper to back up the Big Bad Wolf.

Regulations for the characters have grown stricter and more structured over the years. A "set" is 40 minutes onstage, twenty minutes off. Whereas before characters were left alone in a general area, like Fantasyland or Main Street, supervisors increasingly instruct them exactly where to be and what to do.

But the characters like to horse around as much as the other cast members, and since the shenanigans are done in costume, they sometimes seem in character. Peter Pan and Captain Hook loved to duel on the riggings of the Chicken of the Sea pirate ship and chase each other on and around the Carrousel. A certain Brer Fox was a black belt in karate, and he would put on martial arts demonstrations in New Orleans Square, out of view of supervision. Crowds would cheer as he delivered flying kicks and knocked over Brer Bear.

One Grumpy attached a book light inside his costume so he could read while on the job. Eeyore taped notecards inside his nose to study for college exams. Pluto fit a portable radio inside his head and danced wildly to the music, even though he was the only one who could hear it.

The Three Little Pigs liked to play statue. They'd stand frozen like a suit of armor in the little alcoves in the castle, and guests would feel them, pet them and want to take their picture. Just as they were about to snap the photo, the pig would reach out and grab them. One fourteen-year-old girl was so surprised she wet her blue denim pants.

In 1964 when the Beatles arrived in Southern California to play the Hollywood Bowl, rumors spread that they would visit Disneyland. Employees fueled the rumor by mentioning to guests that John, Paul, George and Ringo might dress up as characters to avoid being recognized. All weekend girls came running up to the characters screaming, and they would pretend to run and hide from them. Confused supervisors finally had to remove the characters from the park.

More often, the victim of the pranks was another cast member. Once Little John playfully bumped the girl playing Robin Hood against a fence. She fell over it into the bushes and partially lost her Robin head. The dwarfs are less expressive because their costumes' hands are too low to reach and must be operated by hooks attached to the hands by Velcro. "Sometimes there are sickeningly sweet Snow Whites," another character recalled. "One Snow White, who just made your stomach turn, said, 'All right, let's all go now!' The dwarfs had all loosened their hands. They threw up their arms and all their hands went flying. They marched off and left Snow White with all their hands there."

But it isn't all rules and regulations, insults and injuries, beatings and bruises. Being a character is one of the most gratifying jobs in the park. They are instantly, automatically loved. The mere sight of them lights up so many faces with joy. One Mickey Mouse was introduced backstage to singer Tony Orlando and his family. Mickey and Tony emerged from behind the scenes at the same time, but all the visitors swarmed the costumed college kid. "See, Mickey," Orlando whispered. "Next to you, I'm nothing."

The strength of that love is incredible. Mickey Mouse was being mobbed near Mr. Lincoln one afternoon, when a small boy broke free from his father, pushed through the crowd and flung himself at Mickey. "Mickey Mouse," the boy said. The child was autistic and those were the first words he had ever said.

Most of all, the characters make the whole fantasy personal to the children. Another grateful father admitted he owed everything to Disneyland. His family had spent a fortune testing and treating his autistic son, but no one could make any progress. Finally, one doctor suggested taking him to Disneyland every day. After many, many daily trips, the boy snapped out of it. He realized it was better living in Disneyland than in his head.

One of the Three Little Pigs said little girls loved to hug "Mr. Piggie," tell him their secrets and say they were going to take him home with them. Two small children from Texas fell in love with Peter Pan and Captain Hook and missed half of Disneyland because all they wanted to do was hang out with them. After their shifts ended, the characters gave the small boy and girl a personal tour of the park and the next afternoon took them to the beach.

Older females are equally attracted to a man in a costume. After visitors hang all over them, many characters have been tempted to break the code of silence and ask them for a date. A pig was once severely reprimanded for setting up a later rendezvous with an adoring guest.

The characters' popularity with the public, though, has a flip-side. It can be impossible to politely make an exit. To make the sometimes difficult escape, they've devised a few tricks, like playing hide and seek or peek-a-boo and then disappearing offstage or calling on co-workers to come to their rescue. One excessively hot day, Winnie the Pooh was desperately trying to get back to the break area but a ring of admirers blocked his escape. A fellow cast member took Pooh by the hand and announced, "Pooh, I saw Christopher Robin and he's got dinner all ready for you!" Immediately, the kids separated and cleared a path to let Pooh through. They didn't want him to go hungry.

Still, among their co-workers, the characters were not exactly the elite. "It was an outsider group," the Big Bad Wolf explained. "You spent all day sweating and you'd stink. It was like the acting club at school. You were all a little bit different, strange."

Ms. Peter Pan added, "There was a definite caste system, and the characters were not high on the totem pole. The characters were sort of short and quirky. Everyone else had their own parties and only Snow White, Alice in Wonderland and I would get invited. One summer we characters decided to start our own parties. Word traveled how great ours were and we moved up (in popularity)."

As well, Disneyland has non-cartoon characters who mill about the park or put on little skits for the crowds. In the early years, there were gunfights in Frontierland and waterfights aboard the Mike Fink keelboats. A swordfight atop the Sailing Ship Columbia commemorated the opening of Pirates of the Caribbean.

One early regular was an older gunman who roamed Main Street dressed all in black. "He was sort of a strange Black Bart, Disney-type villain," a co-worker recalled. "Most of the time he was just harassing people, scaring kids by firing blanks at them. Once he asked some kids why they weren't at Knott's Berry Farm instead:

'You'd like it better. It's practically free down there!' Their mother didn't know what to think. He didn't last too long. People were just kind of dismayed by him." His dismissal also came quickly because he usually came to work intoxicated.

Taller employees dressed as spacemen to greet guests as they entered Tomorrowland. They chummed with the guests and playfully bounced an imaginary ball between them. They would pose motionless in the Bell Telephone Building and pretend to be exhibits. A rosy-cheeked, white-haired sweeper would amble up to the frozen giants and begin dusting them off. As a crowd gathered, he'd explain how Disneyland had invented a special milk formula living tissue. "It feels almost real!" the janitor smiled.

Sometimes the six-foot-six spacemen tried to hide from their supervisors by taking the Skyway to Fantasyland. One spaceman named John Glenn (no relation to the better known astronaut) was fired because he was caught in costume in Frontierland talking to a gunfighter.

After her stint as space girl, six-foot-three Shannon Baughmann won the role of a Submarine Lagoon mermaid. "It was like a dream job," she said. "You could swim within fifteen feet of the subs and wave to the guests. We'd do underwater stunts, synchronized swimming, play and splash each other. I was always the last one out to make sure we didn't forget our oversized combs, necklaces or jewels."

The girls had to be careful lying out on the concrete coral, because when they stood up, their heels had a tendency to tear holes in their rubber tails. Wardrobe then had to patch them up.

Guests passing overhead on the Skyway liked to pitch money down to the bathing beauties. A few were tempted to pitch themselves down. On a dare from his buddies, one man climbed the fence around the lagoon and dove in, coming dangerously close to a sub's propellers. Terrified, he swam to the nearest occupied rock. And the mermaid swam with him over to the end of the dock and introduced him to security.

After a few years of swimming the Submarine Lagoon in the mid-Sixties, the mermaids got the hook, but not due to lack of popularity. They were simply taking too tough a beating from the sun and the chlorine.

At the nearby Matterhorn, mountain climbers continue to scale the peak on not-too-windy days. A favorite stunt was tying off on an overhang and pretending to slip and fall. Onlookers gasped in terror as the climbers suddenly began waving their arms and disappeared over the other side of the mountain. Supervisors put an end to that, as well.

But the mountain really belongs to Tinkerbell, who would signal the start of the nightly summertime fireworks shows by sliding down a cable from the top of the Matterhorn to a tree-shrouded tower in front of Frontierland. The first Tinkerbell was hired in 1961, Tiny Kline, a 71-year-old circus aerialist from Europe whose résumé included hanging by her teeth from an airplane. The white-haired, leathery-skinned woman rode to the park every evening from Brea, then a tiny town in the middle of nowhere, and had to catch the last bus of the night home right after the show. One night Walt was waiting for her at the bottom of the tower. He had a gold Tinkerbell pendant that he wanted to give her, along with a little thank you speech. But as soon as he began his presentation, Tiny's eyes began to bug out with anxiety. She didn't care about Walt or his pendant – she just wanted to go catch her bus.

Tiny was very temperamental and once bawled out the mountain climbers in her thick accent when she noticed a little grease on her wire. She always wanted to go down the cable by her teeth, but the park never let her. Once, early in her cable-sliding career, she got stuck coming down. Tiny was left dangling 60 feet in the air, and no one could reach her. The Anaheim Fire Department finally arrived with a huge extension ladder and pulled her to safety with a rope.

Since Tiny went down without a brake, "Tinkerbell catchers" were positioned at the end of the cable on the landing tower in front. Standing on the six-foot square platform, they steadied a small mattress between them, nervously gripping the rubber handles at each corner. "We'd catch her in the stomach just to slow her down," a catcher said. "There was a rubber foam-padded post that she hit. She was doing about 25 miles per hour and seeing this tiny thing coming and then all of a sudden, the very last second it was a human being coming at you, I never really got used to it. There were always butterflies in my stomach." Still, Tiny was a generous tipper and left the catchers $10 a week to split.

Tiny retired in 1964 due to poor health and passed away soon after. The park hired a replacement and also installed a high-wire hand brake to slow the new Tinkerbell's descent. And, just in case, they still had catchers with a big mattress on top of the tower. One night the catchers taped a poster of Tom Selleck to the mattress and the fairy came flying in with outstretched arms.

To get more mileage out of Tinkerbell's cable, they tried sending down other characters, like Dumbo and Baby New Year. In the mid-Sixties, they also sent up Mary Poppins, but her ascents were quickly stopped for fear that little boys were looking up her dress.

The character department is just one segment of an entire Entertainment Division that stages parades, fireworks shows, concerts and other special events. Walt personally recruited the park's first entertainment director, Tommy Walker, already famous as USC's flamboyant placekicker Tommy the Toe. Tommy was inventive and extravagant, but not always practical.

One spring Walker devised a special way to mark Easter Sunday. He said a friend at the El Toro Marine Base would loan them a helicopter to fly over the park with a rabbit on the pontoon, dropping flowers over Town Square. "Walker," Walt bellowed, "you are out of your mind!"

But Walt got called away to New York on business and Tommy decided he didn't hear him. The big day came. A 100-member orchestra lined the steps of the Main Street Railroad Station, playing "Easter Parade." Guests flocked in, adorned in their Easter's finest. And, precisely on schedule at 11:15, up over the railroad tower appeared the Marine helicopter. But as it lowered, everything went flying into the air – the band's sheet music, trees, women's skirts, everything. The sound of music was replaced by the deafening roar of the copter. Then the rabbit went to toss his flowers. Unfortunately, the orchids were still frozen and, thrown from hundreds of feet in the air, they came down like bullets. Guests ran in fright as the purple and white bombs stained their beautiful clothes.

For the finale, Walker had instructed the rabbit to fly down Main

STUCK UP. 71-year-old aerialist Tiny Kline holds her breath as she is pulled to safety by rope after being stuck 60 feet in the air. (June 27, 1961) *Photo by Anaheim Bulletin. Courtesy Anaheim Public Library.*

Street, and the rabbit wanted to be paid. So as the copter swooped down for one more fly by, winds whipped dirt into all the shops and blew out furnaces and thermostats. And the helicopter from hell disappeared into the horizon.

But for every enormous fiasco, Tommy introduced an enduring park favorite. He dreamed up the Christmas Parade, Candlelight Procession, Fantasy in the Sky fireworks show, Date Night and appearances by dance bands to increase nighttime attendance. The first Christmas Parade in 1955 was a peculiar cross between nativity procession and traveling circus. Braves from the Indian Village led the march down Main Street, followed by wise men, live camels, a llama and trained bears. Four nervous ride operators toted a long board chained to a tiger. Two pairs of employees dressed as Arabs each escorted an awkward ostrich. As they rounded the hub, one of the ostriches broke free and took off into the crowd. Its two handlers were the lucky ones. Ostriches have claws on the sides of their feet that swing outward when they walk and by the end of the parade the second beast's chaperones were bloodied.

Shepherds were soon replaced by Saint Nick in the holiday parade. Earl Harper, who played Santa Claus at Disneyland for seventeen years, said bad weather was a constant worry because, for some reason, the Christmas parade was always held during the winter. "Once it was absolutely pouring rain," Harper recalled. "People were all under blankets watching. I got soaked. My beard was straight down, like Fu Manchu, and the people were all cheering. When I got out of the outfit, the velvet had permanently dyed my longjohns pink."

Walker also instituted summer night Big Band concerts at Carnation Gardens, which continue to attract a loyal following of senior citizens. For them, the music is like a stereophonic fountain of youth, as they are suddenly rejuvenated once they step out onto the dance floor to swing.

Disneyland has brought in Louis Armstrong, Benny Goodman, Harry James, Count Basie, Les Brown, all the top band leaders. If not all the top bands. "Often when they booked a big name, I had to form an orchestra to fit," said the music department's Jud Denaut. "He had his own music and uniforms but not his own band. Nobody knew the difference. I got bands for Cab Calloway, Patti Page, Bob Crosby. But I had to be careful, because the regular patrons would look up and recognize one of the band members and ask, 'Hey, wasn't he here last week?'"

When Tommy came to work for Disney, he insisted that his father, Vesey Walker, be hired as leader of the Disneyland Band. The marching band grew to include incredibly talented and versatile professionals, but it did get off to a rocky start. Vesey quickly assembled a crack unit, but for the Opening Day telecast ABC brought in its own studio musicians and dressed them in the Disneyland Band's outfits. During the park's first weeks, the band attempted to put on old time band concerts, four a day, at a gazebo at the end of Main Street. The concerts had no seating, no shade and no audience. So Vesey decided his musicians had better find an audience before the park decided it didn't need the musicians. He led them in marches up and down Main Street and around Town Square, and had them play at each afternoon's flag lowering. The gazebo was moved to various other places in the park – and finally out of it.

Vesey also thought of splitting the band up into smaller combos, like the Straw Hatters and the Saxophone Four, to play in different areas of the park. This varied the type of entertainment, allowed the musicians to cover more ground and let the conductor take a nap on the couch in his office.

A warrant officer during World War I, Vesey was a stubborn old man who thought music began and ended with John Philip Sousa. "Vesey locked into about three different set programs, and he didn't want to vary them or change them at all," trombonist Jim Barngrover remembered. "Vesey figured that was our best stuff, that we couldn't do any better. It got to where some of us didn't even open up our music books. It could be boring. Musicians are not particularly adaptable to set routines. A guy came up after one concert and asked me, 'Are you kidding? I was out here two years ago and you played exactly the same concert!'"

The crusty old conductor retired in 1966, and a year later his son was released as entertainment director supposedly after trying to make some money off of Walt's secretive land purchases in Florida. But with Tommy's pioneering of computerized firing of fireworks programs, he went on to become "Mr. Fourth of July." He formed his own company and recreated in fireworks the destruction of Pompeii in the Rose Bowl and the San Francisco earthquake in Anaheim Stadium, plus orchestrated fireworks for five world's fairs, two presidential inaugurations, three Olympic games and the Liberty Weekend unveiling of the restored Statue of Liberty.

Walker was succeeded as Disneyland entertainment director by Bob Jani, an equally inventive mind but much more concrete-thinking. His greatest contribution was the Main Street Electrical Parade, a summertime procession of floats and characters decorated with a half million twinkling, brightly colored lights. Unfortunately, most of the floats consisted of flat scenes outlined in lights, so they had to pass right in front of the guests to deliver their full effect. The parade ran from 1972 to 1974, and was reintroduced in 1977 with more realistic, three-dimensional scenes that could be viewed from virtually any angle.

Parade characters also wore lights on their costumes, powered by battery packs around their waists. But the experimental first models caused some serious burns. Once Cinderella was dancing with her prince when her battery pack overheated and ignited her gown. "Is that you?" Prince Charming asked. "Why, you're smoking!" Parade aides instantly jumped out into the middle of the street and grabbed her. In a matter of seconds, they ripped off her dress, threw it to the ground and stomped out the fire.

The technology was transferred to the Christmas parade, with similar results. One of the dancing Christmas trees caught fire after acid from her battery pack leaked onto the costume. Aides immediately pulled her backstage and put out her outfit.

Even under normal conditions, working a parade is a difficult, strenuous job. Performers are in constant motion for the entire twenty-minute trip from Small World to Town Square, some dressed in the already uncomfortable character costumes. There are competitive try outs for every role. When the season's parade ends, the dancers are terminated and then have to audition again for the next one.

But despite thorough training, rehearsals and repetitive performances, the parades don't always run smoothly. Sometimes guests run out to the parade and the characters accidentally trip over them.

Speakers and lights go out. Floats lose power. "If a float breaks down, they want you to stay in character," said one performer. "You keep dancing, but it's hard when they have to bring the tow truck out. If the delay gets really ridiculous, like half an hour, you go out and greet people."

For America on Parade in 1976, many characters performed in stilts and as one headed offstage, a stilt broke and she fell twelve feet down onto the train tracks. She just got a little scratched up, but needed assistance getting off the ground. But the security guard, who had been trained not to move someone who falls, demanded that she not be moved. Even though there was a float fast approaching from behind and a train sure to cross any minute. Fortunately, a few co-workers went against his orders and helped her out of the way.

A square dancer in one parade's "Frontier Days" troupe got her foot caught in the trolley tracks in the middle of Main Street and the parade continued without her. As the other teams danced past her, a parade aide ran to try to free her. After a quick struggle, they finally untied her shoe and sneaked backstage without it.

In the Christmas parade one year, the Cinderella unit featured a glass coach pulled by a dozen baby ponies. Marching down Main Street, one got its leg stuck in the track and twisted its ankle. The horse went wild and threw the other eleven into a panic. Security dashed out and had to tranquilize the pony in full view of the guests. The parade continued on, redirected around the sedated animal like a freeway accident.

Other Cinderella troupe performers danced underneath a tall canopy carried by eight attendants. The carriers were notorious for checking out all the girls along the route and would unintentionally gravitate towards the cute ones. Naturally, the whole canopy and all the dancers would have to follow. Once the attendants strayed so far off course, they got the canopy caught under a tree.

So it's not Broadway. Things go wrong. Some of the actors are in high school. Many make minimum wage. Disneyland entertainers are still very serious about their craft. That professionalism is typified by the Golden Horseshoe Revue. From July 1955 to October 1986, the show ran for more than 50,000 consecutive performances, immortalizing Sluefoot Sue and comic Wally Boag in the

Guinness Book of World Records for the longest running stage production in history. When Disneyland temporarily lowered the curtain on the show in 1986, it wasn't for lack of demand. There were
still lines around the building. They just wanted to install a new
production with fresh faces. And then it was right back on with the
show.

In a way, all of Disneyland is a show. Entertaining the guests is
a part of every worker's job. Only for the characters, actors,
singers, dancers and other performers, it's their only job.

6

Be Our Guest

EACH year about twelve million guests visit Disneyland. They come in all shapes and sizes, nationalities, IQ's, dispositions and moods. It's a cross section of the population of the planet, yet when they enter the Magic Kingdom, they seem to become magically transformed. People from the world around adopt a common mindset and become remarkably similar. It's partly because, for a place originally designed to be educational as well as entertaining, Disneyland actually encourages guests *not* to think. They are subtly urged to suspend their imaginations and let the attractions and the employees do the thinking for them. As the familiar saying goes, "You come to Disneyland, you check your brain at the gate."

Tourists have gotten so caught up in admiring the scenery, they would walk right off a dock. "People occasionally walk right into the water," said one amazed employee. "We'd dry them off, give them ride operators' clothes and send their wet clothes to the laundry to be mailed back to them. One girl walked right between the wharf and the boat, and her husband pulled her out by her hair."

People would always stand in line for the Golden Horseshoe Revue with absolutely no idea what they were waiting for. They were walking in Frontierland and saw a line of people that wrapped around the building, so they would wait in line for two hours and then ask, "What's this?"

One woman, heavily engrossed in reading a brochure, got in a line off Main Street, thinking it was for a ride. She didn't know where she was until she stepped up to a urinal and realized she was in the men's restroom. She fled screaming.

Especially in the park's infant years, when there was no other place like Disneyland, guests thought everything was real. Jungle Cruise passengers were genuinely surprised when the captain pulled out his gun and fired at the hippos. When the submarines "lowered" and the recorded spiel intoned, "Dive! Dive!," people would sometimes dive over each other to hit the deck. Once, an employee slipped between a sub and the dock and tore a gash in his leg. As his blood dripped into the water, many visitors thought it was a shark attack.

A young man stepped onto the wobbly barrel bridge on Tom Sawyer Island and, as it started to bob beneath his feet, he thought it was broken. "Everybody jump!" he cried and dove into the river. His embarrassed girlfriend refused to help him out.

A scare on Space Mountain was much more realistic, horrifying hundreds of onlookers. As two men came down the ramp to the loading area, it was obvious to the attendants that one of them had an artificial leg. But because the rockets are precisely timed, the ride couldn't be slowed down to help the man on. If a sled is sent too late, the computer senses "Potential Catastrophe," sends up all the brakes in the ride and brings the entire attraction to a dead stop. So, the employees asked him if he was able to get in and out of the ride unassisted because they weren't allowed to help. "Yeah, yeah, yeah," his friend assured. "No big deal." Actually, the man had to push a button to get his knee to bend and it took him forever to board the sled. The attendants were absolutely frantic. Finally, the man got in and the tower instantly sent him off. But the crew realized that if it took this guy so long to get in, how long will it take him to get out? The foreman decided to put a hefty attendant on the unload side to give him a hand. But when his rocket came in, the employee didn't think to say, "Excuse me, sir, let me help you get out of the rocket." Instead, he just started pulling him out, but the passenger couldn't get his leg bent. Hundreds of other guests waiting in line looked down on the struggle. The host finally picked the man up, set him on his fanny to the side of the sled and yelled, "Move that rocket!" Unfortunately, the man's phony foot had gotten wedged between the back of the seat and the lapbar. The empty rocket took off, ripping free the man's artificial leg. The man just sat there watching as the sled whipped along the track, dragging his leg. The crowd shook with blood curdling screams. And the next guests were understandably hesitant about asking for loading or unloading assistance.

Ride shutdowns and breakdowns can seriously confuse someone caught up in the illusion. Closing up Adventure through Inner Space for the evening, a hostess waited until the last guests had gotten off and then shut the ride down. As per normal procedure, she flicked on all the lights and began walking the track. At the very end of the ride, below a huge eye looking down through a giant microscope, were three more cars. In one was a little old lady, hysterical and crying. She grabbed the hostess and shrieked, "Oh, my God! Are we going to be stuck in Inner Space?"

Naturally, children are even more frightened. Once Pinocchio's Daring Journey broke down just as a small boy's car neared the Stromboli scene. The lights went black just as the menacing Stromboli lowered a cage and yelled, "This will be your new home!" The child went berserk.

Guests can be so gullible, they'll believe about anything employees tell them. If a ride breaks down, workers can convince them the zipper broke. One security guard liked to confuse guests searching for a restroom by telling them they needed a "P" ticket. A woman asked if the ongoing downpour was real rain. "It's not real," explained a cast member. "Mr. Disney has arranged to have an artificial rainstorm in the park every day at 3:00."

Others have questioned if that's actual water in the Submarine Lagoon. "No," employees have replied, "that's cellophane with blowers underneath." Many wonder if the swans in the castle moat and ducks on the Rivers of America are real. No, employees might explain. The birds have to be wound up every morning.

Tourists regularly ask if all the plants and trees in the park are plastic. One woman told her friend that all the characters and dancers in one parade were mechanical. A little girl pointed to the night sky and wanted to know if that was the real moon. And on stormy days, many guests have complained that Disneyland allowed it to rain.

The dumb questions are endless. People ask, "Where's the bathroom?" while standing under a big restroom sign. One man standing in front of the Electrical Parade had to shout, "Where's the parade?" to be heard over it. Others inquire, "What time is the 9:00 parade?" and "Where's Toiletland?" Visitors walk into the Golden Horseshoe, notice the beautifully decorated saloon with polished floor, long brass railing, chandeliers and tables and chairs to seat 80 and ask, "Are the tables and chairs for sitting?"

Naturally, stories of guest stupidity are good for laughs among the employees. Tales seem to travel fastest through merchandising, where business is either very busy or very slow. So, stock people like to go from shop to shop, chatting with the clerks, and stories circulate around the park. Visitor brainlessness was such a hot topic, the Fantasyland stockroom crew even wrote a book about it. They got an autograph book like the ones guests can sign at Card Corner, attached a Disneyland shopping bag as a dust jacket and affixed a Dopey sticker to the cover. It became the Dopey Book. Whenever a guest did or said or wore something unusual, workers put a line or two in the book.

A typical entry: "Two little old ladies were walking past the Matterhorn and one said, 'Isn't it wonderful how they found a mountain to build an amusement park around?'"

One slow winter afternoon, two operators slid a Frontierland trash barrel to the middle of the keel boat dock and removed its lid. A minute later, a guest walked up and, staring at the garbage can, asked, "What ride is this?" "It's the Can Ride," one of the attendants deadpanned, and then helped the man step into the barrel. And the guest stood there, in the can, on a foot of trash, as a boat full of disbelieving passengers pulled up to the dock.

And then there was the older couple that wanted to ride the submarines and asked the operator how long the ride was. "Two days," he replied. So the couple took the Monorail over to the Disneyland Hotel, went up to their room, packed their bags and returned to ride the subs with suitcases in hand.

But sometimes visitor idiocy can be dangerous. One woman had claustrophobia on the steam train and the attendant had to physically restrain her from jumping off into the Grand Canyon Diorama. Another lady had her two young daughters pose for photos in front of the cartoon mural across the face of the Snow White ride as the mine cars streamed past. When the operator ordered her to get them out of there immediately, mom walked in front of a moving car to do so.

One young couple went to ride America Sings and absentmindedly left their baby at a lunch table. They didn't realize their mistake until the 24-minute ride was over and they couldn't find their child. Fortunately, a sweeper had discovered the abandoned infant.

Once the Monorail broke down on the incline over the Submarine Lagoon. As a tractor arrived to push the cars back to the station, the stunned Monorail operator looked back to see a man holding his son out the window by his ankles to look underneath the car.

In a wonderland, people get curious. A twelve-year-old boy shimmied up the pole at the entrance to Adventureland and stuck two fingers in the eye holes of the skull at the top of the pole. A spider was hiding inside and bit him.

A ticket taker offered to watch a small boy while his parents enjoyed Great Moments with Mr. Lincoln. As soon as they went in, the boy was somehow able to stick his head though the round hole in the ticket booth window. The terrified ticket taker couldn't get him out and nearly had to call maintenance to break him free.

Another guest got her finger stuck in one of the little holes on a Motor Boat steering wheel. A park nurse brought Vaseline out to the boat but still couldn't remove her finger. Finally, a mechanic disassembled the steering wheel from the boat and escorted her across the park to the machine shop, with the wheel on her finger. Machinists cut the wheel off and gave it to her to take home as a souvenir.

Children would often get their heads stuck in slats on the trains. Turnstiles have trapped elbows and even entire bodies. One large woman became so wedged in at the Pirates of the Caribbean entrance that maintenance had to be called to dismantle the turnstiles. A heavyset man got stuck in Injun Joe's Cave on Tom Sawyer Island. Another overweight woman became trapped in a Casey Jr. railcar. Her husband had to brace himself against the back of the cage and try to push her out with his feet.

After buying a lucky rabbit's foot at an Indian Village souvenir shop, an obese woman started spinning it around her finger and it flew off and landed in a round metal trash can. When she couldn't reach it by sticking her arm down the barrel, she removed a sandal, hiked up her dress and stuck in a leg, trying to hook it with her toe. When she couldn't get her leg out, she panicked. "My leg! My leg!" she screamed, as her leg began to swell. Paramedics arrived and had to struggle not to laugh as they lowered the woman onto a stretcher to take her and her new metal appendage to the hospital.

Another time Jungle Cruise operators phoned First Aid to ask if they should move a guest who had fallen and hurt her back. "If she's hurt her back," advised the nurse, "definitely don't move her." But when she arrived at the scene, she discovered the jumbo-sized woman had wanted to have her picture taken sitting on top of one of the barrels. She broke through the top and fell into the barrel, scraping her back. Though she was folded up like an accordion, her feet sticking straight up, no one would help her out of the barrel until the nurse got there.

Guests who get lost in the fantasy of Disneyland have a tendency to lose belongings, as well. A day at the park can be ruined worrying about a lost possession. And the park knows well that a memorable time becomes remembered for the wrong reason. Fortunately, the park's Lost and Found Department boasts an incredible recovery rate. In a way, every employee works for Lost and Found. They're encouraged to turn in items or at least call the office as soon as possible. Every item is logged, and the employees who turn them in can ask for a receipt. If no one claims the object in 90 days, the employee can. Items without receipts are sold at an annual Lost and Found Sale, proceeds going to charity.

On a typical summer day, Lost and Found takes in about 150 pairs of sunglasses, the same number of hats, plenty of cameras and lens caps and about a dozen baby strollers. Other common items are clothing, jewelry, money, wallets, travel bags and souvenirs. But they've also collected dental retainers, full sets of dentures, a wooden leg, a pair of ski boots, a hair dryer, television sets, a drained-out water bed, knives, handguns and a canary.

After riding the Jungle Cruise, an elderly woman realized that her glass eye was missing. She went to Lost and Found, and Lost and Found called janitorial to have them check their pans. Minutes later, in came an eighteen-year-old sweeper, who seemed to be turning green. He dropped off the eyeball he'd found in his pan and headed straight for the restrooms.

Some items are irreplaceable. A family wrote from Denver asking if anyone had turned in a roll of 110 film on a particular day. They had come to Disneyland to get away after their three-year-old daughter died of leukemia. The film had the last pictures ever taken of her. Lost and Found mailed them three rolls found that day. One was theirs.

The system works because of the honesty and integrity of the employees. One afternoon a procession of Fantasyland and Tomorrowland ride operators and sweepers turned in loose $20 and $50 bills that they said "came from the sky." Even some guests turned in money, and several sweepers snatched money right out of other guests' hands because they knew it didn't belong to them. Soon after, a little Japanese tourist came to Lost and Found and explained that he had opened his wallet on the Skyway and the wind took off with all his cash. All but a couple hundred dollars of his $3,000 was recovered.

One couple vacationing from the Middle East suffered a similar mishap on the Matterhorn, but lost even more. All of their valuables fell out of their travel bag – money, passports, airline tickets, everything. The employees spent all day looking, but couldn't find anything. So an operator invited the couple to spend the night at his apartment. The next day, he signed them into the park. He gave them ticket books and told them to go play, but all they did was sit forlornly in front of the Matterhorn, waiting, hoping. Late in the afternoon, a host was walking the track during a breakdown and glanced down, way down, in the middle of nowhere. There, in the dark, underneath the rail, he saw all their valuables. Quickly, the crew packed them up and sent the couple off to the airport.

Then again, there's always the exception. One old sweeper was famous for finding money for himself. Once, he noticed a $10 bill hanging out of a young boy's pocket. The janitor trailed the boy and his father from Small World to Tomorrowland to Fantasyland to Main Street, sweeping all the way. Sure enough, the $10 bill fell out. In a split second, he swept it up into his pan and was off in the other direction.

Disgustingly, one of the most common things guests lose at the park is their lunch. Upset stomachs strike after trips on roller coaster rides like Space Mountain or on the high walkways and swinging bridges of the Swiss Family Treehouse. But the primary illness inducer is the Mad Tea Party, especially back before Fantasyland was redesigned in 1983 when a fast food restaurant exited practically right into the Teacup waiting line. Many guests would gorge themselves on cheeseburgers, sodas and French fries and a minute later they'd be spinning around in a teacup.

On busy days employees try to get the ride's capacity as high as possible. They might get on the PA to encourage more people per cup, so more people are spinning each wheel and the cups spin even faster. With six cups on three tables, each cup spins, each table spins and the master table spins. So when passengers toss their cookies, it flies out and makes a giant flower pattern all over the turntable. They quickly call a janitor to sprinkle on "Barf Dust," green kitty litter-type stuff that soaks up the "mishap" so it can be swept up. But Fantasyland sweepers seem to have radar because whenever someone throws up, they can never be found. And the hotter the day, the more noxious the fumes and the longer the wait for a janitor.

One girl suddenly became sick as she got to the front of the line for Autopia. Instinctively, the hostess flipped open the lid on the ticket box and the girl threw up inside. The attendant quickly closed the box up, leaving a special surprise for the ticket counters who remove the inside liner at the end of the night.

In 1982, mass illness hit the park with an outbreak of the ten day red measles. Apparently, an infected guest came to Disneyland and shared his sickness with nineteen other children. They, in turn, passed it on to more than fifteen others when they returned to their homes across the country.

Ten years later, a huge group of guests got sick simultaneously while riding the Pirates of the Caribbean. A strange, unidentifiable gas was wafting through the final section of the attraction, and as riders floated through it, they began coughing, their eyes stinging. And they were stalled in it as a line of boats backed up at the bottom of the motorized up-ramp. Employees holding handkerchiefs over their mouths scurried by on adjacent walkways. By the time the boats made it to the unloading dock, 30 passengers had to be taken to First Aid. Six of those, nauseated, coughing, their eyes burning, chests tightening and skin blotching, went on to the hospital. Some of the victims' irritations, dizziness and headaches persisted for days. A doctor said it was from a Mace-like gas, possibly sprayed by someone in a preceding boat. Disneyland never called the city fire department's hazardous materials specialists, but did shut down the ride for about an hour to investigate.

Some guests are going to be problems no matter what the park does. Small children who don't know any better will urinate into the Submarine Lagoon or over the rail on the Monorail or Rocket Jets, much to the dismay of the people waiting in line below. Worse are abusive adults. Many grow hot, tired and impatient with the long lines and take it out on the employees. Others are just naturally rude or delight in ruining someone else's day.

Some visitors get a kick out of popping the vendor's balloons with their cigars. One Autopia host asked a man to put out his cigarette before he went on the ride. The belligerent guest put it out on the back of the operator's hand. An employee told a woman she couldn't go back into Fantasyland because the park was closing. She slapped his face. A visitor, informed he couldn't bring his sodas and popcorn into the Haunted Mansion, started screaming, "Why is there a popcorn stand 90 feet away?" and threw his refreshments all over the attendant.

During a private party for a group of inner city kids, eight girls handed the young Haunted Mansion hostess only two tickets. When she said she needed more tickets, the girls just turned on her. They beat her up, pulled out some hair and broke her nose. Coworkers chased the girls halfway across the park before they caught them.

Nightly conflicts arise at closing time when people have to be turned away from the rides. To have the Matterhorn empty by closing on summer nights, the line has to be cut off 45 minutes to an hour early. Those turned away verbally abuse operators, try to bribe them to let them get on or have stories like, "We've come all the way from Paris and this is the only time we'll be here in our lives." One visitor pulled a knife on an employee to let him through.

"People would come up to you and say, 'I pay your salary,'" said one frustrated hostess. "They'd abuse you and call you names. They expected you to pick up after them. On America Sings, I was staring at a woman changing a diaper as she pretended to watch the show. I knew that she was just going to leave the dirty diaper under her seat, so as soon as I did my spiel and the lights came up, I grabbed this woman and said, 'Excuse me, you forgot something.' And she said, 'That's your job.' You were never allowed to talk back to these people. If a guest complained about you, you were always wrong. So sometimes you wore someone else's name tag."

At Disneyland, the customer is always right. The mischievous clerks at the old Merlin's Magic Shop used to get big laughs by stringing up a big black rubber spider and lowering it onto unsuspecting shoppers. But one too many terrorized customers complained, and the spiders were soon gone.

A couple years ago, a small child cut himself on a staple which attached the elastic strap to his Mouse Ears cap. Disneyland had to do away with all the straps.

Guests can register complaints or compliments by completing a form at City Hall. But criticisms far outnumber commendations. And complaints bring instant reprimands, no questions asked. So, employees and leads are encouraged to soothe unhappy customers before they even think about going to City Hall. Leads receive classes in handling complaints: moving the guest to a better environment, using the right words and asking the right questions, finding out what will make him happy. Typical complaints are set up and role played. The main goal is to keep the guest from having a negative experience.

"I was the one who handled guest complaints about employees and usually they weren't the employees' fault," said one lead. "So I had a standard line. I'd listen very intently because they had a horrible time at the park and they wanted to be heard. And I'd say, 'That person has been a troublemaker for quite a while now, so don't worry. We're going to be firing him.' And they'd be so happy. I said, 'What can I do for you? Can I stick you back on the ride?' I'd give them what they wanted and they'd be gone, because those guest complaints were hell on the employees. You'd get fired for having too many of them. And if the employee got mad at me, I'd say, 'Which would you rather have, a guest complaint or me tell them I'm going to fire you? How are they going to know? They're not going to be back.'"

Perhaps the all-time most obnoxious guest was a temperamental paraplegic, who had been born with her hands and feet attached close to her body. She was pushed around in a wheelchair by her blind husband, whose seeing eye dog suffered from a definite bladder control problem. Some attractions cannot accommodate the disabled. Many others can, but require special loading procedures. The impatient woman wanted to get on every ride her way and erupted into a stream of profanities for all to hear when asked to wait, always beginning, "Just because I'm handicapped..." On the People Mover, she made her husband wheel past the attendants who tried to stop them, up the moving ramp. Her husband was in real trouble, though, when he got the wheelchair on the revolving turntable floor at the top. The operators had to stop the ride and call security. An individual guard was assigned to follow the foul-mouthed female as she rampaged across the park, leaving a wake of angry employees and stunned onlookers and a trail of dog urine. Late in the day, she arrived at Storybook Land, cut through the line and demanded to get on. When the hostesses asked her to wait because they needed to take extra care, she began screaming. She finally told her husband to lift her up and set her in the boat. He accidentally dropped her in the lagoon. Employees fished her out, but the woman had cut her head a little and started yelling that she just wanted to leave. Disneyland was pleased to accommodate her request. Security escorted the threesome to her car, rigged with a special system so she could drive. And she peeled out of the parking lot, as her blind husband gave directions to the hospital.

Such stubborn guests can push even the most easygoing cast member to the limit. One party kept demanding to sit in the front seat on Space Mountain, despite the operator's insistence that they go to Row Three. He finally tried to escort them to the aisle, but they dashed for Row One and jumped in the lead rocket. "We wanted to sit in front," they smiled. He glowered back, "Any particular *color* you'd like the rocket to be?"

To protect the pack mules, the ASPCA dictated a passenger weight limit of 200 pounds. And the animals seemed to know it. They had an uncanny ability to sense the limit and would simply lie down if someone was too heavy. To ensure that the limit was followed, operators kept a scale near the entrance. One afternoon, an incredibly huge woman got to the front of the line and squeezed through the turnstiles. A wide-eyed attendant asked, "Ma'am, are you aware we have a regulation which governs the weight these animals can carry? It's California state law." She insisted she was light enough. The limit is 200 pounds, he said, and she answered, "I only weigh 190." He shot back, "Which leg?" Infuriated, she tried to attack him. The fleet-footed host was able to hide from her under a mule, but did receive a written reprimand.

In the parking lot, traffic cone patterns are set up to show drivers where to park. One busy Fourth of July, a guest wanted to park up close, so he broke through the cones and headed for the handi-capped parking area next to the entrance. As the man began to turn into an open space, with a couple of cones under his car, a parking attendant stepped in his path. Angered, the driver started lunging his car menacingly at the young host. The parking lot foreman quickly sped over on his scooter and told the guest, "Sir, if you're not sick, you're going to have to park with everybody else." The hard-nosed driver laid out a few personal invectives, backed up and drove at the foreman to scare him. The foreman ended up on his hood. Rattled and irate, the lead radioed for security. Guards usually want to placate guests, but this time the foreman told them to call the police. City officers arrived and as they led the man, hand-cuffed, into the police car, he yelled at the foreman, "Hey, you're an (expletive)!" The lead smiled back, "At least I'm not going to jail for the weekend." Police booked the man for assault with a deadly weapon and impounded his car. His girlfriend had to take a cab home.

Likewise, a hefty host was standing at the base of the escalator in front of Space Mountain and a guest ran up saying he wanted to join his friends upstairs. "I'm sorry, you'll have to go to the back of the line," the attendant explained. "We don't allow anybody to catch up." The guest started hassling the host and finally spit in his face. The operator, a reserve policeman, decked him. The blood-stain took a full day to wash off the concrete and became, at least for 24 hours, a small symbol of victory by the employees over unreasonable guests.

More often, employees lash out at visitors in subtle ways. On the Jungle Cruise, needling the guests is practically part of the job. "We'd always do things to be vicious to guests," revealed one skip-per. "They'd ask us to take their picture and we'd snap the pictures without their heads. If we found a camera in the boat, we'd snap a few pictures before turning it into Lost and Found. We would bla-tantly single out hecklers and brats and embarrass them or load the gun with the louder emergency ammo and shoot it by their ears."

If it was raining, Jungle captains would fill up their boats' canopies with rain water and then take the corners a bit too quickly, spilling the water down the guests' backs. On slow days, they liked to set up the chains on the bullpen waiting area so guests spent a few minutes twisting and turning through the winding maze, only to end up back at the entrance.

Autopia riders are daily frustrations. They endlessly ram each other or stop to see how many cars they can back up. Other kids would just get out of their cars and wander away, abandoning them in the middle of the course. Before guard rails were installed, trou-blemakers liked to turn cars sideways and wedge them in the mid-dle of the track. Once two large guys picked a car up off the track and had it running up on the landscaping.

Attendants are stationed throughout the ride to keep their eyes on the road. But Autopia workers also devise little tricks to punish the punks. When an attendant jumps onto the side of a particularly rotten kid's cart to guide it in, he might stop at Position 1 and hold the seatbelt across the kid's chest so he can't get out and have the following car rear-end them to shake the brat up. One employee in particular used to get a little carried away. He delighted in sadisti-cally disciplining young drivers. Once he jumped on the back of a car and began bawling the child out. The kid deftly maneuvered his car to the edge of the track and smashed his unwanted passen-ger into a Monorail pylon.

The miniature motorists have also driven off the track without knowing it. A gate off the backside of the course leads to a warehouse where the cars are serviced and stored for the night. A few times operators have mistakenly left the gate open. When no cars returned to the loading area, attendants ran back to discover little drivers riding wild out on the sub dry dock, the Disneyland Railroad tracks and through the garages. They had to frantically chase them all down and redirect them towards the course.

Reprimanding mischievous minors is left up to each ride operator's discretion, whether he should deal with it himself or call security. Scare tactics can be especially effective. When operators caught kids spitting out of the Skyway, they made them stand against the wall and look at a spot. They pretended that the troublemakers were being photographed and said if they made any more trouble, they'd kick them out of the park.

Smoking marijuana has been a common offense on the Skyway. Operators can usually smell it when they swing open the door, because the smoke hangs under the cabin's cover. "We'd pull them out of the car and tell them that we'd have to turn them in if they didn't stand against the wall, empty their pockets and throw the stuff out," said one Skyway customs officer. "And they'd do it! You'd expect them to say, 'Forget you,' and walk away." One particular attendant confiscated dope daily – and stuck it in his own pocket.

Guests get wildest on Grad Nites. In a single location you have thousands of teenagers, celebrating the end of high school and partying until dawn. A few chaperones accompany each bus full of grads, but they are kept out of sight, guzzling coffee and awaiting any serious problems at the Plaza Inn.

For the first Grad Nite in 1961, the park was completely unprepared for the amount of alcohol that the kids would sneak in. Barrels full of booze were confiscated on every ride. All the guests were very happy, and some got very sick.

As the park began patting down guests and searching purses at the gate, the teens got more creative. They visited the park earlier in the afternoon and planted bottles in the lockers. In turn, the park would clear out the lockers before each Grad Nite. Then grads came in early to bury cans on Tom Sawyer Island. So Disneyland got metal detectors. Or they would stash alcohol in the thick vegetation in the back areas of Autopia and try to find it that night. So if cars didn't come back for a while, attendants would go check and find a few kids walking around out of their cars. "Oh, I-ah-I lost my wallet...," they would nervously explain.

Security caught one guy hanging from a tree before a Grad Nite with a bottle in each sock. Another hid a bottle of booze in the Rivers of America to have it chilled. Sometimes the park leaves clever notes in place of the unearthed alcohol.

"It's a game, really," said one guard. "Disneyland will pat down males, visually inspect females and look into purses, yet they always manage somehow to sneak something in. It's difficult when they're inebriated and go overboard. But at Disneyland, they can't go to sleep and they can't leave. In security there's a holding tank – a six-by-eight-foot room with chairs. The problem is on Grad Nites we need about ten of those rooms. So we set up chairs along this long hallway in the basement and we bring them in and set them down along the line. The worst punishment is they get to spend their Grad Nite that way."

Teenagers also try to sneak themselves in by climbing the fence. Once inside, they can usually be spotted because they don't dress up to meet the Grad Nite dress code. The park will also turn on the sprinklers to deter infiltrators or to later identify them by their telltale soaking. A few infiltrators have also been exposed by their torn-up trouser legs, which they ripped in scaling the barbed wire fence.

Getting out isn't any easier than getting in, because the teens aren't allowed to leave until their bus is ready at about 5:00 a.m. About 2:00 to 3:00, Disneyland begins to look like a scene from *Night of the Living Dead*. Visitors start crashing wherever they can find a level surface. Hostesses have to go through the Mr. Lincoln theater after each performance to wake everyone up. The employees as well sprawl out on chairs and tables behind the scenes, making each break area look like a Chinese opium den.

Mischief runs rampant. Vandalism has ranged from small pranks, like squirting packets of ketchup at the Abominable Snowman, to ripping the top off Big Ben on Peter Pan's Flight. Every so often Snow White would lose a few dwarfs. And it became a Grad

Nite tradition that by the end of the night someone would have swiped the poisonous apple from the wicked witch's outstretched hand. To alleviate the problem, when designers overhauled Snow White's Scary Adventures in 1983, they made the apple an untouchable optical image.

"On the dark rides everything used to be real close and people would damage it," said maintenance director Bob Penfield. "When they rebuilt Fantasyland, they put an 'envelope' around it so it couldn't be touched from cars at a certain distance. And people don't know this, but when they're caught, they're billed for the damage."

In the late 1980s, someone actually abducted part of the president. They stole the right hand and face mask of Mr. Lincoln. Fortunately, there were extra masks for the robot. Police caught the thief when he tried to pawn it at a Disney memorabilia shop in Anaheim. The shop called Disneyland and asked, "Would you, by chance, be looking for the face of Mr. Lincoln?"

Graffiti is kept to a minimum, with most of it in the restrooms. Though during one private party, kids took their spray cans to the waiting area of Space Mountain and covered the corridor walls with profanity and even an anatomically gifted Mickey Mouse. Graffiti breeds itself, so if it shows, maintenance takes care of it immediately.

For couples, Grad Nite is more an amorous occasion. "At the end of the night, we'd find pantyhose, panties and condoms all over the Motor Boat ride," said one hostess. "Kids would jump off onto the islands or behind the bushes. It got to where we wouldn't run the Motor Boats or America Sings on Grad Nites because people would only go there to fall asleep or make out."

Guests seem to get most amorous in the late hours of the evening, as the crowds grow thin. Couples will go at it whenever they find themselves alone, whether they're in their own Monorail cabin or on the floor of the submarine, faintly illuminated by red light yet unseen by the operator in the sail. Late at night on the Pirates of the Caribbean, most of the boats are sent out near empty, promising excitement on the control tower monitors as the hidden cameras capture the various stages of passengers' journeys and lovemaking. One summer night near closing time, the dispatcher in the Pirates tower couldn't believe what he was seeing on the monitors. "Get up here, you guys!" he called to his co-workers. Since the ride was empty, the entire crew gathered to watch the couple enjoying themselves from screen to screen. By the time their boat returned to the dock, the couple was fully clothed and all the workers had lined up to meet them. "You know, it's really late," smiled the dispatcher, "and, well, my crew would really like to thank you a lot for making our night. Here are your tickets back." The embarrassed twosome fled.

Adventure through Inner Space was the notorious site for action of all kinds, and quickly became known by employees as "Voyage through InterCourse." Passengers figured it was so dark inside and the clamshell cars were so private that no one could see what they were up to. What they didn't realize was that two employees were positioned inside the ride to watch their every move. Soon, Inner Space, too, would have to be kept closed during Grad Nites.

Inside positioned employees occasionally gave guests a scare at their most passionate moments by tapping on the back of their car or suddenly shining a flashlight on them. One unseen operator tied a passenger's blouse around the outside of the car. Another night three guys had sneaked a bottle of Jack Daniel's inside Inner Space and were passing it from car to car. The hidden employee reached out and took it, and he could hear the trio arguing for the rest of the ride: "I gave it to you, man." "No, you didn't." "I don't have it..."

Another time an obviously amorous couple approached the Inner Space host and nonchalantly asked how long the ride was. "Twenty minutes," he replied, knowing full well the ride wasn't even a third that long. Expectedly, the couple started going at it as soon as they hit the dark, and the attendant ran from ride to ride to spread the word. By the time the car swiveled back into public view, a huge crowd of employees had gathered at the exit to applaud the still contorted, half-clothed couple.

After hours parties closed off to the general public can also get out of hand. In 1978, the Los Angeles Bar and Restaurant Association reserved the park. Two weeks before their private party, Disneyland discovered it was an association of gay bars and restaurants and it had violated the terms of its contract by selling tickets

to non-members of the group. The park could have legally canceled, but decided it would create less controversy just to host the
event.

Disneyland scheduled no bands that evening because they didn't
want anyone dancing. They warned employees ahead of time and
gave them the opportunity to take the night off. That night, Dick
Nunis and other Disney chiefs went to every attraction and every
employee to caution, "Just be cool. Let's get this night over with.
And just act like professionals." Supervisors were more blunt.
They said that, for a night, courtesy was optional. Anything goes.

With about 40 to 50 protesters at the gate, the show went on.
15,000 guests turned out, mostly homosexual, and turned it into
one of the most interesting evenings ever at the Happiest Place on
Earth. The visitors started rhythmic clapping on Space Mountain,
graduated to creative freestyle riding on the Carrousel and finally
to outright lewdness on the Submarine Voyage.

"And we did have a few instances of guests taunting employees," remembered a park manager. "Unfortunately, there were people who took their families. They were very upset. We gave them
readmissions."

While private organizations and corporations long have been
permitted to rent the park for a night, one common request was
always turned down. For its first 40 years, Disneyland didn't allow
any castle-side weddings. A wedding ceremony in the park would
"detract from the guest experience" was the official word. Still,
considering the numerous Saturday afternoon sightings of tuxedo-
and gown-clad congregations, it's a certainty there have been many
in-park weddings, albeit quickies. Wedding parties have hurriedly
gathered aboard the Mark Twain, in inconspicuous corners of
Fantasyland and other lightly traveled locales. Since the services
were short and discreet, security usually wouldn't break them up.

When informed by the park that no weddings were allowed
inside, one persistent couple devised a clever alternative. In 1988,
Anaheim city councilman William Ehrle married his bride, Julie
Johnson, in a five-minute ceremony just outside the gates, yards
from where they first met. Following the speedy ceremony in front
of the kennels, the couple posed for the traditional wedding snapshots – on the attractions they rode the day they met – then took the

Monorail to the Disneyland Hotel for a champagne toast.

To capitalize on the demand for fairy tale weddings, the Disneyland Hotel now offers a "Disney Fantasy" wedding reception package. Priced at up to $80,000, the extravaganza includes horse-drawn glass coach, fanfare trumpeters, strolling Disney characters, costumed servers and a ballroom recreation of Sleeping Beauty Castle. In one ceremony, the groom entered carrying a glass slipper and searched among the guests for the foot that it would fit.

Two other special events at the park were unplanned. On the Fourth of July 1979, Rosa Salcedo went into labor while riding the submarines. As she hurried down Main Street with her husband, the pains increased. She could only get as far as a park bench, where Disneyland nurses delivered her baby.

Five years later, pregnant Margarita Granados had to wait outside while her husband rode Space Mountain with their two sons. By the time he got off, he was the father of three. During the ride, Margarita gave birth in the First Aid station to a little daughter, with the aid of three park nurses, two of whom helped deliver the Salcedo baby.

All kinds come to the Magic Kingdom. Some families have to save up for years to make the trip. One ticket seller was known to let in for free guests short on funds who gave her a convincing sob story. One visitor was so cheap he drove around with a wooden ramp in his trunk. To avoid the then 50-cent parking fee, he laid the board over the spikes at the far end of the lot and drove in the exit.

A bald little Frenchman was riding the bobsleds and, as he took a fast corner, his cheap toupee flew off into a pond. An employee fished it out like a dead rat and handed the dirty, dripping rug to the man. He promptly took it to the drinking fountain, washed it off and put it right back on his head.

Another foreigner had to be restrained from standing up on two of the Carrousel horses. She said she had been a professional bareback rider in Europe and, even with the horses going up and down, would have no problem remaining upright. "Maybe not," the attendant explained, "but you're wearing a skirt."

A woman on the submarines could only see the driver standing in the sail from the waist down and figured he was a mannequin. So on her way out, she playfully bit him on the privates. He suddenly came to life. Another young lady allegedly tried luring guests into the Mickey Mouse Club Theater to swap sexual favors for E-coupons.

To communicate with all the tourists from around the world, employees often have to resort to charades. But on the tour guide staff are "speakers" who know Spanish, French, German, Japanese and other languages. One day the Japanese speaker was ill and a non-speaker was forced to give a Japanese group the tour. She showed them around the park as best she could, but when their tour had ended, they didn't understand that it was over and just kept following the girl. She went back to the break area, and they followed her there. Finally, the tour guide herded the group onto a submarine and, at the last minute, jumped out and ran.

One Japanese tourist wanted to know how to get to Magic Mountain, so a host gave him detailed directions to the Valencia amusement park, 50 miles away. The guy actually only wanted to find the Matterhorn.

A 400-pound man walked up to the hostess at the base of the Space Mountain escalator and asked, "What's the average *wait* on this ride?" Noticing his massive *weight*, she replied, "Don't worry, sir. You can always sit across two seats." "No," he repeated, "how long's the line?"

One night in the late Sixties, the cornet player for a guest band playing at the park, apparently high on LSD, drifted away from his group. Arriving in a far corner of the Indian Village, he took off his clothes, threw his horn and then himself into the river and swam to the back of Tom Sawyer Island. There, he climbed up on the rocks and began directing the river traffic, au naturel. As the keel boat came around the bend, the driver was shining his flashlight on the various sights. "To your right is the burning settlers' cabin, on the left is the Indian Village," he pointed out. "And on your right is a nude man standing on a rock." A split second later, a passenger screamed, "Ahhh! He's real!" At which point, the keel boat driver flicked off his light and added, "Yes, sometimes you see strange things on the Rivers of America," and continued on with the tour. By that time, a Mark Twain operator had already radioed security. A guard took a boat over to the island, threw the exhibitionist over his shoulder and, as he walked him offstage, placed his hat over his rear. A revealing write-up in the morning paper told all: "Nude Dude at Disneyland!"

Perhaps the park's most frequent visitor was an odd old man named Arthur, who spent about eight hours a day at Disneyland, almost every day, for 22 years. Each afternoon, he would take a bus to the park and visit with the employees. He came to know hundreds of them by name, memorizing the names of their boyfriends, girlfriends, interests and troubles. At 10:00 every night he'd wait near the employee exit and a worker would always give him a ride home.

He always carried around a canvas bag and liked to find lost articles and turn them in to Lost and Found. No one knew exactly who he was. Wild stories circulated about him, that he was a former employee who remembered only that he belonged at Disneyland. That he thought his job was to take care of the characters. That he was an eccentric part of the Disney family. In actuality, he was slightly disabled and never worked. And after his mother died in 1970, Disneyland became his life, his family, until he died in 1992 at age 78.

Sometimes celebrities who come to Disneyland just want to be one of the crowd. In the early years, the park gave Gold Cards to certain VIPs. If they flashed them to an attendant, they would be "back doored," or discreetly brought in through the exit. Some, like Fred MacMurray, preferred waiting in line with everyone else.

Others liked the special attention. The first thing one morning, an alert went out that voluptuous actress Jayne Mansfield and her daughter were coming to the park and didn't want to be bothered. "If you recognize her, please don't pester her," warned supervisors. "She's with her family and just wants to be like everyone else." She arrived dressed in a tight pink blouse, pink pedal pusher, large pink bows in her hair, and layers of makeup and jewelry. Three publicity agents cleared a path for her through the crowds, announcing, "Now, please, please, don't bother Miss Mansfield."

Obviously, the plan was to be as noticed as possible, even when no one was interested.

After a trip on the Jungle Cruise, Mansfield wanted to have pictures of herself taken among the trees and animals. Disneyland loaned her and her entourage a little row boat and they went out for their own private photo shoot in the wild.

Singer Michael Jackson loves the Magic Kingdom so much, he built a mini-amusement park at Neverland Valley Ranch, his Santa Ynez, California, estate. Before his multi-million dollar pop successes and plastic surgeries, he visited Disneyland all the time and was rarely recognized. After his *Thriller* album came out, girls began chasing him all over the park and he began dressing up.

His usual disguise includes a hat, a surgical mask, surgical gloves and a wheelchair. "It was so stupid," said one hostess. "Once he crawled out of the wheelchair into the Peter Pan car like some invalid. I wanted to say, 'Come on, get on your feet!' He was slowing everything up. The car returned and he said, 'I wanna go again!'"

Former secretary of state Henry Kissinger was a little better at melting into the crowd. In the early 1970s, stressed by the pressures of shuttle diplomacy and trying to bring the Vietnam War to some sort of conclusion, he liked to come to the western White House to get away from it all. He frequently visited Disneyland, mostly just to walk around and let the tension flow out of his body. He was always escorted by a Disneyland guard, with a Secret Service contingent in the shadows.

One unusually cold evening, after watching the fireworks, Kissinger asked for a coat. The security guard had one like his own brought over, a heavy topcoat with a Disneyland logo. As they continued walking around, a woman stopped Kissinger and asked him where the restrooms were. He looked at the guard, who said they were on the right. Kissinger then turned to the lady and, in his distinctive voice, answered, "They're on the right." The woman gave him a funny look, only half recognizing the newest Disneyland cast member, and thanked him. Kissinger loved it. And from then on, if someone asked them a question, he wanted to answer.

While that was the first night the statesman "worked" at the park, on later visits they let him sell popcorn from a Disneyland stand. And as he said, "Thank you," people usually gave him a hard second look, but couldn't quite put it together.

If ever Kissinger did stand out, it may have been because of the accompanying five man entourage of dark suits and the occasional helicopter circling overhead. The agents insisted on sending out an empty sub before his and one after his. This added precaution didn't work out as well one night on the bobsleds. Since the Matterhorn is run by gravity, the weight in adjacent sleds has to be carefully distributed so they don't catch up to each other. But when Kissinger arrived, his agents came in the back gate and just started getting on the ride. Attendants tried to explain that they had better let them supervise the loading or there would be problems. The Secret Service agents wouldn't listen. Sure enough, as soon as their sled neared the top, the whole ride shut down. And instead of getting on and off the ride quickly and quietly, Kissinger and all his men were stranded in open view at the top of the mountain.

Western White House chief and Orange County native Richard Nixon was also fond of the park. In fact, his press secretary, Ron Ziegler, once worked as a Jungle Cruise captain. One trip back they cleared out a boat for Nixon and his entourage, and Ziegler gave what he could remember of the spiel.

Dignitaries from around the world have visited the park, but the biggest headlines came when one couldn't. In 1959, Soviet Premier Nikita Krushchev made a trip to America and the place he most wanted to see was Disneyland. The park was all set, but at the last minute, the U.S. government canceled his visit for him, fearing inadequate security. Krushchev was furious and newspapers across the globe chronicled his tirades.

Security for international ambassadors seems impenetrable. Dignitaries are invariably accompanied by a wall of bodyguards, police, security, Secret Service agents, helicopters, bomb experts and even SWAT teams.

In about 1970, Kwame Nkrumah, ousted premier of war-torn Ghana, made the trip. "His armed bodyguards thought if anything happened to him they'd be killed so they were all paranoid," recalled one Haunted Mansion attendant. "At first we couldn't get them all in the elevator. It went down with their boss and it came back up empty. Then somebody tripped (on the moving ramp) so we had to stop the ride. It announced, 'Your ride has been temporarily stopped. Please stay in your car.' But these guys didn't understand and bodyguards started running all through the ride. I heard screaming and gunshots. They were scared to death something happened to their boss. Meanwhile, Nkrumah was off the ride, laughing. He had a great time."

Whenever someone famous is in the park, the Employee Grapevine quickly spreads the news and everyone's on the lookout. Performers in the parades compete to see who'll be the first one to spot the celebrity and tell everyone where along the parade route they were sitting. One afternoon the word was out that Barbra Streisand was in the park because there was a limo in the parking lot with "BLS" on the license plate. So the dancers spent the entire parade not doing their routines or mingling with the people, just searching for Streisand in the crowd. After the parade ended, their supervisor bawled them all out. And they later discovered that "BLS" stood for "Butler Limousine Service."

The park's biggest gathering of stars, surpassing even Opening Day, was at a private party for actress Elizabeth Taylor's sixtieth birthday on February 27, 1992. Friends spent over $150,000 to have the entire park closed off from the public and Fantasyland reserved for four hours. The guest list included Michael Jackson (a conspicuous no-show), Roddy McDowall, Robert Stack, Jean Stapleton, Jane Withers, Elton John, Barry Manilow, George Harrison, Ringo Starr, Tom Selleck, Arnold Schwarzenegger, Carol Bayer Sager, Jose Eber, Esther Williams, Robin Williams, Richard Gere, Geena Davis, Delta Burke, Bo Derek, Diane Ladd, Cheryl Ladd, Steven Segal and about 1,000 others. At least a dozen uninvited reporters tried to crash the party. They were caught hiding inside the park or trying to climb the fence and arrested for trespassing.

But for many years, the biggest celebrity wasn't a guest at all. He was the founder. When Walt was in the park, everyone got excited, tensed up. Disneyland Band conductor Vesey Walker kept an eye on Walt's apartment over the fire station, said trombonist Jim Barngrover. "If Walt's curtain was up, we knew someone was in, so Vesey would make sure we went all out."

When Walt would fly in to Disneyland from the studio, a Code W went through the park. The warning went out on security's

SHOOT FOR THE SKY. Walt Disney takes off in a Hiller 12-B helicopter.
Copyright Anaheim Public Library.

radio system that Walt was on his way. Security had a car waiting
for him at the park's own helicopter landing pad and drove him to
the Main Gate. First stop was the security office, to pick up a key
to his apartment. But by that time, news of his arrival had been
disseminated through the park. Everyone was on his best behavior.
After all, if you could please Walt, you could please anyone.

7

The Tragic Kingdom

WHEN Walt came to town in 1954, Anaheim was a sleepy rural community of orange groves and open fields, population 30,000. But his park's incredible success quickly attracted a collection of cheap motels, restaurants, liquor stores, gaudy neon lights and cheesy souvenir shops. And as Anaheim evolved into a big city, all the problems of a big city came with it.

Anaheim was slowly becoming a part of the gritty real world Disney was intent on locking out; there had to be extensive safeguards to keep it that way. Today, the mountainous berm and a barbed wire fence encircle the park. A surveillance tower overlooks the parking lot. Gate personnel may screen or even search guests. A full security force of 300, including undercover officers, patrols the grounds. In the security office sits a hotline to the police department, located just two minutes away on Harbor Boulevard.

What could be more distracting to the Disneyland visitor than an ambulance streaking across Fantasyland? More un-Disneylike than paramedics or policemen? Gunshots? A pool of blood? So, even when violence and crime do seep in, the park is determined to maintain its guise as the Happiest Place on Earth. At all times. And at all costs.

The deadliest price was paid on March 7, 1981 – the life of a teenage boy. Eighteen-year-old Mel Yorba was a burly, curly-haired high school wrestler with tickets to an all night party at Disneyland hosted by a Riverside aerospace firm. He and four friends drove in from Riverside, chugging beer the whole way. By the time they got inside the park, they were really rambunctious. Walking past the Matterhorn, Yorba jokingly reached out and pinched a bypassing woman on the rear. The woman's boyfriend, though, 28-year-old unemployed drywaller James O'Driscoll, didn't care much for the joke. Incensed, he chased after the group and grabbed Mel's skinnier friend Calvin Davis, shoving him against the Matterhorn fence. When his girlfriend yelled that he had the wrong guy, O'Driscoll let him alone. Suddenly, Yorba broke in and punched O'Driscoll in the face, sending him down to one knee.

The teens regrouped and walked away towards the Submarine Voyage, cursing back at the couple. O'Driscoll's girlfriend hurried to his side and told him Yorba was the one who had pinched her. O'Driscoll again ran after the group and this time grabbed Yorba by the shirt. Yorba spun around, struck O'Driscoll in the face and then dove at him, as they tumbled to the pavement. After a few blows, Yorba rolled off the man onto his back, his shirt stained a deep crimson red.

According to O'Driscoll, he had approached the teens merely to demand an apology and brandished an eight-and-a-half inch buck-knife only for protection amid a gang of five. He said he never imagined Yorba would charge an armed man. During the fight, he claimed, Yorba *fell* on the knife. Twice.

But according to Yorba's friends, no one knew the stranger was armed until Yorba, during the struggle, cried out, "He has a knife!" Davis said he saw O'Driscoll lunging the blade at Yorba, so Davis wrenched it free of O'Driscoll's hand and kicked him in the head. O'Driscoll got up as if to come after Davis, but stopped to pick up the weapon and fled. The teens began to give chase until O'Driscoll stopped, turned around and threatened them with the knife to back off.

O'Driscoll sprinted from the scene, intent on sneaking out of the park. But Anaheim police were waiting for him at the front exit and chased him back into the park. They finally trapped him when he crouched to hide behind some bushes near the Disneyland Railroad tracks. Searchers recovered the knife from the moat around the Sleeping Beauty Castle and its sheath from among trash on a nearby bench.

After two trials, O'Driscoll was sentenced to sixteen years to life in prison for second degree murder. But the big controversy would surface over what happened *after* the stabbing.

After abandoning the chase on O'Driscoll, Davis returned to his bloodied buddy. Yorba got up, took a few steps and collapsed. A licensed vocational nurse visiting the park had seen the scuffle and came to help. Noticing the widening blood stain, she quickly removed Yorba's shirt to find a stab wound in the chest and another in the abdomen.

The visitor applied pressure to both wounds with her bare hands to stem the profuse bleeding and thought she had it temporarily under control. She kept reassuring Yorba that help was on the way, but a few minutes later he began coughing up blood and going into shock. His eyes started to roll back, his lips to turn blue, as he faded in and out of consciousness.

By that time, four security officers had arrived, but offered little assistance. Another guest tried to help, but the guards "just pushed me away," he related. "I was so full of blood I could have been the person who committed the murder for all they knew."

About twenty minutes after the stabbing, a park nurse, Elizabeth Micco, finally arrived on the scene. She quickly decided to rush Yorba to the hospital – in the back of a Disneyland First Aid van. She assumed it was not only the fastest alternative, but knew an unwritten general policy said you weren't to call an ambulance into the park. It might detract from other guests' enjoyment of the park.

The van took eleven minutes to reach the hospital two-and-a-half miles away. Along the way, the nurse applied a pressure bandage and, when Yorba stopped breathing, gave him mouth-to-mouth resuscitation. But Mel didn't respond at the medical center. He was dead on arrival, from blood loss and punctured heart and liver.

On the surface, it appeared a life had been sacrificed to preserve the peaceful atmosphere of the park. The press jumped on the story. Within days they unleashed a torrent of harsh criticism of

Disneyland's handling of the situation. First, Yorba was taken to Palm Harbor Hospital in Garden Grove. Although it was the closest medical facility, two trauma centers, trained in handling this type of emergency, were each just a mile further.

Second, they took him in an inconspicuous company van, which had no warning lights or siren and, except for oxygen, virtually no lifesaving equipment. The vehicle was legally slowed by traffic signals, posted speed limits and heavy traffic. Not only could an ambulance have made the trip more quickly and safely, but city paramedics could have taken extra steps at the scene. They could have forced oxygen into Yorba's lungs, administered transfusions of liquids, placed him in a pressurized suit to keep blood in his upper body and would have known to take him to a certified trauma center.

Unfortunately, this wasn't the first time Disneyland had been accused of mishandling an emergency. The uproar surrounding the tragedy revealed that county health officials had long been trying to meet with park officials to discuss their medical treatment policies, to no avail. "We've been talking to people at Disneyland about this for years," one fire department official told reporters. "Something like this is pretty hard to swallow, especially when we had a station just one minute away. Our medical unit was three minutes away."

For at least three years, the county fire department's office of emergency medical services had been urging the park to make greater use of paramedics, but was completely rebuffed. In its defense, Disneyland responded that it had summoned paramedics "about five or six times" in the last year. Anaheim fire department records revealed the park called paramedics just four times in the previous two years, and an ambulance entered the park in only one of those cases, during a special event closed to the public. All too typical was one police call to the city fire department after a traffic accident in the Disneyland parking lot two months before the stabbing. A fire engine arrived, followed by an ambulance. But as soon as the paramedics team got there, the engine company informed them that the park nurse didn't want them around. When the nurse saw the paramedics, she shooed them away quickly, insisting the injuries were minor and being handled.

A year earlier, fire department official Ray Boatright had written

Disneyland pleading for a change in park policy after his father-in-law died during a visit in 1979. Since the man died almost instantly, he knew paramedics couldn't have saved him. But Boatright said the First Aid station manager instructed him that "it was the rule of the park not to use paramedics in any medical emergency" and no one was permitted to call paramedics except a park nurse. The emergency medical services office got hold of a copy of Boatright's letter, sparking an investigation of Disneyland policy by the fire department.

Less than a month after the stabbing, Yorba's mother and stepfather filed a $60 million wrongful death suit centering on the park's reluctance to call paramedics. Four days later, a second suit was filed, by a woman whose husband died eight months earlier of an apparent heart attack at the park. He was walking through New Orleans Square with his family, went into cardiac arrest and was rushed to Palm Harbor Hospital in a Disneyland van.

One week after the second suit was filed, 34-year-old Janet Wallace was standing in line for popcorn near the hub when she went into convulsions and collapsed. Two park nurses examined her, moved her by stretcher to the nearby First Aid station and sent her by white, unmarked company van to Palm Harbor. She died at the hospital of natural causes.

The next day, Disneyland finally agreed to meet with county health professionals. The latest death had no bearing on its decision, they claimed; they always intended to have the meeting. Still, emergency medical services officials reiterated that requests to set up a meeting following Yorba's death had all been denied.

Later that same day, the park announced it had hired an ambulance service to provide full-time driver and fully-equipped vehicle to aid in medical emergencies. They also promised to consult medical officials regarding installation of Code 3 equipment including sirens on company vans. Again, they said they had been contemplating the move for some time and were not influenced by the recent deaths.

It took more than five years for the Yorba case to come to trial. During the two full weeks of testimony, the prosecution called to the stand two visitors, Yorba's mother and stepfather, the park nurse, a trauma specialist who claimed Yorba should have had a 50 percent chance for survival, and a medical services expert who testified that paramedics could have arrived at the park in less than two minutes and gotten him to a trauma center in seven minutes.

For the defense, a fire chief testified that paramedics would have taken much longer than the van did to arrive at Yorba's location, assess his condition and get him to the medical facility. A Disneyland security guard then said he was on the scene within five minutes of learning of the incident. Next up, the surgeon who operated on Yorba concluded the injury was "definitely a mortal wound." A second emergency room surgeon added, "I don't think that he could have survived this wound if he had been stabbed in the operating room." Finally, nurse Micco was recalled to the stand to say there were times when outside help was called in. In fact, the park *did* have a written policy stating that paramedics should be called in life-threatening situations. But the soft-spoken Micco, a twelve-year employee of the park, testified she had never heard of such a rule.

In summation, attorney John Luetto stressed to the jury that Yorba's survival had not been assured, but "Disneyland's failure to provide adequate medical care took away whatever chance he had of surviving."

After deliberating for two hours, jurors found Disneyland negligent in not following its own written policy to summon paramedics and ordered the park to pay Yorba's parents $600,000. Disneyland immediately demanded a new trial. The plaintiffs, faced with a lengthy appeal, decided to accept an offer from the park on the condition that they not disclose or publicize the proposed settlement or its terms. But when the family's attorney mentioned to the press settling for between $100,000 and $500,000, the park threatened to back out before reconsidering.

One charge originally included in the Yorba lawsuit but immediately dismissed claimed the boy's death was partially due to lack of security at the park. Security may not be ever apparent at the park, but it is ever present. It makes its presence felt only when necessary. To perpetuate the carefree atmosphere, guards operate without police-type uniforms, weapons or formal law enforcement training. No instruction in martial arts, no drilling in pursuit tactics. What they do receive is a brief three-to-four-hour indoctrination on how the park runs and what is expected of them in a variety of situations.

Much of the force consists of moonlighting high school teachers. Teachers make ideal Disney guards because they are well educated, know how to deal with teenagers and have school schedules that coincide with the park's busy seasons – weekends, holidays and summertime.

To add to the fantasy, some guards are dressed to fit their area of duty. They might get a striped blazer for New Orleans Square or a pith helmet for Adventureland. They wear cavalry outfits on Tom Sawyer Island and Keystone Kops get-ups along Main Street. For Fantasyland, there used to be a Toy Soldier costume complete with a tall fur hat. Today, guards can be identified by their Secret Service-like ear pieces. "It's mostly public relations," said Fred Hecker, who used to patrol Frontierland in marshal attire with his two-way radio swung low like a six-shooter. "But we're also there watching kids to make sure they don't tear things up. The whole idea is to make sure everybody has a good time, and anyone who's having a good time at the expense of somebody else, that's when we step in."

Stepping in, though, can mean more than calming rowdy teenagers. Disney security nabs drug users, drunks, shoplifters and even gang members, all as inconspicuously as possible. The bottom line: be polite even to potential assailants, but act decisively if the park's tranquility is threatened. When officers first approach suspects, they must be conciliatory, even friendly. "It's better to grin 'em to death than to start fighting," said one officer. Potential troublemakers should somehow be guided offstage, for a talk. Guards are to react physically only if guests become violent. They are then to be "escorted" to the security office. If uniformed city police have to be called in, they aren't allowed in areas where guests may see them or the arrest. Disneyland guards will meet the police in the parking lot or at the security office.

At all times, maintaining the trouble-free image is paramount. Guards are instructed to refer to the holding area for suspects not as the "Whiskey section" but the "William section." Once, in struggling with a huge drunk who had to be evicted, a guard mumbled an obscenity that was overheard by a guest. The officer was severely reprimanded.

When violence does occur, security responds quickly and in quantity. A guest assaulting an officer may suddenly find himself surrounded by ten or more of Disneyland's biggest men. The key is defusal without confrontation. Once, a guard spotted a gathering of teens that had the makings of a gang staking out its turf. Alone and unarmed, he approached the youths. "I hope you gentlemen are enjoying your evening," he said, casually reminding them that Disneyland rules prohibit large groups from congregating. They would be asked to leave if the group didn't break up. After some muttering, the group dispersed without incident.

But one time in particular Disneyland's passive confrontation avoidance strategy backfired, forcing armed riot police to storm the park in full view of the guests. More than twenty years later, many from the park and the police still regret the misjudgment.

The Youth International Party, or "Yippies," were long-haired, shabbily-dressed protesters of capitalism and the Vietnam War, made famous at the Abbie Hoffman and Jerry Rubin-led riots at the 1968 Democratic National Convention in Chicago. In 1970, the Yippies decided to stage an afternoon of "free love, free dope and free fun" at the Happiest Place on Earth.

During the summer, festival organizers distributed about 100,000 flyers across the country announcing the "First International Yippie Pow Wow." The cover of the flyer pictured Mickey Mouse raising a machine gun over his head. The date, August 6, 1970, was selected because it was the twenty-fifth anniversary of the bombing of Hiroshima. The release explained the site was chosen because of some of the corporations sponsoring exhibits there, such as Bank of America which "finances war machines."

Various underground newspapers reprinted the flyer. It promised:

"Nonsponsors offer the following noncalendar of nonevents:

• Admission: all day 'by any means necessary.'

• Black Panther Hot Breakfast: 9-10 a.m. at Aunt Jemima's Pancake House.

• Young Pirates' League: 11 a.m. on Captain Hook's Ship.

• Women's Liberation: 12 noon rally to liberate Minnie Mouse in front of Fantasyland.

• Self-Defense Collective: 1-2 p.m. at shooting gallery in Frontierland.

• Mid-Day Feast: 3 p.m. barbecue of Porky Pig.

• Late in the afternoon Yippies plan to infiltrate and liberate Tom Sawyer's Island. Declaring a free state, brothers and sisters will then have a smoke-in and festival. Get it on over to Disneyland, August 6. YIPPIE!"

As rumors escalated, Disneyland officials met with local authorities to discuss possibly closing the park for the day. They decided to stay open. They figured the whole event might be a hoax and that if thousands of protesters did come to town, they would find a way to make trouble whether Disneyland was open or not.

Police in Anaheim and neighboring cities formulated mutual aid plans. Most officers were ordered to stay close to their phones, ready to roll at a moment's notice. They calculated that as many as 200,000 Yippies from across the country could conceivably converge on Anaheim. Special courts were also set up in case they had to handle mass arrests. The National Guard was contacted as a last resort.

Employees spent the preceding week searching attractions for bombs. They found one smoke bomb on Bank of America-sponsored It's a Small World. Almost every employee was scheduled to work Yippie Day. "The Matterhorn usually had about seventeen or eighteen people working it. We must have had 50," a ride operator recalled. "My job was to stand on the back side of the Matterhorn and watch the fence so no one threw a bomb over."

Two Bank of America security officers were to dress as tourists and spend the day taking photos of people in or near the bank. If there was any trouble, they could use the pictures as evidence. Supervisors, some undercover, were to be walking the park instead of sitting in their offices.

By Yippie Day, officers were prepared for 20,000 radicals to crash the gates first thing in the morning. Police from about every city in Orange County, including helmeted riot squads, packed backstage areas. They converted a backstage bus into a communications headquarters. The backstage area became an armed camp, combustible as a tinder box.

The day started quietly but built slowly, tensely. In the morning a few long-haired youths gathered at Aunt Jemima's Pancake House, presumably for the noncalendar's Black Panther program. There were no panthers and, except for a few clenched fist salutes, no trouble.

Shortly before noon, about 35 youths gathered at the front gate and began clapping their hands and exchanging words with security guards. Anaheim police immediately rushed to the scene to form a line in front of the gate. The kids quieted down, paid their admission and filtered into the crowd.

But from that moment on, security walkie-talkies began crackling with reports of small disturbances from different corners of the park. The first scene occurred at the drawbridge to the Sleeping Beauty Castle. When the Disneyland Band came marching by, the Yippies followed, screaming their own lyrics to "Zip-a-Dee-Doo-Dah": "Ho, Ho, Ho Chi Minh is going to win." They tried to mess up the musicians by running in between their ranks. The band, in danger of getting their horns jammed in their faces, decided to quit playing and unobtrusively retreat offstage.

The activists ganged together in packs of 50 to 75, taking the rides en masse and causing minor disturbances. Guards would disperse the packs from time to time, but they would soon regroup in another area of the park. For many of the Yippies, it was all a show. They would get rowdy and as soon as they were taken backstage, they would instantly calm down.

Executives and supervisors, especially harried park vice president Dick Nunis, mingled with the rebels. Confused and frustrated, he pleaded, "Please, keep it cool." Other managers disguised themselves as tourists and spent the afternoon wheeling around in wheelchairs or talking into paper bags that hid their walkie-talkies. Some of the incognito supervisors, though, stuck out like Eskimos at a nude beach, and Yippies pointed them out and taunted, "Narc! Narc! Narc!"

The protesters grew increasingly uncooperative, cursing, chanting, spitting, snake-dancing through the park, bowling over children. They gathered for sing-a-longs at the Carrousel, Chicken of the Sea pirate ship (where a few climbed up the mast), AT&T

Building, General Electric's Carousel of Progress, Monsanto's Adventure through Inner Space and Coke Corner, where they lampooned the Mickey Mouse Club song. Inner Space became a hazy drug den, thick with marijuana smoke. The employees positioned inside collected all sorts of paraphernalia and had to be relieved constantly because of the intoxicating fumes.

Throughout the day, others similarly clad in blue denim, buckskin fringe and tie-dye shirts milled about outside the front gate. Angry about not having the money for admission, they argued that private property should be outlawed and the park should be open for free to the public. "It's just a lot of people doing their own thing," one told a reporter. "There is no plan of activity, just whatever." A red cross was drawn across his forehead in sympathy of jailed Charles Manson. As he roamed outside Main Gate, he mused, "Man, that's America in there. You can play the game if you have money and look nice. But if you're different, forget about life."

To calm them, Nunis offered to admit them at a group rate of 50 cents each. They declined. Some who had entered got their hands stamped for re-entry and then tried to transfer the stamp onto their friends' wrists.

Most of the other guests struggled to ignore the Yippies, and Disneyland made it well into the afternoon without serious trouble. Rough estimates pegged the Yippie count at a few hundred instead of many thousands. Nunis thought they had averted a major catastrophe and called for a 3:20 p.m. press briefing to commend the long-haired patrons for not getting too out of hand. They're "not greatly different than other kids throughout the country," he told reporters. "They may look a little different, but they are just out here to have fun. Maybe we ought to listen to them a little more."

Nunis spoke too soon. About 4:00 a bunch of Yippies met inside the Main Street Cinema to devise a plan. After rounding up a sizable group, they held hands and began parading single file up Main Street, chanting: "We are marching to Cambodia." More accurately, they marched to Frontierland, where they took rafts to Tom Sawyer Island. The horde chased tourists off the Wilderness Fort and took over, hoisting the Viet Cong flag. They chanted "Free Charlie Manson!" and "Legalize marijuana!," sang, danced and passed around marijuana cigarettes. Allegedly, a security guard on the island even reported seeing a guy running around naked. The park closed up the fort's refreshment stand and temporarily discontinued rafts to the island. Still, no one in the ever visible security force moved in to make an arrest, even though officials feared the Yippies would remain on the island after its dusk curfew.

As it neared 6:00 p.m., the group, tiring and running out of things to chant, sensed itself fizzling out. Then one guy shouted, "Bank of America! Let's all go down Main Street again to Bank of America!"

"Right on!" the crowd answered. Though disorganized, the activities were being instigated by a handful of obvious ringleaders. The Yippies took off single file for the bank off Town Square.

Frantically, Nunis and park security director Al Niemeyer continued trying to deter the demonstrators in one-on-one rap sessions. "No good, man," one rebel replied. "We want some action." Another activist called Niemeyer a capitalist pig.

The Yippies headed for City Hall, forming a chain that would extend the length of Main Street. A few tried to rush City Hall, but employees pushed them back and locked the doors. Yippies camped out on the steps, calling for the liberation of Minnie Mouse. When they began chanting obscenities, a crowd of about 700 visitors responded with a loud rendition of "God Bless America." The Yippies tried to drown them out with boo's. They ripped down a red, white and blue bunting nearby and replaced it with the Yippie flag, which pictured a dark green marijuana leaf in a red star on a black background.

When a tourist tore down their flag, a group of Yippies jumped him. A woman with a baby carriage called for them to stop yelling bad words in the presence of children. Park officials labeled it all very "un-Disneylike."

When the mob decided to march around Town Square and back up Main Street, a wall of security guards tried to close off their path. Niemeyer told the Yippies to break it up. "Fellows, this is it," Nunis added. "We have gone out of our way and now you can leave the park or you can go back on the rides but there's no more mass marching, no more demonstrations and no more singing."

YIPPIE GO HOME. Police officers direct Yippies to the exits after a riot closed down the park. (August 6, 1970) *Photo by Anaheim Bulletin. Courtesy Anaheim Public Library.*

One of the leaders attempted to shove his way through the line of plainclothes personnel. A guard shoved back and the Yippie took a swing at him. Nunis pulled one of the leaders offstage and decked him. Within seconds, several other fights broke out.

Flash point. Riot police streamed out from behind the Main Street facades where they had been waiting all day. The Yippies who had broken the security line in an attempt to run back into the center of the park were met at the end of Main Street by a second police force. About 150 riot police joined the melee, suited in padded vests and helmets with plastic face shields and armed with yard-long batons. They formed an oval riot ring to push the demonstrators back towards the front gate. A policeman tried to grab one of the long-haired leaders by his locks and pulled them off – he was wearing a wig. Backup units arrived, bringing the total show of force to about 300, the largest showing of police force up to that time in Orange County history.

Nunis finally ordered the park closed at 7:10 p.m., section by section, clockwise from Adventureland. The clearing came about six hours before the scheduled closing time. The park had had only one prior unscheduled closure, to mark the death of John F. Kennedy. Some Yippies ran to other areas of the park as each section was closed off. Nearly 30,000 disgruntled patrons with crying, confused children were hustled out the exits, informed that they could get a refund or a rain check (total attendance for the day approached 50,000). It took two hours to clear the park and produced a massive traffic jam that took two more hours to clear out of the parking lot.

Once police had forced the mob outside the gates, Yippies began screaming, "Burn the park! Burn the park!" They lit trash barrels on fire and set off firecrackers. One threw a light bulb at the turnstiles and it exploded amid the exiting crowd. Others tore up flower beds and threw yellow carnations, rocks and other debris at officers and over the spiked fence. Police moved in long formations to the parking lot. Screaming Yippies ran wildly through the parked cars, breaking off aerials. One threw an iron stake at the officers, and four policemen pounced on him and slapped on handcuffs. Through a megaphone, police boomed that the assembly was officially declared unlawful. Police marched across flower beds to sweep the lot clear.

"Let's go to the hotel!" shouted one bearded leader, as the police forced the rioters in that direction. But as the throng streamed on foot across West Street to the Disneyland Hotel, they found nearly a dozen police cars waiting for them. The Yippies dispersed in all directions, as police helicopters circled overhead. At 10:00 p.m., Disneyland turned on all the sprinklers in the park to flush out anyone else from hiding. Sweeps revealed six Yippies hiding in various places throughout the park.

No injuries apart from a few scrapes were reported. Twenty-three of the approximately 300 Yippies, some from as far away as Wisconsin, Pennsylvania and New York, were arrested and held on charges including assault and battery, drug possession, disturbing the peace, inciting a riot, failure to disperse, malicious mischief and trespassing.

Unfortunately, Disneyland had thought it would look best to give the media carte blanche during the day. The results were jarring, graphic pictures on the evening newscasts and in the morning papers. Most reports lauded the park's patient yet forceful handling of the situation. Some of the public and even employees viewed it as a disgraceful, horrifying experience. Some of the college-age workers, though, thought it was cool, just a bunch of kids protesting the war who got a little out of hand and shook up the stuffed shirts. "It was a big joke," remembered one employee. "We got off early and had a big party." Others thought the park let it go a little too far, that they should have nabbed the apparent ringleaders earlier.

Late that evening Disneyland announced a "tough new grooming policy" banning "long-hairs" from entrance to the park. No set hair length was determined, but visitors would also be evaluated on their attire and attitude.

The next morning, six-foot-tall, 200-pound security guards sat by each ticket booth. More than 100 long-haired or unusually-attired youths were turned away after brief interrogations, most of whom would have been admitted two days earlier.

"Those were difficult months after that because we didn't know what was going to happen," said a security guard. "It took a while. There had never been an incident like that. It was so out of place that it was almost surreal. It just didn't fit. It was like going into another dimension. We were prepared but seeing it take place surprised everybody."

For months thereafter, a bulked-up security staff worked around the clock, fearing a repeat performance. And less than three months later, it was nearly déjà vu at Disneyland. A rock concert by Grand Funk Railroad at the Anaheim Convention Center across Katella Avenue attracted an overflow crowd. So when the convention center reached capacity, it closed its doors, shutting hundreds of angry youths outside. They began screaming and cursing. They finally broke in the glass doors and windows and tried to storm the entrance. The sixteen policemen lined up inside the entrance were pelted with rocks, bottles and timbers from broken barricades. When reinforcements arrived, the police drove the mob back out the shattered glass doors.

Nearly 400 officers were called in, swinging batons and arresting 84 rioters. Police formed a "v" to force them out of the parking lot. But their retreat turned into a rampage. The mob ran down Katella Avenue, smashing windows of motels and parked cars, and streamed into the Disneyland parking lot. Suddenly, a mass of humanity was storming across the lot like a tidal wave toward the Main Gate. Stunned, guards and parking lot attendants didn't know if the stampeding teenagers were just trying to get away from the police or if by force they were going to substitute the Disneyland Railroad for the Grand Funk Railroad. And no one had any idea of what they would do to the guests inside. Within minutes, without time to think or discuss, security guards, parking lot attendants, ticket sellers, ticket takers and ride operators rushed to the front of the Main Gate, literally forming a human wall and physically blocking the mob's charge through the turnstiles.

Gradually, fewer guards were stationed at the gate and the grooming policy was relaxed to cover hair styles and attire the park considered "inappropriate." It took nineteen years for the threat of another Yippie Day, Nineties style. A white supremacist group mailed flyers to newspapers and TV stations throughout California advertising May 31, 1989, as "White Workers Day" at Disneyland. The flyer called for "white militant workers, Nazi punks, pro-White heavy metallers, mods, skinheads and regular white youth" to celebrate the ninety-seventh anniversary of the birth of Gregor Strasser, an obscure early German Nazi leader. It offered a free case of beer to the first neo-Nazi to raise a swastika flag over the Wilderness Fort and falsely claimed that the event was officially sanctioned by the park.

This time Disneyland made well known its zero tolerance level. Anyone arriving with any Nazi-like signs, from skinned head down to steel-toed boot, would not be admitted. The park also beefed up its security force and Anaheim police agreed to patrol the area throughout the day. This time, though, the racist rally never mate-

rialized.   A total of one carful of skinheads showed up and they
were peaceably turned away at the gate.

As the youth protests of the 1960s faded, the Seventies ushered
into Southern California an insidious replacement, gang warfare.
General disobedience turned into personal violence. Clenched fists
were replaced by clenched firearms and switchblades, peace signs
by signs of divisiveness, like turf boundaries, colors of clothing,
race. Things got more hateful, more senseless... and bloody.
     Gang violence was another all-too-real evil even the Magic
Kingdom could not make disappear. The first reported largescale
gang fight at Disneyland broke out among 30 to 40 Hispanics from
the San Gabriel Valley near the end of an all-night private party in
1975. Shouting and shoving turned into a wild melee in Tomorrowland that ended with a seventeen-year-old drawing a .22-caliber
handgun and firing indiscriminately into the crowd. Another seventeen-year-old boy was struck in the shoulder, a fifteen-year-old
in the left arm and a twelve-year-old girl in the right side of the
face. Finally apprehended, the gunman explained that he carried
the pistol for protection because he had been beaten up at a similar
party last year.
     Six years later, two teenagers began quarreling over a neighbor-
hood rivalry, touching off a scuffle between their friends near the
Matterhorn. The two instigators pulled out knives and stabbed
each other, the nineteen-year-old knifed in the chest, the seventeen-
year-old in the leg.
     When the Videopolis dance area opened in 1985, officials knew
they would see more large groups of teenagers at the park, including more gangs. They had seen it happen at Knott's Berry Farm
with its two similar dance clubs, Cloud 9 and Studio K. And just
days before the unveiling of Videopolis, bloody clashes broke out
between dozens of Hispanic and Samoan gang members at Knott's
and then at Magic Mountain. Disneyland security quickly began
receiving special police training on how to defuse gang conflicts.
Police specialists instructed guards on gang nicknames, hand signals and how to spot members before they entered the park. They
were then to ask them to remove gang-identifying clothing by cit-

ing a dress code violation.

But none of these efforts was enough to prevent the 1987 murder of a gang member at Disneyland. The park was closing up shortly after midnight following a private party when an argument broke out between gang members outside the main entrance. Sparked by a hat worn by eighteen-year-old Samoan Keleti Naea, the argument was punctuated by epithets over the decades-old animosities between South Pacific cultural rivals Samoans and Tongans. The war of words turned into a fist fight when Tongan Salesi Tai, one day shy of age sixteen, brandished a .22-caliber handgun. The fight was broken up after several blows but before any shots were fired.

The two groups headed for the parking lot, where minutes later Naea and four or five Samoan friends confronted Tai and three or four Tongan gang members. Naea challenged Tai, who drew his gun and fired. A stray bullet struck a fourteen-year-old boy in the arm as he walked with his family about 150 feet away. Several Samoans pounced on Tai and wrestled him to the ground, knocking his firearm to the pavement. As the Samoans pummeled Tai, Naea grabbed the gun and fired five shots, three striking Tai in the side and back. The Samoans and Tongans quickly fled the lot, leaving the critically wounded Tai behind. He was rushed to UCI Medical Center, where he did not respond to treatment and died from loss of blood.

About two hours after the brawl, police pulled over a van and a Cadillac on the freeway. Thirteen Samoans were packed in the two vehicles. The group led officers to Naea, who was tried, convicted of second degree murder and sentenced to seventeen years to life in prison.

For nearly five years, groups of teens, lured by a reduced nighttime admission rate, continued to pack the park after dark. And with the related rise in gang incidents, the park decided to scrap the dance club idea in 1989 and use Videopolis exclusively for stage shows.

The danger could be very real for Disneyland's finest. "I used to bring in shoplifters and drunks and people high on drugs," said former security officer Fred Hecker. "Then a cop from Santa Ana was telling me about dopers being potential killers. I said, 'Run that

past me again. You mean I've been taking them in with just a
Mickey Mouse badge? No backup, no radio, no nothin'?' This
cop, who's six-foot-four, looks down at me and says, 'Fred, you're
nuts.' So I got transferred to maintenance."

In 1976, security guard William Fields caught a man trying to
steal a van in the parking lot. As the van started to speed off,
Fields jumped on the running board and grabbed hold of the thief.
Trying to shake him, the driver rammed the van into a Monorail
pillar, crushing Fields' feet. The officer survived the crash but lost
both his feet. Publicly, he was applauded as a hero. The park
offered him a desk job, but he decided to move on and became a
world class handicapped skier.

But privately, some in management criticized Fields, saying a
Disneyland guard shouldn't act like a cop. Nevertheless, the job
does attract some police department hopefuls and wanna-bes.
Security guard Joseph D'Allura had always wanted to be a policeman or security guard and was once enrolled in the police academy.
In August 1983, he said he was patrolling the far corner of the
parking lot when he spotted a suspicious character looking into
cars. The guard radioed his backups to instruct them to stay back
so they wouldn't scare the suspect away. D'Allura said he made
his move when the man tried to break into a car with a wire coat
hanger, but the man spun around and fired a .22-caliber handgun
point blank at his chest. Fortunately, despite the hot and sticky
weather, D'Allura was wearing his own personal bulletproof vest.
The slug lodged in the first layers of the vest. Suspecting bruises
to the heart, D'Allura was taken to the hospital. Although no
bruises were visible, he complained of chest pains and spent four
days at the medical facility, undergoing tests and recuperating.

The shooting caused a stir in the amusement park industry.
Nearby Marineland and Magic Mountain decided to reevaluate
their current security procedures, though Knott's guards already
carried billy clubs and guns and wore protective vests.

D'Allura spoke to local newspapers, publicly criticizing the
park's not arming or adequately protecting guards "lest we spoil
the image." He said park guards make three to five arrests each
day, mostly for the use of cocaine. He said the only training guards
receive is a tour of the park and their only equipment a flashlight,

which if used as a weapon is grounds for immediate termination.

"Things are pretty tense out there right now," reported another guard. "Park officials are trying to downplay the shooting as much as possible. Like it never happened. So much so that security guards coming on duty after the shooting were told nothing about it."

In response, Disneyland said the guards are there to help diffuse situations; if confrontation and restraint are necessary, they are to contact authorities. "We don't want our people to start thinking of themselves as the Disneyland Police Force," said park spokesman Bob Roth.

Meanwhile, police started getting suspicious when they couldn't find anyone who heard a shot fired in the vicinity. Police experts said the bullet in D'Allura's vest and a shell casing found in the parking lot didn't come from a handgun as the guard had claimed. The slug and the casing came from a rifle, the type found at the home of a relative of D'Allura. Disneyland fired the guard, and police arrested him and charged him with filing a false police report. They suspected that he faked the attack to gain money from the park or because he was distraught over recently breaking up with his girlfriend. But at his 1985 trial, jurors said prosecutors failed to prove their case and found him innocent.

D'Allura meanwhile filed a $5 million lawsuit against the park, alleging Disneyland had wrongfully fired him, pressured Anaheim police to seek charges against him, and subjected him to emotional distress. He claimed the park terminated him because following the incident he had spoken to newspaper reporters. Park policy, he explained, limits an employee's freedom to speak out on topics that management considers "detrimental to its public image." He finally dropped the case.

There have been other shootings to disrupt the tranquil Magic Kingdom that were accidental. In 1984, a woman exiting Small World reached out to keep her five-year-old daughter from getting lost in the crowd and dropped her purse. As it hit the pavement, a .38-caliber double-barreled derringer inside fired and hit her sister in the leg. The following New Year's morning, five minutes into 1985, a woman was struck in the left thigh while sitting atop her boyfriend's shoulders near Sleeping Beauty Castle. The .38-caliber slug was presumably fired into the air by some senseless reveler outside the park. Five years later, another bullet from the sky tore through a Disneyland Railroad car's red and white canvas roof and hit an eight-year-old girl in the back.

Gunfire last erupted at Disneyland in the parking lot in August 1991, after a couple tried to sneak into the park by climbing over the kennels. As the man waited above for his girlfriend, he triggered a silent alarm, alerting security. But as the guards arrived to catch his girlfriend, the man pulled out a gun. He dashed across the parking lot and past the administration building, sporadically firing at the officers. Once outside the lot, he stole a car at gunpoint to make his escape. Police later apprehended the man and recovered the vehicle.

To combat auto thefts and burglaries in and around the parking lot, police experimented with a trial program stationing ham radio operators with binoculars on top of the roofs of nearby hotels. A few years later, officers received customized 21-speed Schwinns. Teams of stealth mountain bikers could now sneak up on criminals preying on tourists in the area. Disneyland security has its own lookout station on top of the Indiana Jones Adventure show building, affording binocular-bearing officers a wide view of the parking lot.

Though heavily patrolled, the Disneyland parking lot has the makings of Car Thief Heaven. It holds 15,000 cars over its 100 asphalt acres and, chances are, the drivers won't come looking for them until late in the day. Yet over the years there have been a handful of more daring parking lot heists. In 1986, a woman was robbed at knife point of her car, purse and two cameras. She had tossed her handbag into the car and was about to enter it herself when a man wielding a six-inch switchblade appeared and demanded her keys. She handed them over to the suspect, believed to be a mental patient who wandered away from a park tour group. The man sped away, about two hours later using her vehicle as his getaway car in a holdup of an Anaheim McDonald's.

Less than a year later, the same night of the Tai shooting but in a different corner of the lot, a sixteen-year-old boy was followed by two men as he returned to get the family car at about midnight. They forced him inside his own car at gunpoint and drove off.

LOOKOUT tower originally atop the main Pirates of the Caribbean show building afforded security guards a clandestine view of the Disneyland parking lot. (December, 1992) *Photo by David Koenig.*

Throughout the ride, one man held a gun to the boy's head until they dropped him off unharmed in neighboring Santa Ana. Two days later, authorities arrested two suspects in Los Angeles.

While this was probably the only abduction at the park, for a full decade rumors had circulated that a black market kidnapping ring operated out of Disneyland. The rumor claimed that 200 children were kidnapped at the park each year. The story usually went like this: a child, typically a boy about two years old, is snatched from a stroller inside Disneyland while his mother is distracted. After frantically searching the park, she goes to the front gate, where she sees a woman carrying a child covered with a tattered blanket. She instantly recognizes her boy's tennis shoes poking out and screams. She yanks the child from the woman's arms and is horrified to discover that he has been drugged and his hair cut and dyed red.

Apparently the rumor stemmed from a short 1978 item in a Utah church bulletin warning parents to keep close tabs on children at amusement parks because of news stories on snatchings. Soon after, Utah police and Salt Lake City residents began calling Anaheim police for more information on the Magic Kingdom kidnappings. Callers were so distraught that the Anaheim police chief issued a formal statement to a Salt Lake newspaper that the rumors were false.

As the story spread, police continued to receive dozens of calls each year, mostly during the summer, from people and news media around the world wanting to know about the child stealing. Accounts of actual abductions in shopping malls and campgrounds and a *60 Minutes* report on kidnappings fueled a full-blown resurgence of paranoia in 1984, causing the Associated Press to nationally circulate a story that reiterated the total falseness of "the rumor that refuses to die."

Most of the calls to the Disneyland switchboard are questions like "How late are you open?" and "Are there fireworks tonight?" Many times the callers are children who want to talk to Mickey Mouse. But, every so often, the usually peaceful park phone lines are rattled by a bomb threat. Some are pranks, others bluffs; a handful have been serious. "We get some kooky calls" from time to time, admitted spokesman Bob Roth. Still, the park takes the threats quite seriously, on occasion evacuating and searching wide areas. Police, park security and even ride operators, who usually know the nooks and crannies of each attraction, have been asked to search for explosives to ensure guest safety.

"We had several bomb threats during the summer of 1971," remembered a former People Mover foreman. "I sent a runner out to walk the track. We did this once a week to remove cars with motors that weren't working, and he found a bomb on the track near the end of the ride in the AT&T Building. He came back and looked real white. I went out and there was a large shoebox with wires sticking out. I called supervision, got the bomb squad and, sure enough, it was a live bomb, sitting between the track and the glass window. I still don't know where it came from."

One series of threats that summer came to the Long Beach Police Department from a caller identifying himself as the Los Angeles area "Alphabet Bomber." First he threatened to blow up the Submarine Voyage, so they evacuated and searched it along with all the nearby attractions. The next day he called back, targeting It's a Small World. "'A' stands for airport, 'L' stands for locker and 'I' stands for It's a Small World. You have twenty minutes," he said. They cleared out Small World, the Skyway and the Matterhorn, but again found no bomb. An hour-and-a-half later, he called back saying he had actually planted the bomb on the Matterhorn and the evacuation and search routine was repeated.

Three years later a caller threatened to set off a series of explosions at Disneyland and Disney World. He instructed police to retrieve a note detailing his ransom demands from a Greyhound Bus depot locker in Santa Barbara, California. The note said he would detonate seven bombs over a fifteen day period if he did not receive $3 million. Half of the money was to be placed in a Santa Barbara railroad yard, the other half in Orlando. Santa Barbara police instead left an empty box at the rail yard and captured the man who arrived on a motorcycle to pick it up.

In 1980, a cryptic caller to the Disneyland switchboard identified himself as "Weatherman." He said he represented a revolutionary group and threatened massive destruction if he didn't get $100,000. To demonstrate his ability to carry out the threat, he planted twelve notes and packages throughout the park. Weatherman made five calls to arrange various rendezvous. He only showed up once, but sped off on a motorcycle before FBI agents could close in. Disneyland, meantime, temporarily stepped up its security force and checked purses, tote bags and camera bags at the Main Gate. Three years later, a man was arrested in Louisiana on rape charges. In his panic, he also confessed to the 1980 bomb threats. Sure enough, his fingerprints matched those on the notes he had hidden throughout the park. He was sentenced to five years in prison on the extortion charges.

A bomb threat the next year again proved to be a bluff. But when the FBI moved in to investigate, everyone started speculating that it was part of a terrorist plot. In 1991, a guest stumbled upon an explosive device in the Grist Mill on Tom Sawyer Island. The park immediately evacuated and sealed off every attraction on the river. Police removed the device, which the county bomb squad later determined to be harmless.

The most common crime inside the park is less dangerous and less premeditated. Shoplifting happens every day and much of it is just impulse stealing. Customers are all handling the merchandise, making it easy for a girl to slip a ring on her finger or into her purse or for a young kid to slip a souvenir under his jacket. And shoulder-to-shoulder shoppers can far outnumber clerks, especially during the last minute rush as the park closes.

To catch the thieves, park security has its own plainclothes officers, called "fox units." They blend in with the crowd, pretending to shop but actually spying on shoplifters. As soon as the suspect leaves the store, the guard moves in. Suspects are taken to the security office and interrogated. If they're minors, they have to stay there until their parents arrive to take them home. Once parents had to drive in from San Diego, over 100 miles away. The kids had to sit in the security office from noon until their parents could pick them up just before midnight.

When suspects can't come up with a receipt or grow hostile, security often turns to the Anaheim Police Department. Most suspects won't admit to stealing and the officer can't back down. "When they say 'no' and I say 'yes,' we have a conflict," an undercover agent explained. "We have to call the police and have a full arrest. If we don't, it's an admission of guilt for wrongful detainer. Our only recourse is to call the police. People don't know if they just would have admitted guilt, they probably would have been kicked loose, out of the park. But they think that at Disneyland security they're in a police department of sorts."

Shoplifters come in all shapes and sizes at the Magic Kingdom. One elderly man bought a shopping bag from the Arts and Crafts store and proceeded to go around the shop filling it up with merchandise. When it was full, he started to walk out the door. Kids have tried to slip out with stuffed animals almost as big as they are. Two young couples each had a stroller and were going from shop to shop, loading them up with pilfered plush toys.

If clerks notice suspicious activity, they'll notify a fox unit who usually is nearby. "I could always spot a plainclothesman even if I'd never seen him before," revealed one clerk. "Guards are issued their plain clothes and the same hard black shoes as with the blue security uniforms. So I could recognize this guy with a bag by himself because he had the stupid security shoes on."

Whereas shoplifting is usually a spur of the moment decision, picking pockets is all business. Pickpockets are professionals who go to Disneyland with the intention of stealing. And the park can be a profitable target because of the thousands of guests, totally absorbed in the experience of Disneyland, bumping into each other and carrying wallets packed with cash. The pickpocket's cost of doing business is the price of admission.

Counterfeiters similarly earmark Disneyland as a good place to conduct business. In reality, it's one of the toughest places to unload funny money. Ticket sellers handle so much cash that a bogus bill stands out. They're trained what to look for by security and soon can tell the difference just by feeling them. Real bills have almost a waxy feeling; the counterfeits are more like paper.

In the 1960s, the park handled so much counterfeit cash that one of security supervisor Larry Miller's main duties was serving as a liaison with the Treasury Department. "In one case we apprehended a couple pushing the money and the Anaheim Police Department was called in," he recalled. "They opened the trunk of their car, which contained two bags. One marked 'Ours' was filled with the counterfeit money and 'Theirs' with the real money. There was over $300,000. It led to arresting the whole ring of three or four and recovering the plates. We were instrumental in that."

No one ever robbed the park's own Bank of America, but there have been some scares. Every once in a while a tourist would walk in and, not realizing it was a real bank, say, "This is a holdup." Even as a joke, that was against the law. Almost instantly, a full security team would swarm down on the poor fellow and scare him half to death. After taking him to the security office and counseling him, security could quickly tell that the man was just kidding. But to the tellers, it was a very serious matter.

One stonefaced young man announced, "This is a holdup," but fled before security could arrive. Officers and tellers ran down Main Street after him. Apparently planning to disguise himself by changing into other clothes, he tore off his hat, then his T-shirt as he weaved in and out of the crowd. Security finally nabbed the bare-chested suspect in front of the Candy Palace.

And, as All American as they may seem, Disneyland's own

employees have been caught stealing from the company. One ride operator used to go outside the Main Gate, pull people out of ticket lines and offer to sign them into the park for a reduced admission. Disneyland eventually caught on and fired him.

Any suspected thievery first merits an intense investigation. When they suspected a fifteen-year arcade mechanic of stealing quarters from the Starcade video games, they set up a special sting operation. Security placed coins in an Air Hockey game specially marked with luminescent, seemingly invisible paint. They caught him with a marked quarter among a stash of coins in his locker.

But Disneyland got big help from the outside in uncovering its biggest ever inside job. For three-and-a-half years, a warehouse supervisor had been stealing videotapes, stuffed animals, toys, stationery, clothing and other memorabilia and reselling them to local shops. He said he had a special deal with the park. He stole $500,000 to $800,000 worth of souvenirs, and his half share of the sales profits netted him an estimated $170,000. But, in 1987, one shopper grew suspicious of a garage sale peddling brand new souvenirs on consignment and asked about the source. The man tipped off Disneyland with the supervisor's name. The culprit was arrested, pleaded no contest, served four months in jail and had to make $200,000 in restitution payments to the park in cash and by turning over his Anaheim home and other property.

Signing out and tracking merchandise at Disneyland's warehouses could no longer be regulated by trust. The philandering supervisor had worked there without incident for nineteen years. His co-workers were stunned. "He was a kid when he came to work here," sighed a longtime warehouseman. "He was a pretty good worker and supervisor. I thought he was a nice enough guy. It was a total surprise to me."

It's most surprising because the crime and violence, so commonplace in the real world, happened at Disneyland.

8

Fatal Attractions

INCH for inch, Disneyland is one of the safest places around. And that's no accident. Of the four essentials stressed to each employee, Safety *always* comes first. Before Efficiency, before Show, before Courtesy. Workers are taught that safety is everyone's responsibility, and they must follow a comprehensive safety policy and complete mandatory accident reports. They're trained in emergency response procedures, on everything from what to do if someone gets run over by a car to how to evacuate in case of fire. Most of the specifics they'll never use, but it does make employees sensitive to potential mishaps. They become so adept at handling the little glitches that happen every day that few guests notice.

"I can't tell you the number of times – at least once a week – employees routinely save someone from serious injury," said ride operator Larry Holmes. "Guests get lost in their own world. They don't pay attention to what's going on around them. Sometimes it's as simple as putting your hand out to keep a kid on the submarines from walking into the water. I've seen little kids go in the water because they're not paying attention and employees go in after them. They didn't report it to anybody. There are no commendations on record. And sometimes it's so subtle the guest doesn't even know it happened."

The park has two first aid stations, Central First Aid between the Plaza Inn and Baby Center off Main Street and a smaller station for busy times behind the Mile Long Bar in Critter Country. Both are staffed by licensed doctors and nurses, ready to remove splinters, bandage blisters or even treat serious guest or worker injuries. What distinguishes the stations most from the average hospital is the patients. In a hospital, people are frightened, worried about why they're there. At Disneyland First Aid, guests are in a good mood, eager to return to their day of fun.

But accidents do happen, even at Disneyland. "Anytime you're around machinery that complex and that many people are involved, it's a miracle you don't have more people injured," said Holmes. "We'll have days when 50,000 people come through the gates. There's a lot going on and you can't physically control people all the time, outside of putting them in cages. If you stay in your vehicle, remain seated, don't hang your arms out or shake it back and forth, you're safe. There are few instances of mechanical failure. Metal fatigue, they call it."

More often, *mental* fatigue is to blame. Guests get reckless, thinking, "This is Disneyland. Nothing bad can happen to me!" In reality, you can get hurt on any of the attractions if you try hard enough. And, sometimes, it can be fatal.

The park's first fatality was Mark Maples, a fifteen-year-old playing hooky from school with friends on a Friday morning in 1964. As their bobsled whipped though the Matterhorn, a companion unbuckled Maples' seatbelt. Nearing the top of the peak, Maples tried to stand up, lost his balance and fell to the concrete below. The impact fractured his skull and ribs and ruptured organs. His brain began hemorrhaging. Disneyland rushed the boy to Palm Harbor Hospital, where he underwent emergency surgery the next day. He died in the hospital three days later. His parents unsuccessfully tried to blame the park in court, but obviously there was nothing Disneyland could have done to prevent the accident.

Two years later, nineteen-year-old Thomas Guy Cleveland tried to sneak into the park on a Grad Nite. He scaled a sixteen-foot fence and climbed onto the Monorail track, planning to walk the rail so he could jump into the back Autopia area. A security officer spotted the teenager walking along the track and a train coming in the distance. The guard shouted for him to leap clear. Instead, Cleveland tried to hide on a fiberglass canopy about three feet beneath the rail. It wasn't low enough. The bottom of the Monorail struck and killed him instantly, tearing his body to pieces and dragging it 40 feet along the track.

"The driver didn't even know what happened," said a fellow Monorail operator. "He never saw the kid. All of a sudden the car just slowed to a stop. He radioed security. It's too bad security couldn't have radioed him, but it all happened so fast. Security was hollering at the kid. He was listening but he was scared. He just laid on one of the plastic panels which hang under the track wherever it passes over a walkway. And the Monorail passes just two inches over that. It just sucked him right under the car. And I had to hose this kid off the bottom of the Monorail."

The high speed Monorail's more sedate Tomorrowland companion, the People Mover, has proven even deadlier. Its blazing average speed of two miles per hour and open-air cars are actually temptations to troublemakers. In 1967, seventeen-year-old Ricky Lee Yama and two friends were jumping from car to car as the ride went through a tunnel. His friends made it, then heard Yama's screams as he fell beneath the wheels of one of the cars.

Within minutes, a security officer was on the scene, but hurrying wouldn't help. "I knew he was dead right away," the guard explained. "I bent down, looked under the car and could see his head was right in two." The ride had to be dismantled to remove the body.

Six years later in 1973, another teenager paid the ultimate price for his mischief. At first, though, his actions didn't seem nearly as dangerous. Bogden Delaurot, an eighteen-year-old New Yorker, was staying with friends in Southern California and wanted to take his visiting ten-year-old brother to the Magic Kingdom. The boys took a raft to Tom Sawyer Island and, as it neared dusk, hatched a scheme. When officials came to clear the island for the day, the boys climbed over a fence to hide in the off-limits area containing the burning cabin. But by 10:00 p.m., the excitement had worn off and the brothers wanted to head back. Since there were no more rafts back and they were afraid to call attention to themselves, they opted to swim. The distance isn't very long, but the younger boy

didn't know how to swim. So his older brother took him on his
back. About halfway across, Bogden went down. His brother dog-
paddled until a boat picked him up. Bogden's lifeless body was
found the next morning.

His parents sued the park, alleging the name *Tom Sawyer* Island
gave their children the idea of spending all night on the island, like
Tom Sawyer and Huck Finn did in the Mark Twain novel. Again,
Disneyland was cleared.

The following summer, Disneyland premiered an automated
musical variety show, America Sings. The attraction wasn't much
different from what the Imagineers had done before, using the
Carousel of Progress' building with its outer ring of six theaters
which rotated around various scenes on a fixed central stage. Yet
the ride seemed cursed with setbacks from Day One. During the
attraction's press debut on June 28, 1974, one of the designers was
posing for news photographers amid the audio-animatronic characters on the Gay Nineties set. As his stage began to lower and the
lights went out, the Imagineer stepped too close to the edge and fell
ten feet down into a stage pit. He landed on one of the characters
and smashed it. They tried to go on with the presentation, but then
encountered problems with the sound.

The ride officially opened to the public the next morning, with a
large American flag displayed. It was accidentally hung upside
down. Nine days later, on July 8, newly-hired eighteen-year-old
Deborah Gail Stone was serving as an America Sings hostess. Her
job was to greet audiences over a microphone from the left side of
the stage and then, after the theater had rotated around the five
musical scenes, to bid them goodbye.

At the end of each 24-minute show, there was a 45-second inter-
val after the audience had left the theater in which the stage moved
into position to start a new cycle. Somehow, Stone got too close to
the passway between the rotating theater wall and the stationary
stage wall. A guest in the adjacent theater heard a scream and
turned to see what looked like a child being pulled between the two
walls. As soon as the theater stopped moving, he notified operators. The two passing walls had crushed the hostess to death.

Stone may have fallen, stepped backwards or tried to jump from
one stage to the other. Fellow operators think she leaned back on

purpose because when the building was used for the Carousel of Progress, it rotated in the opposite direction and it was safe to lean back to talk to co-workers in adjacent theaters. But it was Stone's first week at Disneyland. She had never worked on the Carousel of Progress.

News of the tragedy spread quickly through the park. The first reports were sketchy, causing co-workers to grow sick wondering which of their friends had lost her life. The next day authorities closed the ride to investigate. Hostesses in front of the Rocket Jets had to tell guests that their ride was down due to mechanical difficulties. Actually, reporters and camera crews were crowding onto the raised Rocket Jets platform to film the nearby scene of the accident.

To prevent a second tragedy, the park immediately installed a warning light to alert operators who got too close to the danger area. Soon after, they put in a permanent safety system and replaced the solid walls with breakaway walls.

Stone's parents filed suit against Disneyland, but money wasn't their motivation. They just wanted to find out from the hush-hush park what happened. They settled for what they considered a small amount. The years slowly brought the family solace, drawing them closer to Jesus Christ. Deborah's younger brother was inspired to join nondenominational missions in the South Pacific. Her high school christened its pool the Deborah G. Stone Memorial Swimming Pool and classmates started an annual scholarship fund in her name. After reading about the accident, dozens of people from across the United States, Europe and South America began writing to the Stone family. Ten years after the accident, a man Deborah had befriended wrote to say that her death led him to kick his drug habit. "It is amazing how she had touched so many lives in her death," said her father.

At Disneyland, America Sings' fateful Theater Two was kept closed for the longest time. Years afterwards guests waiting in line at the ride constantly asked about the tragedy. "It was so rude," recalled one hostess. "To shut them up I'd say she was my sister."

Unfortunately, tragedy tends to repeat itself. During a Grad Nite in 1980, the People Mover struck again, in a near replay of the Yama accident. Gerardo Gonzales was trying to climb from car to car when he lost his footing and fell under the following vehicle. It crushed his chest and dragged him underneath for hundreds of feet until someone reported the accident to operators. Unlike the Monorail, the People Mover had no "Dead Man Switch" to automatically shut it down when something went wrong. It would just run over whatever was in its path and keep going until someone shut if off. Gonzales was pronounced dead at the scene.

Three years later, Grad Nite was again the backdrop for tragedy, this time a second drowning. Philip Straughan was feeling good. His class had traveled to Disneyland all the way from Albuquerque, New Mexico, to celebrate the end of high school. The night was also Philip's eighteenth birthday, and he and his buddy had been drinking. Walking through Frontierland, the intoxicated twosome noticed an unattended maintenance boat moored at a dock. They sneaked into the blocked-off "employees only" area, untied the inflatable rubber motorboat and headed out for a late night joyride on the Rivers of America. In mid-trip, the sloshed skippers hit a rock and Straughan was thrown from the boat. His friend tried desperately to find him, but when he couldn't he sped back to shore for help. An hour later, they found Straughan's body, floating in about four feet of water.

The autopsy revealed the teen's blood alcohol level at .19, nearly twice the legal limit for adults. His mother filed a wrongful death suit, accusing the park of negligence in allowing the drunken youth into the park. Her lawyer argued that Disneyland even took extra steps to allow him in: he had arrived without a sport coat or tie, and park officials escorted the teenager to wardrobe and suited him up to meet the Grad Nite dress code before letting him in. The park was again found innocent, but Mrs. Straughan did receive a settlement from the travel bureau responsible for organizing and chaperoning the trip.

Seven short months later, to the day, a much more mysterious accident took the life of a 47-year-old grocery clerk vacationing from Northern California. While riding through the Matterhorn, Dolly Regene Young was somehow thrown from her bobsled. She landed on her back atop the track, directly in the path of an oncoming car. As the half-ton sled pinned her head and chest, the entire ride automatically shut down. Puzzled, the lead sent two young ride operators up to investigate. When they arrived at the sled, they didn't see any blood, just two legs sticking out from under it. She looked like the wicked witch under Dorothy's house in *The Wizard of Oz*.

Cause of death on her death certificate was initially listed as "pending investigation." When Young's sled was examined, her seatbelt was found unbuckled, crossed on her seat. The family's attorney contended this was proof that it wasn't used. She must have lost her balance and fallen when she tried to get up off her seatbelt to put it on, he deduced. Operators, though, found it difficult to believe a sled could be released with a seatbelt unfastened, since a whole line of workers checks every lap. The park speculated that Young must have unfastened the belt herself to tend to her child in the next seat. And if somehow the belt was never fastened, they reasoned, it would be the woman's own fault for standing up. Minutes before the $5 million case was to go to trial, Young's family accepted an undisclosed cash settlement.

The final fatal accident at the park wasn't on a ride. It occurred in 1985 in the parking lot. Seven-year-old Jennifer Faith Reid was with her uncle looking for their car when she fell under a passing tour bus. Its rear wheels ran over and crushed her.

A day at the Magic Kingdom is a great way to make you feel better, but don't expect it to heal all your ailments. Signs posted outside rides like Space Mountain warn passengers with medical conditions to bypass such tumultuous attractions. That didn't stop Sherrill Anne Hoffman and her family from riding Space Mountain on a visit in 1979. During the ride, she became ill and when her car pulled into the unloading dock, she couldn't get out of the car. Employees instructed her to remain in her seat and that her rocket would be taken out of service. Unfortunately, the attendant in the tower didn't get the message and sent the car on a second three-minute trip. He could have shut down the whole ride and helped her out at an emergency unloading point, but then she would have to be carried down 83 steps. He figured it was faster and easier to let the ride continue. When the rocket returned to the station, the woman was nearly unconscious. Attendants carried her to a bench.

A nurse and a security guard quickly arrived with a wheelchair and wheeled her to First Aid. There, park nurses tried to console her husband. "Don't worry about a thing," one smiled. "Your wife's going to be fine. She just fainted." But when she didn't get any better, he demanded they take her to a hospital. A Disneyland van took her to the medical center, where she remained in a coma for a week and then died.

Doctors discovered Hoffman had a tumor in her heart. Presumably the jostling of the ride had dislodged it. The fragments traveled up to her brain, lodged there and killed her. Her husband sued, convinced the second Space Mountain trip had broken the tumor free and the park was negligent in not properly or speedily caring for her. The action was eventually dismissed.

Medically, at least, Disneyland cannot suspend reality. Numerous visitors have dropped dead of natural causes. One man suffered a heart attack while riding the bobsleds and slumped over his small granddaughters. When the sled finally came in, operators had to pry the stricken grandfather off the crying girls.

Veteran operator Hank Filtz had an older gentleman die in his arms as he was helping him out of a Storybook Land boat. Twenty years later, he encountered a second cardiac arrest victim. "I was in the Pirates control tower," Filtz recalled. "There was a Hawaiian group and down the second ramp I could see them waving their arms. One woman was slumped over. Each time they appeared in a monitor, it looked like they were just having a great time. When I saw them standing at the bottom of the up-ramp, I asked them to sit down. Then I knew there was a problem. It was a heart attack, and she was only twenty-something years old. I tried to revive her but she was gone. She weighed about 300 pounds, and we couldn't get her out of the boat."

Once a horse pulling a streetcar had a heart attack and dropped dead in the middle of Main Street. The only way to get the huge animal offstage was to haul it off with a forklift. But the supervisor knew the newspapers would have a field day with that. Instead, they got a big tarp and threw it over the horse. Passersby asked what happened and the staff tried to explain that horses have heart attacks, just like people. Finally they were able to clear the area and bring out the lift.

Falls from rides have caused many extreme, near fatal injuries. Adventure through Inner Space was a constant site of trouble. The clamshell cars were easy to slip out of and the pitch darkness disguised the fact that the track would rise up to twenty feet above the floor. In the late 1960s, a teenage girl was following her boyfriend jumping from one car to another. She missed. The following car ran over her and she tumbled to the ground below. Cut, bruised and broken, the girl got mangled.

In 1972, four teenagers hopped aboard the People Mover. As they passed through a dark tunnel housing the lighted Model City exhibit, a gust of wind blew off one girl's Mickey Mouse hat. Her cousin climbed over the side of the slow moving car to retrieve the cap and she followed. They snatched the Mouse Ears and hurried along the tunnel to catch the next car. The first girl caught it. The second ran out of tunnel. Freefalling out the exit, the fourteen-year-old smashed into a stair railing and the concrete 30 feet below. Her body was badly bruised, her arms cut, a leg broken and her left hip, pelvis and right side of her buttocks crushed. She spent three months in a body cast and afterwards walked with a limp because of the steel plate installed in her hip and the pin in her leg.

She sued the park, claiming there should have been a guard rail at the tunnel exit. At the trial, a People Mover operator testified that throughout the ride a recorded message instructs passengers to keep all parts of their bodies inside the cars at all times and since he'd never seen or even heard of anyone walking around inside the tunnel, there would be no need for a railing. The jury ruled for Disneyland.

But even the employees can unwittingly place themselves in grave danger. In the early 1970s it was standard practice on the Matterhorn that when a rider lost a purse or sweater, to avoid shutting down, two employees got a straightened-out coat hanger and hopped in a sled. When they located the item, one would lean out the back of the sled and try to hook it with the hanger. One day a woman's wig blew off and attendants Cathy Davis and Gary Lucas went up to find it. They quickly spotted the wig and took a second trip to get it. The second time up, recalled Lucas, "Cathy turned around and leaned out the back just as we hit a corner. She leaned out a little too far. She was slipping and sliding and popped out of the sled. The strangest thing was seeing Cathy going over the edge, the expression on her face." She plunged nearly 50 feet through the center of the mountain. And Lucas started wildly waving his arms and screaming to stop the ride, terrified his own sled would strike her body on the way down.

Incredibly, she didn't hit a single I-beam or section of track. She landed on the dirt below and suffered severely broken shoulders, ribs and pelvis. A very athletic woman, she survived. "It was a miracle," Lucas said. "If it were a tenth of a second different she would have been killed. I walked the track many times after that and there just weren't that many spots that could happen. One, maybe none."

Doctors told Davis she would never walk again. Today, she not only walks, she has three children and still works at Disneyland in the parking lot.

In 1979, a four-year-old boy from Oregon climbed into a People Mover car ahead of his parents. When he saw them catch the next one, he began to climb out of his car as the tram continued on its way, 30 feet above the Tomorrowland Complex. He plummeted down to the pavement near America Sings and Mission to Mars, landing on the left side of his head and suffering a double skull fracture.

Four years later, eighteen-year-old James Higgins and two friends visited the park, having had a little to drink before they came in. They boarded Space Mountain and somehow during the ride Higgins was thrown from his seat. His body was hurled against a wall and fell five feet below the track. When the ride was over, his friends realized someone was missing and notified operators. Comatose for four weeks, Higgins finally awakened... with severe spinal injuries and some brain damage.

How he actually was able to tumble from the car no one could say. Higgins remembered boarding the ride and then waking up, paralyzed, almost a month later. His lawyer claimed that either a mechanical defect caused the lap bar to lift or his outraised, waving hands hit a low-hanging steel beam and pulled him out. Disneyland, though, had caught the trio drinking beer in the parking lot and behaving wildly before and during the ride. The park was convinced Higgins had intentionally wriggled free of the restraining bar. They even brought one of the rockets into the Santa Ana Courthouse so an employee could demonstrate how a determined guest could quickly work free of the restraint. Jurors and the court of appeals believed Disneyland.

Guests have also been bounced from Big Thunder Railroad by working their way under the safety bars, but these victims have been more fortunate. In the early 1980s, a high school student stood up in a rail car and was thrown out, onto a ledge. He was taken to the hospital and sustained no lasting injuries. In 1991, a 40-year-old Romanian visitor was found lying on the catwalk along the track where the train passes through a dinosaur skeleton. He spoke no English but was able to tell a Romanian park mechanic that the last thing he remembered was feeling faint during the ride and that he may have passed out. He suffered only a broken leg.

Guests and employees alike have fallen off most of the boat rides. The most common victim seems to be the Storybook Land hostess, who helps passengers on board while she stands with one foot on the dock and one in the drifting boat. A few girls slipped off the back of the boat in mid-trip, but their passengers were so absorbed in the ride that no one noticed their guide was missing.

The Disney fleet also suffers an occasional sinking. A few canoes have sprung leaks, run into rocks or been flipped over by rocking riders. After a recent canoe sinking, operators tried to blame it on some splashing kids. A few witnesses, though, thought the attendants had erred in the passenger selection process and packed the boat with overweight riders.

Late one summer night, the Storybook Land lead was demonstrating to a trainee how to throw the switch to Never Neverland. What he didn't know was one last boat was still out. When it came in, the switch was out of position and ripped open the bottom of the boat. The ship sank to the bottom, bringing with it nine passengers and one woman's fur coat. Disneyland quickly installed a red and a green light that shows if the track is open or closed.

Even though the submarines are on a rail, they've found a way to sink. The first system was more of a free-wheeling track, so a sub's wheels might pop off the track and send the boat out floating on a brand new route. One subdriver in the mid-1960s took the corner into the caverns a little too fast. The side of the sub hit the entrance and smashed two portholes. As the vessel began filling up with four feet of water, employees rushed the passengers out onto the scaffolds inside the caverns.

The park revamped the track so it couldn't happen again. But it would, on December 7, 1974, Pearl Harbor Day. Veteran operator Vince Sweeney was demonstrating to a trainee how to bring a new submarine on line while a co-worker was ready to take off at the dock with a second sub filled with 38 Japanese tourists. Sweeney had a reputation of putting a boat on rather quickly, so when the second driver saw who was driving, he figured the new sub would whip right onto the track. But since he was training, Sweeney put the boat on much slower. The second pilot let his craft drift out and it got whacked by the back of Sweeney's. The impact popped the first few portholes and water started gushing in.

OUT OF ORDER. An uncharacteristic admission of problems at the Magic Kingdom. *Photo by Ron Harris.*

The guests, all in suits, all with cameras, stood up on their seats to try to keep their heads above water. Some climbed up into the sail with the driver and, in total panic, started diving out into the lagoon. Luckily no one was hurt because the boat only sank down about three feet onto the track. The supervisor, though, was fired, and the sub stayed half-submerged for three days, with scuba divers going in and pumping all the water out. And everyone joked that it was Disney's revenge for Pearl Harbor.

Employee error was also to blame for a pair of derailments of the Disneyland Railroad. The first incident occurred the first week the park was open. As the train neared the Main Street Station, an operator flipped the switch between two wheels of the rear car and sent it tipping. The car, filled with guests, leaned perilously over the ledge, about to fall, with dozens of others all around below it. Within minutes, employees had the car shored up and evacuated.

About ten years later, the crew was taking the train into the Roundhouse at the end of the night when someone threw the switch before the train was fully on the side track. Half the train backed over sections of double track and it jackknifed. The top heavy engine came close to tumbling, which could have caused the boiler to explode and killed the engineers. The ride was down the whole next day so cranes could be brought in to lift the cars back onto the track.

In 1989, some teenagers rocked their Skyway cabin so violently that one of its guide wheels jumped off the cable near Toad Tower in Fantasyland. The entire ride automatically came to a stop and it refused to start back up again, leaving dozens of passengers trapped 40 feet in the air. City firefighters arrived to help lower the guests, one by one, with extension ladders. It took over four hours to reach the last of the imprisoned visitors. The park tried repeatedly to restart the Skyway but minor problems and strong winds kept it down for three more days.

The very next week on the adjacent Dumbo attraction, a bracket connecting one of the fiberglass elephants to its supporting arm gave way. Tenuously held by a safety cable, the elephant tipped about 45 degrees and, still rotating, dragged and scraped a passenger along the elevated concrete walkway surrounding the ride.

A year later, a thirteen-year-old girl was injured when the support arm on a second elephant collapsed. Disneyland immediately shut it down and began its three-to-four-week annual maintenance check a little early. After closer inspection, they finally decided to entirely scrap the aging 35-year-old attraction. The Dumbo ride built for EuroDisneyland was sent to Anaheim and a new one was ordered constructed for the Paris project, then still two years away from its grand opening.

During their opening months, many of the roller coaster-type rides offered occasional unexpected thrills. Cars would barrel into each other time and again while programmers tried to work out all the bugs. Crashes on the newly-unveiled Space Mountain and Big Thunder Mountain injured dozens of passengers. But the most celebrated smash-up involved the People Mover. During its nightmarish first summer, the attraction broke down about every twenty minutes. This was nothing compared to the evening in November of 1968 when it suddenly started to rain. As one train of cars neared the top of a bend, its tires lost traction on the newly-wet track and the train began rolling backwards. The sliding cars smashed into the front of the next train of cars, and then the next train plowed into them from behind. And then the next. As if in slow motion, the chain of impacts threw screaming passengers from their seats and against car walls, steel poles, the floor and each other. One woman knocked heads with her daughter and tore her cheek on a metal barrette in the child's hair.

Disneyland spent thousands of dollars settling with the injured parties, 23 in all, and immediately installed slip-free, pneumatic tires on the cars.

Since most of the accidents at Disneyland are caused by guest carelessness, sometimes the employees view the mishaps with a cynical eye. The night of the second People Mover fatality, Jungle Cruise drivers were suggesting their passengers check out the new ride in Tomorrowland: the People *Re*mover. Within days of Dolly Young's death on the bobsleds, the Matterhorn crew had nicknamed the site of the accident "Dolly's Dip" and put the entire tragedy to song, played to the music of "Hello, Dolly." Once after Casey Jr. derailed, the ride was down for the summer to replace much of the track. The workers rewrote the Casey Jr. theme song: "Casey Jr.'s coming off the track! It's time for ribs to crack! It's time for broken backs!"

Yet actually, despite all the training and emphasis on safety, cast members may be in even greater danger than the guests. They work with, on and in that complex machinery eight hours a day. And they have to go where the guests aren't allowed to be to get the job done.

Disneyland constantly strives for a safe work environment, but a 1987 investigation by the Occupational Safety and Health Administration revealed just how many little hidden hazards can lurk behind the scenes of such an elaborate operation. Prompted by complaints from employees, OSHA conducted a series of inspections exposing 36 violations of worker safety rules. They were little things like unguarded openings where people could fall and difficult accessways between backstage catwalks. In a Small World attic, parts of a motor used to lift props weren't shielded to prevent employees from getting caught in the machinery. One side of Big Thunder Mountain didn't have a fixed stairway. The park explained that no one had ever questioned the dangerous conditions before, paid the fines and quickly remedied the danger areas.

But that year alone OSHA would record 1,450 occupation-related injuries at the park. "Employees get banged up all the time. It's an occupational hazard," explained one well-battered worker. "If you're working the parking lot, odds are you're going to get hit by a car, maybe brushed, tapped, even knocked down. If you're jumping cars on Autopia, you're going to fall, twist an ankle or get knocked down. On the subs, you can fall off a boat or on the dock. If you're running inside the caverns there are low overhangs and you can get knocked down. On Matterhorn, you can slip and fall."

During breakdowns on the Matterhorn, each sled had to be manually released from its brake zone. Employees would run down the often slippery catwalks alongside the track, dodging low overhangs.

Space Mountain has similar walkways parallel to the track. "We tried to make the breakdowns as short as possible because guests were waiting," said hostess Elizabeth Hayes. "We would take unbelievable chances in order to take shortcuts, swinging from the rafters from one place to another, walking across beams." On Autopia alone, Hayes suffered a broken finger, broken foot, crushed toes, fractured pelvis, run-over knee and sprained ankles.

Before TV cameras and gantries were installed along the People Mover, an employee was positioned as a lookout far out on the track, which had electricity continuously flowing through it to power the cars. At the end of the night, the sentry would hop on the back of the last car and ride it in. One night a lookout jumped on the back and it inexplicably sent a 200-volt electrical shock through his body. He was okay, but plenty shaken up.

Close calls in the line of duty have been countless. One Skyway worker's job was to shut and lock each cabin's door after the guests got in and slide the cabin out onto the cable. One time a handle was already in the lock position, so the door popped back open. He slammed it again, and again it boomeranged back at him. As he ran down the ramp trying to close the door, his hand slipped through the rung and caught. The bucket started going out across Fantasyland with four frightened guests inside and an attendant hanging on the side. Luckily, the cable passed right over the Mad Hatter Shop. The operators stopped the ride and the hung-up host was able to drop down onto the hat shop roof. He returned to his buddies to join them for a good laugh – until someone wondered aloud, "Hey, what if you had to ride it through?" The gravity of the situation finally hit him and he just turned white.

Employees have so many routine, monotonous chores, sometimes they try to take shortcuts. One of the responsibilities of opening foreman on Rocket Jets was walking around the perimeter of the ride before sending the jets up for one quick test run. They did that for about the first week and from then on would just lean over and take a quick glance. One lead started the ride up for a check run without walking around it and all of a sudden heard screaming. She quickly pressed the Emergency Stop button and ran to see a little maintenance man straddling an upraised rocket, holding on for dear life.

In the 1950s, a fire broke out aboard the Mark Twain that the captain swears could have blown up the ship. The fire started in the engine room and spread to within a sheet of plywood of a 60-gallon gas tank. The ship came steaming into the dock, with security, First Aid and fire department waiting, and was evacuated in record time. Fortunately, the automatic fire extinguisher system put the blaze out and that very night the park installed a new four cylinder generator in the stern.

Because fires are a very real threat at Disneyland, the park maintains its own professional fire department, complete with contemporary engines and 30-some fully qualified firefighters. Retired firemen usually hold the full-time positions, while part-timers are often active in local fire departments. The park's first fire marshal was the retired city fire marshal for Omaha, Nebraska. Every morning he drove around the park on a cart with a hose, personally checking everything out.

The department's main responsibility is preventing fires and accidents. Regular duties include maintaining and inspecting fire extinguishers, checking alarm and sprinkler systems, ensuring nothing is blocking accessways, inspecting kitchen, warehouse and storage areas and standing by during fireworks shows, welding, soldering and other potentially hazardous work. They respond to minor emergencies, such as grease or motor fires, but call the Anaheim Fire Department if it's more serious.

And there have been a few memorable blazes. In 1971, a fire broke out beneath a stretch of bobsled track in the middle of the Matterhorn. As one family's sled reached the bottom of an incline and entered a tunnel, five-foot-high flames shot through their car. The man and his wife were doused with a greasy substance that stung their eyes and caused chemical burns on their hands and face. The sprinkler system quickly extinguished the fire, after it had burned a small section inside the mountain. Its cause was never determined, although one passenger said he saw what looked like a flare burning beside the bobsled track.

The toasted twosome sued. "We could see flames coming on either side of the track," the man explained, "so I felt rather sure this wasn't part of the ride." Disneyland settled the suit for about $1,000, covering their medical costs.

One December an electrical short ignited the year's huge Christmas tree in Town Square. The fire department quickly doused the blaze, but not before it burned the top off the tree. The ingenious crew cut the top off a smaller tree and, using a crane, attached it to the top of the burnt one.

In 1993, an electrical fire broke out on the People Mover in the Tron Tunnel that passes through the America Sings building. Operators quickly evacuated the ride and closed off all of Tomorrowland. Automatic sprinklers were able to contain the blaze, and city and Disneyland fire crews extinguished it in 25 minutes. No guests were injured, but six employees suffered minor smoke inhalation.

On the Fourth of July 1967, the fire scene in the newly-opened Pirates of the Caribbean really caught fire. It started from a short or a break in the hydraulic line of the drunken pirate leaning against a lamppost and began to spread. Yet the realistic fire effects made it hard to tell there was an actual fire. At the end of the ride, disembarking guests told attendants that it looked like the burning city was really burning. "Yeah, it's supposed to look like that," the operators smiled, blissfully unaware.

Fortunately, a lookout positioned nearby smelled smoke. He was able to wade through the water, intercept boats before they got to the fire and help guests out the emergency exit. Eventually, the smoke triggered the sprinklers, which hadn't been tested yet and also contained an oily preservative so the pipes wouldn't rust. Riders were doused with water and oil.

The section of the set surrounding the lamppost was severely damaged, and the drunken figure charred so badly it looked like a real human, all burnt to a crisp. One of the melted posts blended so well with the scene, they never replaced it. It's still there. The park did install a special button so they could shut off the fire effects in case of future emergencies.

Then in the mid-1970s, a Pirates of the Caribbean boat passenger flicked a cigarette into a basket of plastic fruit in the wench auction scene. The plastic caught fire and smoke started spewing from the basket. Quickly contained, the fire didn't present any real danger, but as smoke began filling up the ride, people started panicking. Attendants in waders went down into the water to calm the passengers, but one hysterical woman handed a knee-deep worker her nine-month-old baby. "Please save my baby!" the mother cried, as she and her boat continued on into the smoke.

Nothing else caught on fire, but burning plastic turned everything in the scene black. Each figure, costume, wig and prop had to be cleaned or replaced.

In 1985, two kids on Adventure through Inner Space tossed a firecracker out of their car and set part of the fiberglass structure on fire. The blaze sent draperies falling down onto four cars, injuring some of the passengers inside. Others were hurt trying to scramble from their cars. Five guests had to be treated for bruises, eye irritation and smoke inhalation.

The next summer a blaze erupted in a backstage storage lot, caused by sunlight reflecting off a mirror-covered *Return to Oz* parade float. The fire quickly spread to nine other Christmas parade floats before firefighters finally contained it.

But every summer, it's the nightly fireworks shows that present a special challenge for the park's fire crew. For the first Fantasy in the Sky fireworks show in 1956, employees used hand flares. Now they're staged by state-licensed pyrotechnicians, firing from cylinders buried in the ground behind Small World, linked to a twelve-volt battery and Mickey's Match, a computer about the size of a washing machine. Fireworks programs are stored on a small computer circuit, half the size of a matchbook. An average summertime show includes about 200 shells, shooting as high as 800 feet into the sky. The computer system allows the shells to be fired at a rate of one every few seconds, perfectly synchronized with the music on the park PA system.

Every employee is on alert. Falling embers can get into brush or a trash area, so the force tries to keep all containers covered. Four or five firemen are positioned in different areas of the park throughout the presentation and they comb the grounds after every performance. At certain intervals before each show, the firemen send up helium balloons to see where they drift. If one drifts back over the park, they may have to clear out entire areas to protect people from fireworks fallout or, on especially windy nights, cancel the entire program. If the wind starts blowing back into the park after the show starts, the first place fallout strikes is Small World. So Small World attendants are armed with walkie talkies and at the first sign of falling embers, they'll radio to stop the show.

More often the embers fall outside the berm, to the chagrin of local homeowners. Over the years, residents in the Disneyland neighborhood have periodically complained about fireworks fallout and noise. In the summer of 1991, angered by ashen debris burning into their car paint, residents filed a formal petition. The park responded by flying in its Disney World fireworks expert and canceling the most elaborate portions of the show.

The biggest deluge of phone calls from locals demanding the shows be stopped came after a spectacular blaze in 1984. A stray rocket from the summertime show flew off course into a fenced-off, outdoor storage area and landed amid a group of wooden pallets and cardboard boxes packed with stuffed animals. Soon gigantic flames were leaping up to 300 feet into the air, shrouded by plumes of dark black smoke. The 36 firefighters responding had to don special breathing devices to combat the possibly toxic fumes. The fire and the water it took to put it out destroyed about $430,000 worth of plastic shopping bags, printed material and 82,000 character dolls.

For a special smaller pyrotechnic presentation in the mid-1970s, fireworks were set up on barges along the Rivers of America. One errant rocket crash landed in the muck on the banks of Tom Sawyer Island and set the reeds afire. "There were firemen on the island," recounted an eyewitness. "One grabbed his hose and ran toward the fire but his hose wasn't long enough. Unfortunately, the two guys who arrived on a raft docked at the far dock and then left their fire extinguisher on the boat. By now a nice little blaze was going. Finally a fireman got an extinguisher out of a shed and put it out. It took longer than it should have, with about 10,000 people watching."

The park has only had to close up about a dozen times due to bad weather, usually because attendance is so low. Many attractions can operate in the rain and Disneyland quickly learned that with the unpredictable Southern California weather, it can be pouring one minute and clear and sunny the next.

Bad weather makes for extra difficult working conditions. Poor drainage used to turn Main Street into a lake, with water washing over the curbs. The park provides employees with raingear, hoods, scarves, mittens, rubber pants and galoshes. Huge gas heaters are set up in the breakrooms.

During one heavy storm, a bolt of lighting struck the fence

around the flagpole in Town Square and zapped around the wrought iron. During another downpour, lightning hit a power transformer and instantly shut down all the rides on the west side of the park.

The 1982-83 winter was unusually harsh. Torrential rains had kept down the number of guests, usually huge during the holidays. Then three days before Christmas, at 4:34 p.m., powerful winds toppled a major Northern California powerline linked to Anaheim's city-operated power system. Just as the last traces of daylight were vanishing, everything stopped and went black. Disneyland management made the quick decision to evacuate the park. Several hundred flashlights were handed out to employees, who lined Main Street directing guests to the exits. In the suddenly darkened shops, clerks clutching flashlights had to both help and keep an eye on customers, hurriedly writing sales receipts on notepads.

Patrons had to be plucked out of Matterhorn bobsleds and Space Mountain rockets. Rescue workers in battery-powered maintenance tractors pushed Monorail cars back to their stations. They used an emergency generator to reel in the wire cable with the Skyway buckets.

One of the most precarious situations was on the Pirates of the Caribbean, which begins and ends in the higher level bayou, using gates to keep all the water from rushing down to the lower level. Without electricity, the foreman couldn't raise the gate, so all the water flowed downstairs. Below, the water level rose so high that boats began to float out of the flume. Freefloating through the pitch darkness, the passengers were all too terrified to move.

The crew went into standard evacuation procedure, taking flashlights, putting on waders, getting into the much deeper water and directing boats to the nearest evacuation point. Guests in the boats stalled on the chain-pulled up-ramp had to be carefully led up the stairway along the side of the ramp. Disneyland would later install automatic emergency lighting unattached to the main power line.

Fortunately, no one was hurt in the blackout. Many were so shaken up they had to be taken to First Aid to lie down and catch their breath. And just as the last of the 7,700 patrons were herded out of the park, less than two hours after the outage, the power came back on.

The unusually harsh winter ended with a bang a few months later. It began like a perfect day at Disneyland: big, happy crowds in sunglasses and shorts under clear, sunny skies. Then, in the middle of this idyllic afternoon, the sky suddenly turned jet black, filling with thunder, lightning and powerful 60-mile-an-hour winds. And guests and attendants alike stood motionless, their mouths hanging open, as a freak tornado ripped through Tomorrowland. It blew out a window and sent trash cans dancing around the park. Umbrellas flew everywhere. The twister-power gusts also knocked the Skyway's cable off a car's guide wheel, shutting down the ride. Firemen with cherry pickers responded, but this time they had to deal with the pounding rain and dangerous winds. The Skyway had become a completely different kind of thrill ride, as dozens of passengers huddled on the floors of the wildly swaying buckets.

Management closed down most of Tomorrowland to allow the emergency equipment to reach the stalled Skyway. Some considered it part of the adventure, dropping their cameras down to ride operators to snap pictures of them climbing down the cherry pickers.

Evacuees were taken to First Aid and given free Mickey Mouse sweatshirts and passes to the park. The staff wrapped recovering guests in dry blankets and yellow raincoats, then had some of the costumed characters entertain them. And in the middle of a tornado, you could hear the laughter of children. Only at the Magic Kingdom could you hope to snatch hundreds of people from a harrowing, life-threatening ordeal and send them home safe – and smiling.

9

Lawsuit Land

IN today's world, people who suffer serious injuries typically pursue two types of therapy. They try to get better and they try to get even. Filing a lawsuit has become almost as common as filing a tax form, and about as truthful. But when the defendant is Disneyland, you'd think people would have reservations about suing. It's as if they're taking on an almost-saintly favorite uncle, and a quite wealthy one at that.

Think again. Precisely because it's so big and so image conscious, dissatisfied customers have been dragging Disneyland to court for nearly 40 years. More than 1,500 lawsuits have been filed against the park over the years, at a pace of about 40 suits a year. At any given time, they're juggling at least 100 active cases.

Despite the large number of challenges, it's extremely difficult to beat Disneyland in court. According to Orange County Superior Court records, less than a fourth of all resolved cases made it to trial, and the park has won over 80 percent of them. In other words, a suit against Disneyland historically has about a four percent chance of making it to court and winning. And the chance decreases daily, since the park has gone to trial only a handful of times in the last ten years.

If the park knows it's at fault, it will usually try to settle before

or soon after the suit is filed. But unlike many other huge corporations, Disneyland won't settle suits just to make them go away, no
matter how Mickey Mouse they may be. The park has much deeper pockets than the average plaintiff and can drag a case on for ten
years if they have to. More importantly, they're willing to spend
more time and money fighting questionable suits than it would take
to settle them in the first place. "If we think we are not in the
wrong, we're going to fight," said the late W. Mike McCray, the
hometown lawyer who represented the park during its first 30
years. "It's the only way to keep 50 lawsuits a year from becoming
500. It took a long time for people to realize that we meant business."

Sometimes parties are so set on going to court or obsessed with
the dream of a big pay day that they reject fair settlement offers. In
1960, a woman was climbing up the ladder through the hatch when
her submarine was rear-ended by a second craft. She was thrown
back down into the sub, landed on a set of seats below and suffered
bruises, cuts and a sprained neck and back. She retained flamboyant defense attorney Melvin Belli, who advised she demand no less
than $100,000. Disneyland offered her $35,000. He laughed at the
offer and flew down from San Francisco with his entourage. The
trial court delivered a judgment of $36,500.

A year later another woman was climbing out of a sub and
pinched her right hand between the hatch and the dock. She
claimed the incident caused a flare-up of her muscular dystrophy.
In court, McCray conceded that Disneyland was at fault but disagreed as to the extent of her injuries. She asked for $500 for her
medical costs and $50,000 for her pain and inconvenience.
McCray pulled out copies of her doctor bills and told the jury she
deserved just $32.50, the cost of her x-rays and emergency treat-
ment. The jury awarded her $32.50.

Some guests just flat out refuse to settle. Disneyland was able to
strike agreements with all the parties injured on the chain reaction
People Mover crash of 1967, except for one woman from Monro-
via, California. She absolutely would not settle and demanded a
trial. When the jury handed down a judgment for $37,740, the
judge ruled the figure excessive and ordered her to relinquish
$25,000 of it or face a new trial. Again, she chose the trial.

Before the retrial, her attorney sought to force Disneyland, the park's lawyer or its insurance company to turn over films of the woman taken by a private investigator. Disneyland acknowledged that the woman had been under surveillance, but refused to say who hired the detective, since they thought she was just looking for an excuse to file an invasion-of-privacy suit.

To avoid a second trial, Disneyland representatives raised their settlement offer to $17,000. They would have even gone as high as $20,000. They didn't have to. The second jury found in favor of the woman for only $4,500 plus court costs.

People think Main Street is lined with gold, that the park is a soft touch, that they can get something for nothing. Many "victims" fake or orchestrate their own accident. They'll stage a fall, or deliberately step in front of a streetcar.

One young woman was taken to First Aid after falling off a Frontierland barrel, a prop she never should have been climbing on. She claimed an assortment of injuries, but park nurses couldn't find anything wrong with her. So they sent her to the hospital for a medical evaluation and told her to rest and not return to the park. Three hours later, she was again being wheeled into First Aid with a new injury from another area of the park.

Disneyland wins most of the cases because a majority of them fail to show any liability by the park. Some are just plain frivolous. One woman tripped while alighting from the Monorail. She said her fall was caused by an exit ramp which was "defective" because patrons were forced "to be brought out into the bright sunlight."

A pregnant woman got claustrophobia while inside a Casey Jr. cage and demanded that operators unhitch her car from the train. When they refused, she decided to unhitch it herself. In trying to uncouple the car, she tripped and tumbled out.

And the family of a man who was killed by their neighbors' pet lion sued the park, claiming the neighbors were unable to control the beast because they were spending the day at Disneyland. The plaintiffs alleged that when the African lion next door first escaped from its backyard cage, they phoned Disneyland to have the animal's owners paged. With attendance in the tens of thousands, the park explained that there was no way of tracking down the neighbors. And by the time the neighbors got home, it was too late.

Expectedly, Disneyland was cleared.

Many times the judge will inform the plaintiffs during the settlement conference that they don't stand a chance. But, at least in the days of lighter traffic at the Orange County Courthouse, when some parties insisted, judges felt obliged to grant them their day in court. In 1959, a woman sued claiming she was traumatized by a ride on the Matterhorn bobsleds. She said she never would have boarded if she had known it was a "roller coaster" ride because they frightened her. After she lost the trial, she accosted McCray in the hallway outside the courtroom and put a curse on him which she said would keep him from ever winning another case.

Ten years later, a 25-year-old woman walking along Main Street was knocked down to the ground by a Clydesdale pulling a streetcar. She said the beast then started kicking her, walked over her and pulled the wagon over her hip. She received bruises all over her body, a scar on her hip, a swollen foot, torn-up shoes and hoof prints on her slacks. All the witnesses testified that the woman wasn't looking where she was going and walked into the oncoming horse.

Another woman, who wanted to watch her daughter riding Dumbo, selected an odd vantage point: right outside the attraction's iron exit gate. Not unexpectedly, someone opened the gate to exit and decked her.

Unhappy guests aren't the only ones pushing for frivolous suits. "A lot of lawyers apparently aren't that busy," McCray said. "They sue us when they have no case. They are convinced they can beat us, and they convince the client. But it doesn't happen very often."

Disneyland has proof on film. During the making of an in-park training film depicting what employees should do when a guest spills something, an actor was to walk out of a Bear Country saloon with a tray of sodas, trip, fall and spill his drinks. Security was to keep people away from the spill and call for a wheelchair, but the instant the actor hit the ground, a bystander handed him his business card. "I'm an attorney," he whispered. "I saw the whole thing. It's Disneyland's fault. I can sue them for a million dollars." As security guards helped the actor into a wheelchair and wheeled him off-camera, the lawyer followed them right into the lights. The shameless shyster even agreed to film a second take.

Another attorney paid for a round on the Frontierland Shooting Gallery with a C-coupon. Afterwards, he noticed a sign which said you could use a C-coupon or a quarter. But the coupon he had used was imprinted with a value of 40 cents. He felt that Disneyland had cheated him and thousands of others out of 15 cents apiece. He filed a class action suit for $1 million in punitive damages, plus his lawyer's fees and his 15 cents.

The lawyer and the park exchanged about every possible argument. Disneyland said the lawyer never paid 40 cents for the ticket. He bought a ticket book at a discount price that worked out to about 24 cents per C-coupon. And he suffered no damages since he had the choice of using his C-coupon for the Shooting Gallery and was allowed to do so. Citing *Blue Chip Stamp v. the Supreme Court of Los Angeles County*, the attorney claimed the park did receive added benefits by selling the tickets by the book since the books gave them non-refundable money up front for tickets visitors might lose or not have the chance to use and forced patrons to visit less popular attractions. In truth, the park classified the Shooting Gallery as a C-ticket attraction to guarantee it made about a quarter off the ride whether patrons paid cash or used tickets purchased in discounted ticket books. Even today the Shooting Gallery is the one attraction not included on the all-day pass. The case was eventually dismissed.

People don't beat the park that often, mostly because it's basically a safe place, with a reputation for being meticulously maintained and refuse-free. Every inch is constantly cleaned, with every attraction inspected and repaired on a regular maintenance schedule. It is difficult for a plaintiff to paint a picture of a dangerous environment at a place where there's always a sweeper within sight. Disneyland often submits safety records as evidence to show a ride has accommodated millions of other visitors without incident. Employees are trained to detect potential hazards. If someone does drop an ice cream bar, an employee stands over it until a janitor arrives.

People also don't realize how well everything is documented by park nurses. The view of the legal profession is if it isn't documented, it wasn't done, so nurses take innumerable notes on every detail. One woman sued for a new cashmere sweater. Unbeknowst to her, at the time of her accident the nurse had noted that she was wearing a cotton sweater.

Another suit said a woman got dizzy watching the 360-degree "America the Beautiful" presentation. She teetered out of the Circle-Vision Theater and tried to lean against a railing, but fainted back over the railing and struck her head on the ground. Obviously the attraction was unsafe because it made her dizzy. The day of the accident, though, she had casually mentioned to a park nurse that she tripped over the railing trying to take a short cut. The judge declared it a "non-suit."

Nurses make key witnesses in trials, but other Disneyland employees prove equally valuable on the stand. They're usually well educated, well groomed and articulate, promoting an All-American image.

In addition, Orange County cases fill jury boxes with local citizens, who typically are more easily influenced by the Disney reputation. Disneyland is a top employer, moneymaker and taxpayer for the area. To dilute this home court advantage, many lawyers seek a change of venue. Opponents reason that a case transferred to, say, Los Angeles County may wind up with a jury less likely to take Disney's side. Cases aren't easily transferred, but one Los Angeles lawyer got a case moved by suing both Disneyland and Bank of America, the non-Orange County corporation that sponsored the injury-causing attraction. He successfully repeated the strategy when another client was injured at a Carnation Co.-sponsored site.

Another advantage for Disneyland is its fine legal staff. For its first 30 years, the park was represented by McCray, a World War II veteran turned private attorney. A Donald Duck plaque on his office identified him as "Disneyland's mouthpiece." He also earned the nickname "Iron Mike" for once in his pre-Disneyland days trying 36 cases before juries in one year and later "Perry McCray" for his unusual Perry Mason-style tactics.

In cases involving the Autopia, the wily character would bring actual cars into the courtroom's basement for the judge and jurors to examine. Other times, when he thought the jury could benefit from seeing the attraction in action, he took them to the park. For a

1960s bobsled injury suit, McCray had jurors climb the Matterhorn, leading them up the maintenance stairway inside the mountain to view the ride in action. Disneyland won the case. A similar
strategy also won a case in which he took the jury to inspect the
Mad Tea Party. To demonstrate, he had the Superior Court judge
and his bailiff get into a teacup and asked the bailiff to spin the cup
as fast as he could. The bailiff had the teacup spinning so fast, the
judge nearly became ill.

McCray died of cancer in 1985, seven months after successfully
defending Disneyland against the man who was paralyzed after he
was thrown from a Space Mountain rocket. The park continues to
rely on McCray's one-time partner Richard McCain and a battery
of other top legal pros based at Burbank headquarters.

Competing lawyers claim that Disneyland's advantage stems
more from a fantasy perception than reality. After all, it's the Happiest Place on Earth and Mickey Mouse is an international symbol
of good. "You have to have good and clear evidence," said one
opposing attorney. Juries demand "a little bit more proof against
Mickey than against other people."

Disneyland is run by people. People make mistakes. And many
disgruntled guests contend that the park's homecourt advantage
discolors the truth and results in miscarriages of justice. "The situation with Disneyland, to put it bluntly, is that you can't sue God in
heaven," said the husband of plaintiff Sandra Varela. In 1975, she
had to bring her Autopia car to a quick stop because the seven cars
in front of her were backed up behind a twenty-foot eucalyptus
branch that had drooped into the roadway. The car behind Varela's
didn't stop. It rammed her from behind, causing whiplash and
severe back injuries. She had to undergo several operations, cost-
ing a total of $120,000. McCray argued that all the operations
aggravated her injuries and turned a "psychologically neurotic hysterical woman" into a "surgical invalid." Varlea said that if Disneyland just paid her medical bills, she wouldn't have to sue, even
though she lost another $50,000 in earnings as an executive secre-
tary. They wouldn't pay.

Her only chance, her lawyer stressed, was getting a change of
venue. They couldn't. During the three-and-a-half-week trial, she
thought her case had been proven beyond a reasonable doubt. But

the jury deliberated only two hours before awarding her nothing. They ruled for the park because, according to Varela, the jurors were "so against anybody not from Anaheim or against anybody who was against Disneyland. We had the case won hands down and we lost it."

Most of the suits are personal injury complaints. The most common cases have always been falls. Guests have slipped on things like frozen bananas, tripped over curbs or lost their footing on cobblestone walkways or the rougher terrain of Tom Sawyer Island. When McCray was faced with such suits, if the plaintiff was a woman, the lawyer would first find out what type of shoe she was wearing, hoping to be able to blame the loss of balance on high heels. If it was a child, McCray would accuse the kid of being careless or unsupervised.

In most cases, the best defense is that no one would have gotten hurt if they would have exercised reasonable caution. People who trip over curbs or low garden fences should look where they're walking. Expectedly, many falls occur when people's minds are elsewhere, such as when they're engrossed in watching a parade. One guest tried craning her neck for a better view of the Christmas parade and tumbled off the sidewalk. She suffered multiple injuries and required hip replacement surgery. The woman insisted that she fell because the parade route was so poorly lit. But McCray got her to testify that she was surrounded by so many people, she couldn't see the ground in front of her. "So what good would better lighting have done?" he asked the jury. Disneyland won the case.

Another guest said he got caught in the middle of a "dangerous crowd" that was shoving to get a better view of the Christmas parade. In trying to protect his wife and three children from the mob, he was pushed over crowd control ropes. A mob scene at the Magic Kingdom? The jury couldn't imagine such unruliness at Disneyland and found in favor of the park.

In 1990, a woman stumbled after stepping off a curb near the hub and fractured both legs. A longtime sufferer of "lack of depth perception," she couldn't tell the street was lower than the curb.

She charged that Disneyland was at fault for not painting the curb and street different colors to accentuate the height difference. But her suit mentioned the curb was light gray, the street was dark gray and the accident was caused by her own vision problem. She dropped the case.

Other victims have tripped over chairs or had their seats collapse beneath them. A few submarine passengers fell to the floor after missing their flip-down seats, which had flipped back up. One woman said she rented a wheelchair from the park because she was pregnant. Allegedly, a rod between the chair's wheels broke and she fell. The woman was rushed to a nearby hospital, where she miscarried.

For others, the objects fell on them. Pendleton Woolen Mill customers have been bumped on the head by tumbling display mannequins and falling bolts of clothing. One woman was buried by an avalanche of umbrellas. A lady and her son riding the Disneyland Railroad past New Orleans Square while the area was under construction were injured when plumbing installers dropped copper piping onto and into the train. And a jury awarded a Club 33 diner $15,000 after an ice sculpture fell on her foot and fractured her ankle.

Another woman claimed severe injuries when a restroom soap dispenser broke apart and powder flew into her eyes. A man strolling below the Monorail track said he was struck by a Monorail brake shoe, claiming the 40-pound hunk of metal struck him on the head and shoulders. After another man was diagnosed as having cataracts, he said they must have been caused nine months earlier when he was riding the Monorail and an unidentified object flew through an open window and struck him in the right eye. The cases were handled out of court.

Also airbound and dangerous, stray Shooting Gallery pellets led to two lawsuits. In three other cases, passersby blamed the loud roar of the sailing ship Columbia's cannon for causing shock and puncturing ear drums. And over the years Jungle Cruise captains' pistols have given one man shock, a woman an "ear concussion" and another woman blurring, burning eyes, powder burns, night blindness, photophobia and headaches. She said she walked around virtually blind for ten days. Her case was settled.

The park had been open to the public only three days before an accident occurred on an attraction that led to a lawsuit. A small girl driving an Autopia car hit a curb, slamming her jaw against the dash, fracturing two teeth and cutting her mouth. The suit became the park's first court trial and its first court victory. And Autopia would go on to cause more lawsuits than any other attraction.

Three months later, a 55-year-old housewife was injured on Mr. Toad's Wild Ride when a stack of barrels that lunges forward and almost hits patrons really *did* hit her. A safety cable broke and sent the barrels crashing down on her head. A few months later, a Snow White rider received a nice settlement following a three-car pile-up. When his car suddenly stalled, the following vehicle plowed into his from behind. As his cousin went flying by the wayside, his car jumped the track and started to smolder. The driver suffered back and neck injuries, compounded when a third vehicle rear-ended the second.

A power failure on Alice in Wonderland turned off all the cars and all the lights. When one small girl's car lurched to a stop, she struck her head on the back of the car and fractured her skull. Trapped under the car's safety bar in pitch darkness, the girl went berserk. Mom said her daughter remained sick for a long time and then starting acting really strangely. Disneyland settled for $737.35.

One woman said she was thrown from a Dumbo elephant into the pit below. As she lay helpless on the concrete below, a barrage of bypassing elephants repeatedly struck her in the head, shoulders and back. Besides her pain, suffering and medical bills, she asked to be reimbursed $51 for her broken sunglasses, ripped hose and torn sweater. The jury decided the woman was at fault and voted in Disneyland's favor.

Plenty of Mad Tea Party passengers have sued after being "violently" whipped around in or thrown out of the teacups. The mother of an eleven-year-old boy said his cup was spinning so fast, he began rising out of his safety belt and over the lip of the cup. His friend tried to grab his legs but couldn't. The boy was hurled from the cup and then struck repeatedly and knocked unconscious by the other cups spinning by. He sustained a swollen face, black eyes for two-and-a-half months, numerous cuts and bruises and a series of migraine headaches. The park settled for $1,500.

Most of the suits involving the Fantasyland rides have been considerably less dramatic. Passengers simply slipped in trying to get in or out of a car. Sometimes their cars were rear-ended; more often, they began moving before guests were fully in or out. Likewise, dozens of suits were sparked by loading and unloading mishaps on the Jungle Cruise, Small World, Storybook Land and Pirates of the Caribbean boats, as guests tried to bridge the gap between the dock and a boat with often slippery seats inside.

Most troublesome was the Haunted Mansion's tricky Omni-Mover system, in which passengers are loaded and unloaded between a moving walkway and continuously-moving cars. "People were falling out about every fifteen minutes," recalled one attendant. "Disneyland tried all sorts of things. There was an unnatural step, with people tripping on the ledge of the bucket's shell, so they cut out part of the bucket. They put white and yellow dots on the walkway. They had more people to help you out."

Suiting Up

Attractions cited in the most personal injury lawsuits based on 650 O. C. Superior Court cases filed from 1954 to December 31, 1992.

1. Autopia – 67
2. Matterhorn Bobsleds – 45
3. Haunted Mansion – 20
4. It's a Small World – 19
5. Pirates of the Caribbean – 18
6. Parking Lot Tram – 17
7. Mad Tea Party – 16
7. Jungle Cruise – 16
9. Alice in Wonderland – 15
10. Space Mountain – 14
10. People Mover – 14

A dozen near identical suits were filed during the attraction's first five years of operation, and the park only lost one. Clumsy guests got the point. In the next fifteen years, only two more such suits were filed.

Other rides have also been altered following serious accidents. The prototype Autopia cars had no bumpers and the designers had their children try them out. The young test group delighted in slamming into each other at full force and demolished most of the cars. By Opening Day, Disneyland added spring-like bumpers. Still, many riders got hurt when their cars slammed into the curb and their jaws slammed into the steering wheels. A guide rail along the center of the roadway was added in 1965 to keep drivers on course and away from the curb.

In the mid-1970s, the People Mover received a slight alteration following three similar suits. In 1972, a five-year-old boy was exiting a People Mover car when his left foot got caught under the car. The front metal wheel crushed his foot, severely damaging his foot muscles and nervous system. He had to have his three middle toes amputated and had to undergo two skin grafts. The family's lawyer said he obtained park First Aid files detailing more than 75 similar accidents from 1967 to 1972. Then, a year later, a five-year-old girl broke her foot under the ride. The next year, a twelve-year-old boy had to have two toes amputated after an identical accident. In 1976, before the cases were decided, the park installed a protective flange next to the track to keep feet away from it. They later settled with the three families for about $15,000 each.

Other rides were so liability prone, Disneyland just got rid of them. The horses pulling the Frontierland stagecoach got regularly spooked by the Mine Train whistle. They would run wild through the forest and flip the coach over. Midway through one ride in 1957, a horse gave a leap and scared the others. The entire team broke into a run and, trying to make too wide a turn, tipped the stagecoach. The passengers riding on top were thrown off. One struck his head and was knocked unconscious. The passengers inside were thrown about the cabin and trapped inside as it was dragged along the ground on its side. After a 200-yard sprint, the horses ripped the front wheels off the coach and broke free.

When three passengers filed separate suits over the incident,

Walt demanded that the stagecoaches be scrapped. Disneyland settled one case and took two to court. Their defense: the passengers should be responsible for their own injuries since overturning is a normal risk of riding a stagecoach. One man collected $5,000, the other $17,500.

It was worth a try. The argument had worked before. In fact, four times passengers sued after the Main Street vehicles they were riding went out of control and tipped over or collided with other vehicles. In one, the surrey horses were scared by some workmen and ran out of control down Main Street. A wheel finally struck a curb in front of City Hall, and the coach tipped over against a lamppost. The case went to trial and Disneyland won, thanks to the testimony of a young boy who was thrown out of the surrey. Asked if he was scared, the lad replied, "No! I thought it was fun!" A judge then threw out a fellow rider's suit over the same incident.

In another case, a horse was frightened by a collision between the Omnibus and a streetcar and bolted. The first jury ruled for the park, but the plaintiffs received a retrial and won $5,500. And a final surrey suit sounded so implausible – the horses were spooked by the firetruck carrying the Three Little Pigs – it was quickly dismissed.

The pack mules also had a history of legal problems. Thirteen Superior Court cases were filed by guests who fell off mules. The ones that Disneyland was not able to settle went to trial – and the park lost them all. "We used to shudder when we saw a mule train case coming," said McCray.

In 1962, one rider's mule suddenly began "jumping, lunging, rearing, shying and bolting." The man was thrown off to the side and dragged through bushes and over rocky terrain before he was finally torn free. The court awarded him $4,000.

Then came the big money cases. In 1971, a mule bucked off its female rider while crossing a bridge. The woman slammed into a fence, rolled underneath it and down the side of a hill. A year later, another female passenger was thrown to the ground and trampled by the entire pack. The woman, a Berkeley fashion model, charged she was "jostled, dislodged, knocked to the ground, stomped upon, kicked, bitten and in other ways injured." One mule even left a permanent horseshoe-shaped scar on the small of her back.

The woman said she also suffered psychological injuries, and so did her child. "My son also seems to be frightened of animals, something he had never had before the accident, undoubtedly brought on by the fact that he was there when his mother was injured," she testified. "I often have dreams and hallucinations of animals, especially mules, in which I fear bodily injury. I cringe in fear whenever I am on the street and a dog or a cat is in the area. I was never like this before the accident and I am very disturbed over it."

During the trial, handlers of Ruth, the 8,000-pound mule, admitted the animal was "goosey" and that the other mules liked to nip at her. In its defense, Disneyland secretly shot movies of the woman briskly walking around town, with no visible handicap. The jury still handed down a $41,084.03 verdict.

In 1973, a rider's "rotting away" saddle strap broke, and he fell off the mule, onto his backside and slid down an incline. The injury required major back surgery. The jury handed down a $130,000 judgment and the park closed down the mule train.

The largest settlement following an attraction accident was granted to a 28-year-old former employee. In 1980, Denise Guerrero was working the Space Mountain loading dock, checking to make sure passengers' safety bars were secure before the ride began. In pushing one bar down, she got caught. The car dragged her 25 feet and inflicted severe bruises, cuts, a broken pelvis and ankle, and injured back. Disneyland agreed to pay out $154,000 in cash plus $240,000 in an annuity program to give her tax-free payments for the rest of her life. For a normal life expectancy, payments would exceed $1 million.

The parking lot tram may be a most unsuspecting "ride," but it has sparked more than a dozen lawsuits. The first tram suit involved a woman who, in heavy fog, began stepping off while the tram was still moving. Another woman walked between the tram's cars, tripped over a coupling and broke her knee. One tram passenger said he was hurt when the tram crashed into a large cement planter. A woman was riding the tram to the park from the Disneyland Hotel when the parking lot's automatic gate closed on the tram – and her.

And a 58-year-old filed suit after her eleven-year-old grandson missed the tram. The boy ran after them and after about 100 yards finally caught up. Grandma held out her hand but just as he grabbed it, he was pulled underneath the tram's wheels. Still holding tight, granny was pulled off the tram, smacked her head on the pavement and was knocked unconscious. The case and three others involving the trams made it to trial, and Disneyland won them all by proving recklessness on the part of the passengers.

A few visitors have accused tram drivers of crashing into their cars, but in most of the parking lot accidents, guests smash into each other. That doesn't stop them from trying to blame Disneyland, for things like poor lighting or badly situated hedges cutting down on their visibility. Again, the park has won all these cases that made it to trial. Even motorists driving outside the park have tried to pin the blame for their accident on the Magic Kingdom. In 1965, a woman filed suit after her husband was killed in a car crash on West Street, which runs between the park and the Disneyland Hotel. The widow claimed that the Monorail pillar in the center divider, "commonly known as the Pillar of Death," obscured the view of motorists. She said Anaheim Police Department records showed at least 22 prior collisions at the same location, but could not get her case to trial.

Employees named in lawsuits are usually pictured as careless. But when they're characters, plaintiffs typically try to paint them as psychos. There was no disputing that the first suit involving Disneyland characters was an accident. Marching in a parade in 1960, the Mad Hatter sideswiped a woman with his oversized hat. She said her entire body instantly became sore, from head to toe. The bump left her with a stiff back, cervical sprain, muscle spasms, neck traction, recurring headaches, numbness in the arms and hands, difficulty in sleeping, even arthritis.

But most of the time, guests contend that the costumed crew was after them. One character reportedly twisted a small boy's nose. Another scared a little boy so badly, he ran into some crowd control ropes. Mary Poppins attempted to pull a woman out of her chair and worsened her back problem.

In 1986, a twelve-year-old girl went to have her picture taken with Brer Bear in Frontierland. Supposedly, the bear grabbed her around the neck with both hands and started violently shaking her. She cried for him to let go and tried to break free from the choke-hold, but he tightened his grip, the suit said. She suffered soft tissue neck and back injuries. The suit portrayed John Doe Bear as "a violent and maladjusted individual and a danger to the safety of individuals visiting Disneyland... (he should not be) permitted to have contact with and mingle amongst children while wearing a costume which disguises his (or her) appearance and countenance." The case was eventually dismissed.

Five years earlier, another young girl dragged Winnie the Pooh to court for hitting her in the face. She said the beating gave her deep bruises, recurring headaches and eyeaches, and possibly even some brain damage. An arbitrator awarded her $1,000, but Disney-land demanded a jury trial. McCray's first witness was Robert Hill, the actor who portrayed Pooh bear at the park that day. Hill testified that while in costume, his vision and movements are severely restricted. The girl, then nine years old, was tugging at him from behind and, in turning to see who it was, he accidentally struck her with an ear. "We're trained not to retaliate," he said.

McCray then asked for a brief recess. After jurors returned to their seats, Hill reentered the courtroom in costume. Taking the witness stand, Pooh answered the lawyer's questions by nodding his head and stomping his feet. "What do you do at Disneyland?" McCray asked. Pooh got up and did a jig down the aisle. The courtroom audience burst into laughter. "Have the record show that he's doing a two-step," noted the judge. By calling Pooh to the stand the attorney was able to present a lovable, sympathetic witness who wouldn't – and couldn't – hurt anyone. The bear demonstrated that he couldn't have slapped the girl in the face as she claimed. The costume's arms were too low to the ground. The jury took just 21 minutes to acquit Pooh on all charges.

But no case can compare in sheer bizarreness to the overweight woman who in 1976 said she was molested by one of the Three Little Pigs. The 240-pound woman said she was near Small World when a sailor-suited piglet ran up to her and started playing with her breasts, squealing, "Mommy! Mommy!" Her $150,000 damage claim accused the character of assault and battery, false imprisonment (the pig grabbed her and wouldn't let go), and humiliation from onlookers laughing and ridiculing her since, according to the suit, the pig's actions were "asserting that the plaintiff was mother to a pig."

"She claimed later that the whole thing made her so nervous and upset that she gained 50 pounds," McCray said. "Why she filed that suit I'll never know. It had to be a phony." The woman gave up on the case after McCray showed her a photo of the pig that revealed the costume had no working arms. They were inoperable stubs.

A recent case surrounded a character not on the payroll. A young man who resembles pop singer Michael Jackson and works as a celebrity impersonator came to Disneyland in costume and started dancing in front of the just-opened Captain E-O attraction. He attracted a huge crowd and a few security guards, who promptly kicked him out of the park. He returned two weeks later, but this time when security tried to escort him out, he put up a fight. After the scuffle, he sued for assault and battery, $2,000 in doctors bills, a busted camera and broken sunglasses. Disneyland filed a countersuit, accusing him of conducting commercial activities in costume in the park without permission and using the park's "name, goodwill, property and publicity" for his own commercial benefit.

He wasn't alone. Five years earlier, a Lincoln lookalike was strolling around Town Square, signing autographs and handing out photos to the guests. Security showed him to the exit. The man claimed he couldn't help it if he looks like Lincoln, but admitted he did use the resemblance to attract business to his barber shop. That day at the park, in addition to his beard, he was wearing a black suit, wire-rimmed glasses and top hat. The park pointed to its long-standing policy refusing admittance to people in costume and added that the presidential impostor was competing with his audio-animatronic counterpart.

The E-O impostor would have his gloved hand full in court because Disneyland is virtually unbeatable in cases involving false arrest and the related charges of wrongful detainment, assault and battery, humiliation, defamation and malicious prosecution. Seven such cases have made it to trial and the park has won every one of them. In all, more than two dozen guests have sued after being

held by Disney security and then kicked out of the park or forward-
ed to an Anaheim jail. Guests have been nabbed for jumping from
car to car on the People Mover, smoking on the Skyway, being
drunk or on drugs and, most commonly, shoplifting.

Among the more interesting accusers:

● A woman who said her family was harassed by *eleven* hulk-
ing security guards after her three-year-old son lifted a bag of
candy from a Bear Country vendor.

● A young lady who left the park to get her medicine but forgot
to get her hand stamped for re-entry. When she tried to return to
the park to get a soda to wash the medication down, the ticket taker
naturally wouldn't let her in. "In pain and frustration," she ducked
under his arm and headed for Coke Corner. Guards then approached her "in a menacing manner which frightened" her. And,
though she said she would leave, they forced her into a wheelchair
and carted her off.

● A suspected shoplifter who said officers threw her to the
floor, beat her, handcuffed her and pulled her hair.

● A man high on drugs who said a guard punched him out then
battered him with a walkie talkie.

● A feisty drunk who said officers chained his wrists and ankles
and dragged him to jail for the night.

● A woman who said she was jailed for instructing her three
children to shoplift. Security found about 30 items from various
shops stuffed in a shopping bag with no receipts.

● And in two different cases in the mid-1980s, Hispanics arrested for shoplifting who said their captors threatened to call immigration and intimated that they must have sneaked into the park by
jumping over the fence.

Most of the cases were dismissed, but at least twice the park has
been forced to settle. In 1989, a family visiting from Idaho was
wrongfully arrested for shoplifting a $2.50 coin bank. Although
they were later freed after producing a receipt, during questioning
guards repeatedly told them they weren't in Idaho anymore. They
were interrogated backstage, where the two young daughters
caught glimpses of characters filing into the dressing room areas
with their heads off. The mother said her four-year-old was terrified at the sight of headless characters because they wore what

appeared to be breathing and cooling devices underneath that made their heads look like skeletons. She said the girl had nightmares that she was being chased by headless giants and required psychiatric treatment for three months. The family sought more than $1 million in damages. Disneyland settled the case for an undisclosed sum.

The second time they paid up even though the woman admitted to stealing a Mickey Mouse T-shirt. "She pleaded guilty to shoplifting, but later she sued Disneyland for the treatment she received," said the arresting guard. "Some months later I was informed her case was settled for $25,000 to make it go away. Supervision had not given her normal rights, they didn't even let her make a phone call or contact an attorney. This lady could have been treated a little better. A lot of it is ego by the supervisor in charge. It's the police mentality that led to the Rodney King beating. You think you're above the law. We're not policemen. They knew it, but thought they could fake it."

Disneyland expects its guests to act within certain guidelines and to look a certain way. "We do reserve the right to ask people to leave if we feel their appearance would be offensive to others at the park," said park spokesman Bob Roth. Those wearing unacceptable clothing may be asked to remove it or cover it up. Guests with unusual hair styles or colors might be turned away or asked to wear a hat. A few of these "head cases" have filed discrimination suits. Most recently, a teenager was denied entrance because her hair was dyed pink and purple. She showed up at court as a brunette, and the judge awarded her $250.

Disneyland's most famous discrimination case was filed by a couple that was ousted during an end-of-the-summer Date Night in 1980. The pair held hands on the Matterhorn and had their arms around each other on Space Mountain. The trouble came when they tried to dance together at Tomorrowland Terrace. They were both male. Andrew Exler, age nineteen, and his date, Shawn Elliott, seventeen, hurried past a security guard to the center of the dance floor where a disco band was playing. The guards caught up with them and suggested that the men find female partners. Exler asked why, and an officer replied that it was Disneyland policy.

When the couple continued dancing, guards again asked them to find new partners. When the dancers refused, the guards tried to cut in on them, and the boys danced around them. Two officers finally marched Exler off the floor. A third instructed Elliott to follow. "This is a family park," one guard said. "There's no room for alternative lifestyles. Two men can't dance together, that's our policy."

"We make our own rules," a second officer added. "This is a private park."

At the security office, officers took down the boys' names, addresses and ages and told them they were welcome back any time except that evening. They stamped their hands to make sure. "They treated us like we were criminals," said Exler. "We just wanted to dance."

A week later, the boys filed suit, seeking actual and general damages of $10,250 apiece and an injunction to prevent the park from prohibiting dancing between members of the same sex. They cited the Unruh Civil Rights Act, which permits anyone to use business facilities without regard to such factors as sex.

Disneyland countered that its long-standing policy calling for ejection of "individuals or groups who may by their actions, dress or attitudes interfere with or jeopardize the enjoyment Disneyland gives to others," said Roth. The "modest" regulations included bans on necking and petting, smoking by minors, alcoholic beverages and group activity that could be interpreted as gang-related. Dancing regulations: "Couples only are allowed on the dance floor (male/female)." They said the rule was designed to prevent singles, trying to pick up a girl, from bothering other dancers.

The Superior Court judge ruled the guards' actions were allowable and reasonable to protect the interests of other patrons. Within days the boys appealed the decision, since the judge, as Exler explained, "made a ruling based on his own belief that Disneyland did not have to go by the law." But when the Court of Appeals heard the case a year later, it upheld the lower court's decision.

Actually, Disneyland was set up. Beforehand, Exler had written to the park inquiring about their same sex policy. He attended Date Night specifically to challenge the ban, assuming he and his date would be bounced. Exler would also file similar suits against Chippendale's nightclubs and their male dance shows, become a paralegal, be fired as a county government clerk for wearing a gay rights button to work, and sue Disneyland again twelve years later over a discount ticket promotion for Southern California residents. He claimed it discriminated against people without a driver's license, but Disneyland responded that residency could be established with a utility bill, student ID or even a library card.

Although Exler and Elliott could not receive any damages, Exler continued to pursue the case to overturn park policy. In 1984, he finally got his day in court. Disneyland called to the stand president Dick Nunis and three typical guests, all of whom testified they had been to Disneyland many times and considered it a clean, wholesome, family-type attraction.

Exler gave his side of the story. Jurors deliberated for less than one day before deciding that the men were discriminated against. The judge stood behind the verdict and struck down the ban – but only as it applied to the plaintiffs. Though the same sex rule would still hold against all other individuals, Exler and Elliott could dance together at Disneyland. Unfortunately, they had broken up months after Date Night. The real winner was Exler's attorney, Ron Talmo, who received attorney fees of $25,000, to be paid by Disneyland. "Quite frankly," he later admitted, "I didn't think we had a chance of winning." Talmo warned that other suits would follow if Disneyland didn't change its policy.

Although the new injunction applied only to Exler and Elliott, Disneyland quietly dropped its same sex dancing ban about a year later. They said it was because of all the requests by youngsters at the newly-opened Videopolis. "We discovered via Videopolis that with the modern styles of teen dancing, you can't really tell who is dancing with whom. It's now more popular for people to dance more to the music than with anybody in particular," Roth told reporters. "Any interpretation that the decision had anything to do with the lawsuit is inaccurate." Talmo, for one, didn't buy it.

Yet another suit would arise, in 1988. Three gay UCLA students were dancing to fast numbers for about an hour without incident. But when a slow song played, security quietly intervened. "Touch dancing is reserved for heterosexual couples only," instructed one guard.

The trio sought unspecified damages and a permanent injunction applying to all Disneyland guests. They agreed to drop the suit a year later, after the park reaffirmed that its written policy prohibited discrimination based on sexual orientation.

Much more than the guests, employees have an image to live up to. An eighteen-year veteran stage manager sued saying he was unfairly fired because he has AIDS. He said he had worked his way up from pageant helper to assistant stage manager to stage manager, until 1985 when he was diagnosed with the disease. After that, he found himself denied advancement, training, pay and benefit increases and, finally, in 1989, his very job.

For another employee, it was age discrimination. A 55-year-old Golden Horseshoe trumpet player accused the park of demoting and then firing him because they thought he was too old. When Disneyland fired the entire band in 1986 "to keep things fresh," each member had to reaudition for his old position. The trumpet player was the only one over 40 to be retained and was appointed lead. He would be twice demoted before being released in 1990, again with the entire cast. The trumpet players that took his place were 27 and 35 years old, with less experience, training and education for the position.

When Wheeler Kelly was hired as a carpenter in 1966, he became the first black among the park's 400 skilled craftsmen. As the only black, he was subjected to racial jokes, comments and name calling by co-workers. When Kelly complained to his supervisors, they ignored him or told him to follow the example of Jackie Robinson and remain "bigger than some of the remarks and incidents." And they refused him overtime pay on the same basis as white workers, assigned him to less desirable shifts and passed him over for promotions in favor of less-experienced whites.

In 1969, Kelly filed a discrimination complaint with the state against the park. One month later, he was fired. He had been assigned to repair some huts along the Jungle Cruise. When his supervisor didn't show up immediately, Kelly and a gardener started talking about repairing other huts across the river. The next thing he knew his bosses stormed on the scene, acting as if they had been looking all over for him. The foreman swore at him and the next day handed him his walking papers.

The state eventually dismissed his complaint. He filed related charges with the federal Equal Employment Opportunity Commission. After an investigation, they discovered "probable cause" to believe Disneyland had discriminated against Kelly and other blacks. Instead of taking formal action, the agency suggested Kelly file his own lawsuit. He did so in 1980, asking for lost wages, benefits, attorney fees and his old job back.

His 1985 trial lasted nine days. The U.S. District Court judge ruled that indeed Kelly had been fired for "racially discriminatory and retaliatory purposes." The park was ordered to pay more than $100,000 and rehire him to work long enough to quality for a pension. He wanted to return on principle, he said, "to prove my point – mainly that I wasn't wrong to start with."

Disneyland also vowed to hire more minorities, echoing an agreement they had signed with the NAACP two years earlier to work with minorities in banking, advertising and purchasing. Still, Kelly feared upon his return he would still find discrimination at the park. "A black person would have a better chance of being a federal judge or winning a gold medal in ice skating in the Olympics or being an astronaut than being a carpenter at Disneyland," he told the media.

Two months after the verdict in the Kelly case, the Equal Employment Opportunity Commission filed a similar suit after the Disneyland Credit Union terminated a black financial analyst. She claimed that just before she was fired, she overheard other employees telling a "discriminatory joke." The commission claimed Disneyland had maintained a "racially offensive work environment" even long before she was hired.

Disneyland said they were in the right firing the woman six months after they hired her. "She had already been sanctioned for not performing her job before she made any complaint," said the credit union's attorney. "She was still on probation. She just wasn't doing the work."

Disneyland had tried to reach an agreement with the commission soon after the firing. When negotiations broke down, the agency decided to file suit. They sought back pay and reinstatement for the woman and a court order forcing the company to "eradicate effects of past and present unlawful employment practices."

Then in 1988, a second black carpenter tried to duplicate Wheeler Kelly's courtroom success. He said he, too, was wrongfully released "based on a discipline and promotion system that denied black employees equal employment opportunity solely because of their race." His union contract said he was guaranteed full carpenter's pay two years after completing a 90-day probation period. Disneyland fired him just seven weeks before the anticipated promotion, a job level he alleged that no black carpenter had ever reached. The park said they released the man because he falsified his timecard to get a day off. The carpenter responded that it was an honest mistake since the alteration resulted in no difference in hours or pay. He said a white employee caught with repeated falsifications received only a warning notice. No matter, park policy clearly states that such violations are to result in termination. The arbitrator ruled for Disneyland.

But there are some areas where you just can't win. In 1984, a white Disneyland landscaper filed suit claiming *reverse* discrimination by his Hispanic foreman. The employee was working along the western perimeter of the park when he saw U.S. Immigration and Naturalization Service agents conducting a raid on a strawberry field across West Street. Five migrant strawberry pickers ran from the field and climbed over a fence to hide. At the agents' request, the landscaper led them to the suspects, who were arrested. The next day, the man told his supervisor what happened. A day later, the man's foreman told him he had been transferred to removing tree stumps. He would do the work, now performed by three-man crews using mechanized equipment, alone and by hand. Two days later, he severely hurt his back. He also charged that the predominately Hispanic landscaping department regularly discriminated against the white workers, even failing to discipline one Mexican laborer who presumably choked a couple of Caucasians. The judge ruled for Disneyland.

People from all over are claiming to be victims. It is a small world, after all.

10

Sequels

AFTER the incredible success of Disneyland, Disneyland II became inevitable. Walt, though, wasn't interested in doing the same thing twice. The money men wanted an East Coast Disneyland. Walt wanted more. If there was going to be a next time, it had to be bigger, better and entirely different.

He agreed to remake Anaheim's Magic Kingdom only as a bargaining chip for EPCOT, the Experimental Prototype Community Of Tomorrow. Disneyland was the perfect playground; EPCOT would be the perfect community, a new kind of city – clean, attractive, safe and stimulating. A planned and controlled environment, a showcase for the latest in industry, technology, education and culture. Slums wouldn't be allowed to develop because no individuals would own land; they would rent homes, at modest rates, work gainfully and help keep the city alive.

Driven by the desire to be creator and king of his own real, live city, Disney began secretly buying up large tracts of swampland in central Florida in 1964. Walt's World wouldn't be surrounded by any of the cheap Las Vegas strip-type motels and other businesses that had sprung up around Disneyland. In Florida, Disney would own all the surrounding land – and the hotels and restaurants on it. Before Walt died in December 1966, the company had acquired

27,443 acres over two counties and submitted plans for the first phase of the massive project.

The ball was rolling. In the spring, Florida's governor signed into law a bill establishing the Reedy Creek Improvement District, a single, unified governing body to facilitate the passing of new methods and materials outside existing building codes and zoning ordinances. It would provide the property with public services and the legislative and regulatory atmosphere necessary for a private company to build a "City of Tomorrow."

They used many of the innovative new techniques in construction of the Magic Kingdom, a more spacious knock-off of Disneyland. First, they built nine acres of "basements" for office, storage and employee support areas, linked by a mile-long network of corridors. Actually, the underground city was constructed at ground level and then buried with the dirt excavated from the Seven Seas Lagoon. The theme park was built as the second and third stories.

The subterranean tunnels are high and wide enough for delivery and maintenance trucks to drive beneath the buildings. They can replenish supplies and make repairs completely out of view to the guests above. The underground halls are also lined with electrical power conduits, water pipes, natural gas lines and a vacuum collection system pipe which whooshes canisters of garbage at up to 60 miles per hour to a central compactor station. A custom sewage treatment plant produces water clean enough to drink – though it's actually used for watering the grounds.

The labor pool in Florida at the time was a sharp contrast to that in more sophisticated Southern California. Orlando was a farming town, slower paced, innocent, lightly populated. About 150 Disneylanders were transferred to Florida to indoctrinate the new recruits into the Disney Way. The first workers were eager to learn, and the Californians tried to impart to them both the job knowledge and the camaraderie of back home. The transfers even borrowed the Banana Ball.

Walt Disney World opened October 1, 1971, a smash from the start that has grown into one of the top vacation destinations in the world. But despite everything the Imagineers and employees had learned and all the precautions they took, they couldn't avoid many of Disneyland's problems. There would still be mechanical difficulties: The opening of Disney World's Space Mountain came before Disneyland's and suffered just as many technological setbacks. Exactly a month after the ride's official unveiling, a computer malfunction caused three sets of rockets to crash into each other. Forty-one riders were injured and the attraction was closed for ten days. Another time a Monorail car caught fire. They had to evacuate all 200 passengers from the elevated cars and have six of them treated for smoke inhalation.

There would still be employee error: Once a Rivers of America raft driver drove his raft in front of the Mark Twain. The paddle-wheeler smashed into it and sent dozens of raft passengers flying into the water.

And there would still be unhappy customers: Parents of a six-year-old New Jersey boy sued Mickey Mouse. They said that when their son went to ask Mickey for his autograph in front of the castle, the character picked the boy up and threw him against a wall. In an effort to get the case moved to New Jersey, their attorney served a complaint on an unwitting actress who dressed up in a mouse suit at a local shopping mall.

Disney World has the room and the demand to keep expanding. There's always something under construction or opening – new lands, attractions, facilities, hotels, camping areas, golf courses, the Disney/MGM Studios, adults-only Pleasure Island nightclub complex, zoological park, lakes, water parks. The grounds have so many amenities and amusements that many tourists enjoy an entire week's vacation without ever leaving Disney property.

Walt's EPCOT opened in 1982, but it turned out to be nothing like its inventor had imagined. The living City of Tomorrow gave way to a theme park, entertaining, innovative and educational, but still a theme park. The 260-acre complex includes Future World, a high-octane Tomorrowland filled with corporate-sponsored pavilions, and World Showcase, a permanent, sanitized world's fair. Another amusement park just made more cents.

The natural next step was recreating Disneyland in other parts of the world. For Tokyo Disneyland, which opened in 1983 in a little town on land reclaimed from the Tokyo Bay, designers took the Magic Kingdom model and skewed it slightly to accommodate the different language, culture and climate. Main Street gave way to a World Bazaar, protected from the elements under a glass cover. Their Big Thunder Mountain is in Westernland. And since it snows more in wet and windy Tokyo than in Anaheim, the Japanese close their park more often.

The third time was the charm. For once everything was ready by Opening Day. In fact, everything was ready two months before Opening Day, but they waited until the set date of April 15 because of the weather. Everyone was trained, everything was organized, everything seemed to click.

"It was the easiest opening," said maintenance chief Bob Penfield, who has helped set up all the Disney parks. "We learned from our earlier mistakes. And the Japanese are easy to work with. They are very organized. They really get in there and get it done. They're good on electrical and sound, machinery and animation. But we taught some things to the Japanese. They don't practice preventive maintenance. When something breaks, they replace it. They don't do repair checks. They're very weak on painting, mill-work, welding, manual labor. And I didn't think they were superior on landscaping."

Again, Disneylanders were sent to help open the new park and many Tokyo workers were trained at Disneyland. Language and culture differences provided some barriers. Some Japanese characters put parts of their costumes on wrong. One had his vest under his shirt; another had all his clothes on inside out. The Americans showed them how to sign autographs but, since the Japanese character for the "R" sound looks like an "L," one character spent the day signing "White Labbit." And the Japanese were so polite they couldn't bring themselves to leave the crowds. They had to be dragged offstage.

The second international target, though, would be more like a mouse trap. Everyone thought it would be a smash: a European Disneyland, twenty miles east of Paris, the most-visited tourist destination on the continent. In an area so rich with tradition and history and so close to so many other countries, they decided to combine the Disney theme with the heritage of Europe. Tomorrowland became Discoveryland, more a history of the future, focusing on famous Europeans like Leonardo da Vinci and Jules Verne. Fantasyland's subdivisions would evoke the land from which the fairy tale came, Italy for Pinocchio, England for Alice in Wonderland. The Sleeping Beauty Castle would be reminiscent of a French chateau. In the end, though, Disney may have been trying to please too many people. The usually focused Disney vision gave way to a clash of a dozen different cultures. Instead of peace and harmony, there would be conflict and tension.

To the Parisian intellectuals, Disneyland was a symbol of everything contemptible about America: artificial, unstimulating, crass, crude, for the masses. Yet here was a 5,000-acre Disneyland springing up half an hour from the Louvre.

A few months before Opening Day, police began investigating charges that the EuroDisneyland dress code banning facial hair and certain apparel violated France's work code. An employee was fired for wearing a yarn bracelet. Rumors persisted that the park couldn't keep a full staff. Contractors began demanding an additional $150 million for work they claim was added to the project after the initial contracts were signed.

But EuroDisneyland opened on time, in fact a half-hour ahead of schedule, on April 12, 1992. A handful of protesters carrying signs with slogans like "Mickey Is a Rat" marched out front and the night before the opening two bombs damaged nearby electricity pylons. And the intellectuals wrote their criticisms of the "horror made of cardboard, plastic and appalling colors, a construction of chewing gum and idiotic folklore taken straight out of comic books written for obese Americans."

Disney smiled. Let the crowds speak for themselves, they said. Unfortunately, during its inaugural year, there wasn't much of a crowd to do the speaking. Held down by Paris' rainy winters and high prices, attendance and spending for the first six months (the first fiscal year) were well below projections and the park lost more than $35 million. Angry local investors, promised by Eisner that EuroDisney would post a profit from Year One, saw stock prices dive. And shareholders were warned that the prognosis for Year Two wasn't much healthier. Indeed, losses for fiscal year number two topped $900 million, prompting severe cutbacks and rumors of declaring bankruptcy and closing down the park.

Meanwhile, back in Southern California, Disney's increasing economic muscle has earned it more power and more criticism. During negotiations in 1987 to buy the Disneyland Hotel and entertainment rights to the Queen Mary from the Wrather Co., Disney threatened to drastically hike the modest fees Wrather was paying for use of the Monorail to transport visitors between the hotel and the park if Wrather didn't lower its asking price. Wrather caved in. The first thing Disney did was put a fence around the Disneyland Hotel. Then came enforcing the Disney Way inside the gates, beginning with the dress code at the Disneyland Hotel and Queen Mary. After warnings to ship out or shave, Disney suspended then fired five hotel workers and four ship workers.

In working up its latest Southern California project, Disney pitted two cities against each other, insinuating that whichever city would make things easiest would get the new $3 billion resort complex: a marine-oriented Port Disney built around the Queen Mary in Long Beach or a "second gate" in Anaheim. Infuriated by the red tape of county commissions and city regulations and ecological groups, Disney abandoned all plans for Long Beach including dropping its lease option for the Queen Mary.

Next proposed was a 470-acre resort to be built over Disneyland's existing parking lot and surrounding areas that would bring up to 28,000 new jobs to the area. Westcot Center would be a take-off on EPCOT, a world's fair-type theme park with plenty of shops and hotels. Borrowing Disney World's strategy of an entire vacation in one place, it would spearhead an area-wide improvement campaign.

But residents were worried about the increased traffic, need for housing and capital improvements, overcrowding and all the big city problems that come with it. And, local taxpayers wondered, what favors would Disney require? The project has now been transformed into Disney's California Adventure, a smaller scale park celebrating the sights and heritage of the Golden State.

Whatever happens outside its gates, the original Disneyland will

BOYCOTT DISNEY. Everyone excited about Disney's proposed Westcot Center is not necessarily in favor of the $3 billion project, as evidenced by this billboard paid for by Anaheim homeowners. As soon as the message was taken down, a pro-Westcot group used the same billboard to advertise reasons to *support* the project. (June 17, 1993) *Photo by David Koenig.*

continue to evolve as it was always supposed to. The drawing boards reveal all sorts of innovative new adventures planned well into the new millennium:

● New attractions – Disney takes every opportunity to cross-merchandise with its latest movie releases, so look for promotions, parades, stage shows or even attractions based on new and upcoming features.

● Updated attractions – Imagineering is ever devising new ways to keep existing attractions as fresh as possible. Sometimes, to improve the show, they'll just add small elements, such as additional animatronic characters at the Pirates of the Caribbean. Other times, they'll totally rework rides to create a very different attraction. Figuring that most young children didn't know who the Swiss Family Robinson was, designers recently recrafted the Swiss Family Treehouse into Tarzan's Treehouse

The shelves at Imagineering are filled with new concepts for remaking such favorites as the Enchanted Tiki Room, the Submarine Voyage, and Star Tours.

● New lands – With the addition of gigantic new offices and parking facilities beyond Toontown and the acquisiton of surrounding acreage, Disneyland may be able to open entirely new lands in areas now used for backstage operations. Possible locations include areas between Main Street and Tomorrowland and beyond Critter Country and Big Thunder.

The Imagineers will continue devising technological innovations and entertaining creations to produce a dazzling show for all to see. And promising an equally dizzying show of hard work, mistakes and out-takes that most of us will never see. It's because this Fantasyland was built and is operated by and for real people. And the shortcomings and selfishness that go along with being human don't disappear just because you visit or even get a job at what may well be the Happiest Place on Earth.

Notes

Squawking José: *Register* 7-14-85
30. Saucers: *The "E" Ticket* Winter 89-90, *I* Church, *I* Lovegren, *I* May
Hurricanes: *I* Filtz
Concerns, sheared pole *Q*: *I* Waite
Force out lessees: *I* Filtz, *I* France
World's Fair: *American Original*
32. Extend Cruise: *I* May
Redo Storybook: *I* Filtz
Tree: *I* P. Brooks, *I* May, *I* Newman
Bayou: *I* Sunderman
A.m. Walt: *I* May
Instinct: *I* Corson
33. Cautious council: *Wall Street Journal* 2-16-72
Disliked Pirates: *Register* 7-14-85
What would Walt do?: *I* Wheeler
Move Abe: *Inside Story*, *Register* 8-15-90, *I* Penfield
37. Wall St.: *Storming the Magic Kingdom* (John Taylor, Knopf, 1987)
Ferris wheels: *I* Marshall
State Fair: *I* Dayna Budde; One hostess heard that management considered making the midway games permanent fixtures on Main Street.
38. Splash Mt. delays: *Register* 1-31-89, 6-21-89, 7-18-89
1st giveaway: *I* May
Money *Q*: *I* Schlicter
Popcorn: *I* Calabrese
Early Birds: *I* Penfield
39. Filming: *I* Lacagno
Promotions *Q*: *I* Lewis

Chapter Two

41. Main St.: *WS Journal* 2-16-72
Vents: *I* Don Budde
Corners: *California* 3-80
Columns: *New West* 12-4-78
Forced perspective: *Register* 7-14-85, *Disney News* Spring 1989
42. Vehicles: *I* D. Miller
Upper floors: *I* Kehoe
Mud: *Register* 7-14-89
Toontown: *Register* 1-22-93

Artists: *I* Campbell
Artifacts: *Disney News* Spring 1989, "Facts & Figures" press sheet
43. Sub caverns: *Inside Story*
Fantasmic!: *Register & Times* 5-14-92
44. Main St. windows, links to past: *Disney News* Spring 69, Summer 87 & Spring 89, Facts & Figures
45. Zoo: *Disney News* Spring 89
Real gators: *I* Ligthart
46. Catfish: *I* Bowman, *I* May, *Disney News* Spring 1989
Dead ducks: *I* Leslie
Fried: *Register* 5-27-92
Swans: *I* Ligthart, undated *Times* clipping
Spider Patrol *Q*: *I* Perkins
47. Flies: *I* Palmer
Rats: *I* S. Steele
Trapped: *I* Jett
Cider: *I* L. Wettengel
Stomper: *I* Dowd
Mickey's friend, Rat bait *Q*: *I* Jett
48. Wild cats: *I* Don Budde, *I* Haller
Castle cats: *Inside Story*
49. Kennels: *I* M. Smith
Maintenance, divers: *Register* 7-12-90 & 7-23-91
Electricians/gardeners: Fact Sheet 88
Cleaners: *Register* 1-12-90
Mansion dust: *Birnbaum's Disneyland* (Hyperion, 1993)
Olive trees: *Register* 7-14-85
50. Rehabs, droughts: *I* Penfield
Wardrobe: Fact Sheet 88, *I* Iantorno, *I* J. Wilson
Paint: Fact Sheet 88
Fans: *I* Schwartz
51. Backstage: tour of park
Under Fantasyland: *I* Don Budde, plans of park, *Times* 6-12-86
52. Neverland, tunnel: tour of park, *I* Don Budde, *I* Hall, *I* Haller, *I* May
Attic: *Times* 6-12-86, *I* Lucas
Cameras: *I* Don Budde, *I* George
53. Mats: *I* Holmes

Lights, Pan camera: *I* Dayna Budde
Lilly Belle: *Birnbaum*
Fire Dept. apartment: *I* Kehoe, tour of park, *Inside Story*
Disney Gallery, apartment: *Disneyland Line* 7-23-87, concept drawing
54. Club 33, wait: *Register* 11-17-90
15 year wait: *I* Elliot
Conception: Club 33 Fact Sheet
Lessees: *I* Ward, lessee brochure 68
Name, no map: *Register* 11-17-90
No publicity: *Orange Coast* 8-84
Cost: Price Sheet 1992
55. Routine: *Register* 11-17-90, visits
56. Decor: Fact Sheet 1988
Original furnishings: *I* L. Blackburn
57. Animate *Q*: *I* Ward
Microphone: *Register* 7-14-85
Decor: *Register* 11-17-90
Matches: visits to Club 33
Service: *Register* 11-17-90
Tips, mature *Q*: *I* L. Blackburn
Discussing secrets: *I* Anonymous

Chapter Three

59. 30,000 apply: *Times* 7-12-70
Personnel dept. criteria: *Times* 7-2-69, 7-14-85
60. Guides/operators: *I* Landgren
Foods: *I* McClaran, *I* B. Thomas
Class system: *I* Landgren
Guides: *I* Bryant, *I* Thompson, *I* Lefebvre
Sorority *Q*: *I* Aldecoa
Jealous ticket sellers, animosity: *I* Passo, *I* Scillieri
Operators: *Register* 6-30-63, *I* Paschal, *I* Wheeler
Lot: *I* Hellyer, *I* M. Smith
Tan: *I* Fred Fischle
Driver *Q*: *I* M. Smith
61. Fast drivers: *I* Fred Fischle
Janitors: Hall
Film: *I* Leslie
Marines: *I* Moersch
Marine call: *I* T. Foster, *I* Newman
Disney University: *Register* 8-27-89

& 10-17-93
62. Attitudinizing: *Disney News* Summer 1969
"Brainwash": *I* May
Look: "The Disney Look" handbook
Haircuts: *I* Schaefer
Bras: *I* Persons
Wig: *I* Hellyer
Moustache *Q*: *I* Craig
Confining: *I* Alder, *I* Schweppe
High school *Q*: *I* Scillieri
64. I'd go back *Q*: *I* Don Budde
Moonlighter *Q*: *I* D. Miller
Reunions: *I* Wheeler
Ticket sellers: *Register* 8-19-90, attended luncheon
Retirement program: *I* May
Subculture: *I* Dunham, *I* DeLucia
Rapport: *I* M. Smith
Own business: *I* Alder
Sure hire: *I* Kehoe
Taught me *Q*: *I* Jett
65. Walt solicits opinions: *I* Burroughs, *I* Manning
Cheeseburger: *I* Mann
Day Walt died: *I* Cashin, *I* Evans, *I* Lefebvre, *I* Rochelle
Lost father: *I* May
Coffee chats: *I* Stanley
Christmases: *I* Lucas
Many kingdoms: *I* Solorio
66. Disney World drain: *I* Lucas
Restructuring: *I* France, *I* Holmes, *I* Leach, *I* Palmer
Less flexibility: *I* Beaver, *I* Haller, *I* Hore, *I* Stanley
Babysitters: *I* Beaver, *I* Wheeler
Duck winders: *I* Hore
SOP: *I* Holmes
Greatest asset *Q*: *I* Stanley
Yes men: *I* Fritz Fischle, *I* Foss, *I* Pruitt, *I* Stanley
Supervisor *Q*: *I* Brent
67. Miss communication: *I* Foss
Veterans, Idea program: *I* Holmes
Disney $ lawsuit: *Register* 5-14-87
Coupons eliminated: *I* Deck, *I* Lyles

Chapter Four

McDonald's: *I* Hensley
Main Street: *I* D. Miller
Retlaw: *I* Dowd, *I* Goltz, *I* L. Johnson, *I* Mills, *I* Perkins
Christmas party: *I* Newman
Snob *Q*: *I* Dumas
81. Ride count rivalries: *I* Lance
Photos: *I* Dunham, *I* Holmes, *I* Landgren
Canoe races: *I* various, Kruger letter
Guinea pigs: *I* various
Setting Space Mt. *Q*: *I* Holmes
82. Basics: *I* various
83. Loading *Q*: *I* Filtz
Intentional breakdowns: *I* Gorham, *I* Leslie
Autopia game: *I* Alder, *I* Healy
Skyway: *I* Belz
Jungle Boat: *I* Leslie
84. Omnibus: *I* Schlicter
Small World: *I* Landgren
Jungle spiel: *I* Wheeler
Spinner: *Register* 2-24, 3-4 & 23-93
Slow raft : *I* Jett
Snow White: *I* Penfield
85. Skiff races *Q*: *I* Leslie
Pan: *I* Penfield
Matterhorn: *I* Carman, *I* Craig, *I* Harris, *I* Holmes
Autopia: *I* DeLucia, *I* Holmes, *I* Schweppe
Busy season: *I* Belz
Shelter, shots at Monorail: *I* May
86. Vietnam: *I* Goodwin, *I* Landgren
Less paranoid: *I* Pratt
Extinguishers, etc.: *I* various
Resident pranksters: *I* Lovegren
Behind the scenes: *I* Belz
Closing Autopia: *I* Holmes
Mansion exhibitionist: *I* Schaefer
Ex-Lax cupcakes: *I* Lucas
87. Sail pranks: *I* Alder, *I* DeLucia, *I* Harris
Diving for mermaid: *I* DeLucia; *I* Healy, *I* Holmes
Send help!: *I* Wheeler
Animation, native dancer: *I* Leslie

Fire at driver: *I* Waite
Pet hippo: *I* Deck
88. Keel spiel: Herold letter
After dark spiels *Q*: *I* Goodwin
Mars ad-libs: *I* DeLucia
Soaked send-offs: *I* Carman, *I* Holmes, *I* Leslie
89. Riding doll: *I* Belz
Small World raft: *I* Belz, *I* Kessler
Boxer revue: *I* Leslie
Hippo attack: *I* Landgren, *I* Leslie
Tarzan: *Times* 7-14-85
Bubbles: *I* Anonymous
Control room remodel: *I* Hayes
Roundtrip raft: *I* B. Wettengel
Tram on freeway: *I* L. Wettengel
Mad dog: Skretvedt
Mylar over Main Street: *I* Hellyer
90. Tie to tracks: *I* Holmes
Refrigeration Guy: *I* Fritz Fischle
Condom: *I* DeLucia
Harrass bosses: *I* Alder, *I* DeLucia
Wallpaper: *I* Fritz Fischle
Defective bucket: *I* Hofstetter
91. Stolen Monorail: *I* Newman
Harrass maintenance: *I* Landgren
Leave guests alone: *I* Holmes
Cardinal rule *Q*: *I* Bradley
25¢-to-floor: *I* various
Magic Shop: *I* Haller, *I* Matas
Martin: *Steve Martin: An Unauthorized Biography* (Greg Lenburg, Randy Skretvedt and Jeff Lenburg, St. Martin's Press, 1980)
Doubled-up straws: *I* DeLucia
Jello: *I* Carman, *I* George, *I* Hayes
92. 914: *I* Carman, *I* DeLucia, *I* McCormick
Gumby: *I* Carman, *I* McCormick
Train robberies: *I* Landgren; In the late 1960s, Imagineers proposed a Western River Expedition, a "rip roaring western style adventure" in which masked bandits would interrupt the guests' stagecoach ride – an idea this prankster and Knott's Berry Farm already had.

People Mover robot: *I* Dennison
93. Mars hostess: *I* Gorham
A.Sings co-stars, remodel: *I* Bopp
Easter with Abe: *I* Dow
Snow White: *I* Kessler
Pampered elephant: *I* Nichols
Bra: *I* Hofstetter
Bottles: *I* Persons
Ice bucket, soup: *I* Carman
Space Mt. saboteur: *I* Schweppe
Beheaded mud hen: *I* Carman
94. Canoe close call: *I* L. Wettengel
Spiking: *I* Hellyer, *I* McDermed
Hang-outs, parties: *I* various
Apartment owners: *I* Dunham
Party *Q*: *I* Jett
95. Drunk worker: *I* Leslie
Custer's: *I* Belz, *I* Dunham, *I* Jett
Banana Ball: *I* Carman, *I* Leslie, *I*
Jett, *I* Wheeler
Pirates: *I* Dunham, *I* Lance, *I* Pratt
Sweepers: *I* Jett
Come Park: *I* Lucas
Romance: *I* Holmes
96. Inner Space: *I* Alder
Mansion: *I* Hellyer
Castle: *I* Persons
Treehouse: *I* Dunham
Top of Mt. Club: *I* Gorham
Wheelhouse *Q*: *I* Landgren
Getting dates: *I* Wheeler
Multiple dates: *I* Manning
Hustle *Q*: *I* Dennison
Mansion, Mark perverts: *I* Landgren
97. Cameraman: *I* Holmes
The obsessed: *I* Anonymous
Daily visitor: *I* Leslie
Sub/Autopia pain: *I* DeLucia
98. Company D: *Register* 1-13-92
Bootlegs *Q*: *Register* 10-7-90
Mementos: *I* B. Berry, *I* Carman, *I*
Landgren
Supervisors: *I* Alder

Chapter Five
99. Tips: *I* Burt
Official position: *Times* 1-21-88

Put head on *Q*: *I* Bals
Ice Capades: *I* Waite
Costume changes *Q*: *I* Castle
100. Lysol: *I* Damico
Cheeks: *I* Barth
Early years: *I* Castle
Subs: *I* Waite
Costumed hostesses: *I* Burroughs
Girls *Q*, tenure, weight: *I* Castle
Chiropractors: *Register* 5-14-91
101. Talk *Q*, heat, sweat *Q*: *I* Castle
Pig down: *I* Carman
Sticky: *I* Damico
Tablets *Q*, fantasize *Q*: *I* Rondeau
Tooth, pinning Pluto: *I* Barksdale
Forget people inside: *I* Mann
Chica?: *I* Barth
102. Photo session: *I* Holmes
Chip attack: *L.A. Weekly* 3-27-92
Pull heads, stab, smoke: *I* Castle
Lighter fluid: *I* Damico
Pluto, Alice attacked: *I* Barksdale
Minnie molestor: *Bulletin* & *Register* 9-19 & 20-92
103. 16-yr-old, croc decked: *I* Castle
Crippled wolf: *I* Dowd
Clever kids: *I* Gorham
Bloody nose *Q*, groups, most vulnerable, chaperones: *I* Barksdale
Kick pig *Q*: *I* Rondeau
104. 6th sense, fighting back subtly: *I*
Barksdale, *I* Mann, *I* Rondeau
Crazed Mickey: *I* Castle
Troublemaker trashed: *I* Matosich
Fighting father: *I* Barksdale
105. Stricter, playful Pan: *I* Mann
Karate fox: *I* Damico
Booklight, Beatles: *I* Mann
Notecards: *I* Barth
Radio, statue: *I* Barksdale
106. Robin falls: *I* Dayna Budde
Sickening Snow White *Q*: *I* Barth
Tony Orlando: *I* Burt
Autistic boys: *I* May
Mr. Piggie: *I* Rondeau
Day with Pan: *I* Mann
107. Flirt: *Times* 7-14-85, *I* Rondeau

Exits: *I* Burt
Dinner for Winnie: *I* Don Budde
Outsider *Q*: *I* Damico
Caste *Q*: *I* Mann
Black Bart *Q*: *I* Burroughs
108. Intoxicated: *I* C. Blackburn
Spacemen, mermaids: *I* Baughmann
Men jump: *I* Lovegren
Given hook: *Disney News* Spring 89
109. Climber stunts: *I* Barksdale, *I*
Mahoney
Tinkerbell Tiny: *I* Filtz, *I* Mann
Pendant: *I* Filtz
Greasy wire: *I* Baughmann
Stuck: *I* Mahoney, *I* Paschal
Catchers: *I* Filtz (*Q*), *I* B. Wettengel
110. Selleck poster: *I* Don Budde
Baby New Year: *Times* 1-21-88
Dumbo, Mary Poppins: *I* Paschal
Tommy Walker, Easter Bunny debacle: *I* C. Blackburn, *I* France
112. Christmas parade: *I* Filtz, *I* May
Santa *Q*: *I* Harper
Bands *Q*: *I* Denaut
113. Vesey: *I* Barngrover, *I* Strimple
Opening Day band, gazebo, smaller combos, Sousa *Q*: *I* Barngrover
Tommy fired: *I* Anonymous
114. Tommy bio: *NY Times* 5-18-86
Electrical Parade: *Register* 7-12-91
Burns: *I* Adams
Smoking Cinderella: *I* Williamson
Tree on fire: *I* Lacagno
Try outs: *I* McGrath, *I* Williamson
115. Parade problems: *I* Williamson
Breakdown *Q*: McGrath
Stilt fall: *I* Gorham
Dancer in track: *I* Williamson
Pony: *I* Lacagno
Canopy carriers: *I* Williamson

Chapter Six

117. "Check your brain": *I* Jett
Walk off dock: *I* S. Steele
Into water *Q*: *I* Ligthart
Horseshoe Revue: *I* Birnie
118. Into men's room: *I* Lemmon

Dive!: *I* Persons
Shark attack: *I* Church
Bridge: *I* S. Steele
Severed leg: *I* Gorham
119. Inner Space close: *I* McDermed
Pinocchio prisoner: *I* Don Budde
Zipper broke: *I* Hofstetter
"P" ticket: Robert Wachter
Is it real?: *I* Jacobs, *I* Bopp, *I* Harris,
I Gorham, *I* Schmidt
120. Storms: *I* Bixler
Where's bathroom?: *I* M. Foster
Parade?: *I* Schmidt
When's parade?: *I* various
Toiletland: *I* McCormick
Chairs for sitting?: *I* Birnie
Merchandising gossip, Dopey Book:
I Matas, *I* Schmidt
Matterhorn: *I* Schmidt
Can Ride: *I* Landgren
Sub trip: *I* Hayes
Jump into Canyon: *I* T. Foster
121. Snow poser: *I* Dayna Budde
Forgot baby: *I* McDermed
Dangling from Monorail: *I* Goltz
Spider: *I* Green
Stuck in Lincoln: *I* P. Brooks
In wheel: *I* Green
In slats: *I* Adams
Pirates turnstiles: *I* Pratt
Caves: *I* S. Steele
Railcar: *I* Cornwell
122. Trash can: *I* L. Wettengel
Barrel: *I* Green
Lost & Found: *Disneyland Line* 6-25-87, *Times* 11-15-92
123. Eye, film, cash: *I* McFaul
Lost bag on Matterhorn: *I* Sweeney
Sly sweeper: *I* Hall
124. Sick on Treehouse: *I* Hall
On Teacups: *I* Heileson
At Autopia: *I* Hayes
Measles: *Times* 10-1-82
Sick on Pirates: *Times* 3-9 & 10-92,
Register 3-9 & 11-92
125. Urinators: *I* Goltz, *I* McDermed
Angry guests: *I* Holmes

"BLS": *I* Gorham
Taylor's birthday: *Times* 2-24 & 28-92, *Register* 2-26 & 28-92
Walt, apartment *Q*: *I* Barngrover
Code W: *I* Dowd
Copter to security: *I* Watson

Chapter Seven

143. Yorba: *Register* 3-9-81, *Times* 3-10-81, *Register* & *Times* 10-6 & 14-82, *Bulletin* 10-7-82, 4-4-83
144. O'Driscoll trials: *Times* 10-26-82, 5-6-83, *Bulletin* 11-1-85
Nurse, 2nd guest *Q*: *Times* 7-11-86
Van: *Times* 4-11-81
145. Criticism: *Register* 4-12-81, 7-16-86
Fire official *Q*: *Times* 3-11-81
Paramedics in past, Boatright incident: *WS Journal* 3-25-81
146. Accident call: *Register* 4-4-81
Yorba suit filed: *Register* 4-4-81, *L* Reynolds 1981
2nd suit: *Bulletin* & *Register* 4-8-81
Wallace death: *Herald-Examiner* & *Register* 4-17-81
Agree to meet: *Times* 4-20-81
Hire ambulance: *Times* 4-21-81
Prosecution: *Register* 7-16-86
147. Defense: *Register* 7-17-86
2nd surgeon *Q*: *Register* 7-22-86
Micco: *Times* 7-15-86
Decision: *Register* 7-23-86
Settle: *Register* 9-12-86
May back out: *Bulletin* 9-15-86
Reconsider: *Register* 9-23-86
Security charge: *Register* 12-18-82
148. Train, teachers: *Times* 1-12-81
Costumes: *I* Harper
P.R. *Q*, stepping in: *I* Hecker
Grin 'em *Q*: *I* Kehoe
Offstage, W section: *Times* 1-12-81
149. Guard curses, Yippie regrets: *Times* 1-12-81
100,000 flyers: *Bulletin* 8-11-70; Five days after Yippie Day, police uncovered another 50,000 copies of

the brochure at the Anaheim home of a Cal State Fullerton physics teacher, suspecting the known activist's home served as a central distribution point for the leaflets.
Flyer, noncalendar: copy of flyer
150. Authorities: *Register* 8-5-70
Bomb search: *I* Hofstetter
Smoke bomb: *I* Belz
Matterhorn *Q*: *I* McCormick
Bank tourists: *I* Young
Yippie Day a.m.: *Anaheim-Fullerton Independent* 8-6-70
Backstage: *I* Druitt, *I* Strimple
151. Pancake House, rides en masse: *Register* 8-7-70
Band: *I* Barngrover, *I* Strimple, *Times* 8-7-70
All a show: *I* Boag
Executives plead: *Tribune* 8-7-70
Managers in disguise: *I* Persons
Narc!: *I* France
Uncooperative, sing: *Register* 8-7-70
Climb mast: *I* Leach
152. Inner Space: *I* Alder
Outside gate, Manson follower *Q*, Nunis briefing: *Bulletin* 8-7-70
Cinema meeting, fort, head for bank, rap sessions: *Tribune* 8-7-70
153. Fort: *I* Kilpatrick, *I* S. Steele
Naked man: *Daily Pilot* 8-7-70
Lock City Hall: *I* Marshall
154. Showdown, flash point: *Pilot*, *Register* & *Times* 8-7-70
Nunis decks Yippie: *I* B. Berry, *I* Eagen, *I* Anonymous eyewitness
155. Clear park, wig: *Tribune* 8-7-70
Clear lot: *Bulletin* & *Register* 8-7-70, *I* Barngrover, *I* Harper, *I* May, *I* McNell
Sweeps: *Tribune* 8-7-70
156. Arrests: *Register* 8-13-70
Media: *Bulletin* 8-7-70
Joke *Q*: *I* McCormick
Grooming policy: *Pilot* 8-7-70
Next a.m.: *Times* 8-8-70
Difficult months *Q*: *I* Baker

Grand Funk RR: *I* Baker, *Bulletin* 11-2-70, *Tribune* 11-4-70

157. Skinhead Day: *Register* 5-27-89, 6-1-89

158. 1st gang fight: *Bulletin, Register & Times* 1-13-75

Knifing: *Times* 9-22-81

Knott's/Magic Mt. incidents, police training: *Register* 7-4-85

159. Tai: *Register & Times* 3-8-87

Videopolis shut down: *I* George

Danger *Q*: *I* Hecker

160. Fields incident: *I* Foss, *I* Watts

Fields criticized: *Times* 1-12-81

D'Allura, stirs industry, Tense *Q*, Roth *Q*: *Register* 8-17-83

Police, fired, suit: *L* D'Allura 1988, *Times* 5-3-88, 7-20-88

161. 5-yr-old shot: *Register & Times* 8-20-84

Pellets from heaven: *Bulletin* 1-2-85, *Register & Times* 2-12 & 13-90

162. Gunfire in lot: *I* Fritz Fischle, confirmed by one of guards involved

Hotel roofs: *Register* 9-8-86

Bike patrol: *Register* 7-11-92

Lookout tower: *I* Kehoe; The station was relocated from the main Pirates show building to atop the Indiana Jones building in late 1994.

Knifepoint robbery: *Bulletin* 7-23-86

Kidnapping: *Bulletin* 3-9-87

163. Kidnapping ring rumor: undated 1984 *Register & Times* clippings

164. Phone threats: *I* Fitzgibbons

Roth *Q*: *Times* 1-1-85

Bomb *Q*: *I* Burdick

ABC bomber: Undated *Times* clip

165. Bus locker bomber: *Tribune* 12-21-74, *Register* 12-22-74

Weatherman: *Bulletin & Register* 8-22-80, *Times* 4-27-83, 5-25-83, *Bulletin* 4-28-83

Plot: *Register & Times* 1-1-85

Mill bomb: *Register* 8-19-91

166. Shoplifting: *I* Hecker, *I* Oder, *I* Willoughby

Foxes: *I* Fran Fischle, *I* Solorio

Hold for parents: *I* Oder

Undercover agent *Q*: *I* Solorio

Shoplifters: *I* Fran Fischle, *I* Matas, *I* Townsend, *I* Willoughby

Security shoes *Q*: *I* Fran Fischle

167. Pickpockets: *I* Solorio

Funny money: *I* Lyles

Counterfeit ring, bank: *I* L. Miller

Streaker: *I* J. Young; Disneyland closed the in-park Bank of America 7-28-93, announcing it would be replaced with a Disney-operated financial service center. Relations with B of A had become strained after the bank withdrew its sponsorship of Small World a year earlier.

168. Gate cheat: *I* Carman

Arcade crook: *L* Small 1983

Stealing supervisor: *Register* 9-22 & 23-87, *Bulletin* 2-26-88

Trust, *Q*: *I* D. Campbell

Chapter Eight

169. Safety policy: "Working Our Way," "Safety Awareness" manuals

Emergencies, glitches: *I* Budde

Routine rescues *Q*: *I* Holmes

170. First aid: Working Our Way

Different from a hospital: *I* Green

Complex machinery *Q*: *I* Holmes

Maples: death cert., *Times* 1-4-84

Cleveland: *Register* 6-19-66, *Times* 1-4-84

171. Monorail operator *Q*: *I* Perkins

Yama: *Times* 1-4-84

Guard *Q*: *I* Oder

Delaurot: *Times* 9-28-75

172. A.Sings debut: *Register* 6-29-74

Flag: *Times* 7-10-74

Stone: *Times* 7-9 & 10-74

173. Jets cameramen: *I* McDermed

Safety systems: *Times* 7-11-74

Suit, effect, dad *Q*: *Register* 7-25-89

Theater closed, rude *Q*: *I* Hayes

174. Gonzales: *Bulletin, Register & Times* 6-8-80, death certificate

People Mover won't stop: *I* Holmes

Straughan: *Register & Times* 6-5-83, *Bulletin* 6-6-83, *Register* 3-27-84, *L* Straughan 1984

Young: *Register & Times* 1-4-84, death certificate

175. Hosts sent up, operators' suspicions: *I* George

Attorney's contentions, park's speculations: *Register* 3-15-88

Settled: *Bulletin* 3-16-88

Reid: *Bulletin, Register & Times* 9-15 & 16-85

Hoffman: *Register* 8-19-79, 1-24-80, *L* Hoffman 1980

176. Bobsled coronary: *I* Lance

On Storybook, Pirates: *I* Filtz

Horse: *I* Lemmon

Inner Space fall: *I* Jett, *I* Mahoney

177. P.Mover teen fall: *L* Ogle 1973

Mt. fall: *I* Lucas, *I* McCormick

178. Davis recovers: *I* DeLucia

People Mover boy fall: *Bulletin & Register* 1-29-79, *I* Dumas

Space Mt. fall: *Bulletin* 2-21 & 22, 3-4 & 10-83, *Register* 2-21 & 22 & 23 & 27-83, *Times* 2-21-83

Lawsuit, trial: *Bulletin* 3-2-85, *I* Fritz Fischle

179. Lost appeal: *Times* 5-27-87

Big Thunder falls: *I* Flanagan, *Times* 6-17-91

Storybook falls: *I* Baldwin, *I* Goltz, *I* Thomas

Canoes sink: *I* Alder, McClaran

Overload: *Register & Times* 5-31-90

Storybook sinking: *I* Filtz

180. 1st sub sinking: *I* Jacobs

Pearl Harbor: *I* Carman, *I* DeLucia, *I* Harris, *I* Seifert, *I* Sweeney

181. 1st RR derailment: *I* Lemmon

2nd derailment: *I* Perkins

Skyway off cable: *Register* 3-19 & 21 & 22 & 23-89

1st Dumbo: *Register* 3-30 & 31-89

182. 2nd down: *Register* 4-1 & 3-90

Borrow EuroDumbo: *I* Penfield

Space Mt.: *Bulletin & Times* 8-26-78

Big Thunder crashes: *Times* 5-30-80, *Bulletin & Register* 6-3-85

P.Mover crash: *I* Boag, *I* Church, *L* Strauss 1969, *L* Frederickson 1969

Settlements: *Times* 9-28-75

Sick jokes: *I* Leslie, *I* George, *I* Dayna Budde

183. OSHA: *Times* 4-15-88

Banged up *Q*: *I* Holmes

Matterhorn, Chances *Q*: *I* Hayes

184. Lookouts, electrocution: *I* Hayes

Skyway daredevil: *I* Belz

Jets shortcut: *I* Bopp

Mark fire: *I* B. Berry

Fire dept., duties: *I* Blakely, *I* Chandler, *I* Watters

1st chief: *I* D. Campbell

Matterhorn fire: *I* Chandler, *L* Epperson 1972 (victim *Q*)

Tree fire: *I* Hore

186. P.Mover fire: *Register* 6-26-93

1st Pirates fire: *I* Hintz, *I* Pratt

Lookout, sprinklers: *I* Wheeler

Kill switch: *I* Landgren

2nd Pirates fire: *I* J. Wilson

Infant hand-off: *I* L. Wettengel

187. Inner Space firecracker: *Bulletin & Times* 7-5-85

Float fire: *Register* 6-7-86, *Bulletin* 6-9-86

Fireworks: *Register* 7-14-89 & 7-4-91, *I* Belz, *I* Don Budde, *I* Watters

188. Neighborhood complaints, petition: *Register* 7-26-91

Expert called: *Register* 7-30-91

Storage area fire: *Bulletin, Register & Times* 9-7-84

Island fire *Q*: *I* McClaran

Bad weather: *Times* 12-8-92, *I* Hayes, *I* Holmes, *I* May

189. Transformer hit: *I* Mills

Blackout: *Register* 12-23-82, *I* Filtz, *I* Miller, *I* Townsend

190. Tornado: *Register* 4-6-83, *I* Fritz Fischle, *I* Hayes

Take our picture: *I* Fritz Fischle

Chapter Nine

191. Suit stats: O.C. Superior Court cases 1954–1992, *Register* 8-8-82

192. Settle: *I* Solorio, *Register* 8-8-82

Fight *Q*: *Times* 2-28-82

Belli case: *L* Sherwood 1960, *Times* 9-28-75

$32.50 sub case: *L* Fitzjerrells 1961

People Mover crash: *L* Frederickson 1969, *Times* 9-28-75

193. Fake accidents: *I* Adams, *I* May, *Register* 8-8-82

Accident-prone lady: *I* Adams

Blinded by light: *L* Carlson 1968

Casey Jr.: *L* Williams 1962

Pet lion: *L* Simonsen 1977

194. Day in court: *Times* 2-28-82

Bobs: *L* Mogul 1960, *Times* 9-28-75

Clydesdale: *L* Lee 1970

Dumbo gate: *L* Hill 1978

Lawyers *Q*: *Times* 2-28-82

Proof on film: *I* Schwaer

195. C-coupon: *L* Campbell 1976

Records: *Bulletin* 6-18-81

196. Documentation by nurses, cashmere cheat: *I* Andrews, *I* Green

Dizzy visitor: *L* Hovespian 1973

Good witnesses: *Bulletin* 6-18-81

Disney influence: *Register* 8-8-82

Change of venue: *Times* 2-28-82

McCray bio: *Register* 8-8-82

197. Field trips: *Bulletin* 6-18-81

Representation today: McCain

Opposition *Q*: *Bulletin* 6-18-81

Whiplash: *L* Varela 1976, *Bulletin* 12-12-80, *Register* 8-8-82 (*Q*)

198. Check shoes: *Times* 9-28-75

Badly lit parade: *Times* 2-28-82

Mob scene: *L* Rataezyk 1962

Curb fall: *L* Smookler-McCole 1991

199. Sub seats: *L* Kapigan 1961, *L* Sterett 1962, *L* Sye 1965

Wheelchair: *Register* 11-16-93

Tumbling mannequin: *L* Sloan 1958

Clothing: *L* Jalbert 1967

Umbrellas: *L* Kemp 1979

Piping: *L* Fairhurst 1966

Ice: *L* Gribin 1976

Soap: *L* Greenberg 1973

Brake shoe: *L* Katje 1960

Cataracts: *L* Tischer 1988

Shooting Gallery: *L* John 1965, *L* Petrantoni 1969

Cannon: *L* Wright 1959, *L* Mosher 1962, *L* Gzaiel 1990

Pistols: *L* Daly 1960, *L* Tomino 1973, *L* Gardner 1969

200. Car accident: *L* Marshall 1956

Mr. Toad: *L* Fowlkes 1956

Snow White: *L* Jordan 1957

Alice: *L* Duarte 1964

Dumbo pit: *L* James 1968

Teacup: *L* Keidser 1971

201. OmniMover *Q*: *I* Landgren

202. Autopia test, rail: *Inside Story*

People Mover crushings: *L* DeLuise 1979 (cites safety records), *L* Franklin 1976, *L* Sparks 1975

Stagecoach: *I* T. Foster, *I* Moersch, *L* Ruegsegger 1958

$5,000 winner: *L* Horner 1957

$17,500 winner: *L* Norton 1958

203. Surrey: *L* Ure 1958, *L* Kohl 1958 (child *Q*)

Other surrey suits: *L* Marsh 1966, *L* Perry 1960, *Register* 8-8-82

Shudder *Q*: *Times* 2-28-82

$4,000 mule case: *L* Niemet 1963

Roll down hill: *L* Hammersley 1972

Model mule case: *L* Eldridge 1972, *Times* 9-28-75

204. $130,000 mule case: *L* McKinney 1974

Space Mt. accident: *Times* 2-18-84

Tram in fog: *L* Goodman 1956

Coupling: *L* Schramm 1968

Tram vs. planter: *L* McCreary 1967

Vs. gate: *L* Hagar 1977

Goodbye, grandma: *L* Kennedy 1972

205. "Pillar of Death": *L* Sanders 1965

Mad Hatter sideswipe: *L* Gurll 1961

Twisted nose: *Times* 9-28-75

On ropes: *L* Cretaro 1990
Mary Poppins: *L* McClain 1975
206. John Doe Bear: *L* Stormer 1987, *Bulletin* 8-17-87
Pooh: *Times* 4-17-80, *Bulletin* 6-18-81, *Register* 8-8-82
Pig masher: *L* Mick 1976, *Register* 8-8-82 (McCray *Q*)
207. E-O imposter: *L* Evans 1987
Lincoln lookalike: *Bulletin* 7-3-81
False arrest suits: *Times* 2-28-82
208. 11 guards: *L* Fittro 1983
No stamp: *L* Kwiatkowska 1987
Beaten shoplifter: *L* Lewis 1978
Walkie talkie: *L* Lee 1980
Anklets: *L* Trejo 1976
Shoplifting family: *L* Giroux 1979
Racial slurs: *L* Christo 1985, *L* Zavala-Hicks 1987
Idaho family: *L* Boozer 1990, *Register* 9-26-92
209. T-shirt lifter: *L* Ravindran 1983
Guard *Q*: *I* Solorio
Dyed hair: *Register* 9-3-88
Date Nite: *Times* 9-15-80
210. Gays file suit: *Times* 9-23-80
Disney counters: *Bulletin* 9-23-80
Initial ruling: *Bulletin* 11-14-80
Appeal: *Times* 11-20-80
Decision upheld: *Bulletin* 10-21-81
Other Exler suits: undated 1989 *Times* clipping, *Register* 1-9-92
211. Trial, *Q*: *Register* 5-19- 84
Payout: *Register* & *Bulletin* 6-30-84
Drop ban, Roth *Q*: *Register* 8-15-85
2nd suit: *Bulletin* & *Times* 2-26-88
212. Suit dropped: *Register* 10-1-89
AIDS employee: *L* Campbell 1990, *Register* 6-22-90
Aging trumpeter: *L* Olson 1992, *Register* 3-3-92
Kelly: *Times* 9-20-85
213. Analyst: *Bulletin* 11-19-85
214. 2nd carpenter: *L* James 1991
White landscaper: *L* Collins 1984, *Register* 4-13-84

Chapter Ten

215. EPCOT, Secret land purchases: *American Original*
216. Reedy Crk: *American Original*
Underground: *N.Y. Times* 3-28-71
Labor pool: *I* Elliott, *I* Healy
California transfers: *I* Curry
Banana Ball: *I* Beaver
217. Space Mt. crash: *St. Petersburg Times* 3-6-75, *St. Petersburg Independent* 3-7-75
Monorail: *Bulletin* 6-27-85
Raft: *I* Garland
Mickey Mouse suit: *Bulletin* 7-22-85
218. Tokyo, opening *Q*: *I* Penfield
Japanese characters: *I* Burt
219. EuroDisney: *Register* 2-17-91, *Times* 4-10-92
Culture clash: *Register* 11-4-92
Dress code: *Register* 11-4-92
Contractors: *Register* 2-12-92
Opening, protests: *Register* 4-13-92
Horror *Q*: *Register* 4-12-92
Losses: *Register* 11-4 & 18-92
Investors warned: *Register* 1-16-93
220. Wrather deal: *Times* 7-8-90
Hotel/ship dress code: *Times* 3-8 & 18 & 30-88, *Register* 4-21-89, 12-28-89
Port Disney, cities compete: *Register* 1-13-90, 12-13-91, 3-7-92
Westcot: *Register* 5-9 & 10-91
Worries: *Register* 6-6-91
Virginia project: *Register* 11-12-93
221. Coming attractions: *Register* 1-13 & 7-15-90, *FantasyLine Express* 4-95
222. Shortcomings of humanity: The Bible – Romans 3:9-12, 23-24

Index

Order Form

Quantity   Amount

_____   **Mouse Tales: A Behind-the-Ears Look at** _____
Disneyland (softcover) @ $13.95

_____   **More Mouse Tales: A Closer Peek Backstage at** _____
Disneyland (softcover) @ $14.95

_____   (hardcover, *personally autographed by the author*) _____
@ $24.95

_____   **Mouse Under Glass: Secrets of Disney** _____
Animation & Theme Parks (softcover) @ $14.95

_____   (hardcover, *personally autographed by the author*) _____
@ $23.95

Total for book(s) _____

Postage: Add $2 for first book, _____
$1 for each additional

Sales Tax: **California residents only,** add 7.75% tax _____

Amount enclosed (U.S. funds) _____

Ship Book(s) to:

_____

_____

_____

IF THIS IS A LIBRARY COPY,
PLEASE PHOTOCOPY THIS PAGE

BONAVENTURE PRESS
P.O. Box 51961
Irvine, Ca. 92619-1961
www.bonaventurepress.com